Institutional Change and Performativity

"Accounting standards have fundamental effects in shaping economic life. Okamoto's fine book combines his theoretical sophistication with his in-depth understanding of the Japanese context. Altogether a tour de force!"

—Prof. Donald MacKenzie, *University of Edinburgh, UK*

"Is it possible for a book to embody both scholarly depth and engaging relevance while exploring theoretical concepts? Consider a work that delves into the financialization and accounting standards of a particular nation, navigating through the cultural traditions that shape its economic landscape. Discover how these themes connect with Searlean theories of institutional reality and social ontology. Your enthusiastic exploration of this volume is encouraged as a rewarding intellectual inquiry."

—Gary John Previts, *E. Mandell deWindt Professor Emeritus, Weatherhead School of Management, Distinguished University Professor Emeritus, Case Western Reserve University*

Noriaki Okamoto

Institutional Change and Performativity

The Impact of Globalization and Financialization on Accounting in Japan

palgrave
macmillan

Noriaki Okamoto
College of Business
Rikkyo University
Tokyo, Japan

ISBN 978-3-031-53392-1 ISBN 978-3-031-53393-8 (eBook)
https://doi.org/10.1007/978-3-031-53393-8

This Palgrave Macmillan imprint is published by the registered company Springer Nature Switzerland AG
The registered company address is: Gewerbestrasse 11, 6330 Cham, Switzerland

Paper in this product is recyclable.

Preface and Acknowledgments

This book is a compilation of some of my previous research. As a Japanese researcher, I have long dreamed of publishing a book in English. Now, it has finally come true. Long before, especially as a graduate student, I was deeply interested in trends in accounting standards and practices outside Japan. To be honest, I was obsessed with the idea that the Western accounting model was superior to the Japanese model and that Japan needed to catch up with global trends.

However, as I continued my research life, I began to wonder about the unique characteristics of accounting in the country where I was born and raised. How do they differ from the rest of the world? How have they evolved and changed? As I have taken interdisciplinary approaches to accounting issues in my research, this book addresses the dynamics of accounting in Japan from multiple perspectives. Although this interdisciplinary approach and the study of accounting in Japan may halfway between each other, the cross-disciplinary integration of different perspectives makes this book unique, and I believe it has some implications for future research on institutional theory, social ontology, social norms, and performativity beyond the sphere of accounting research.

I have consistently explored how accounting institutions have evolved. In particular, I have focused on the changes in formal accounting standards. Various stakeholders surround corporate accounting standards, which are set, revised, or abolished through the standard setter's political decisions. Hence, it is useful to theorize what drives these institutional changes. This book addresses the fundamental questions of what institutions are and how they are constructed within society. It introduces different theoretical perspectives, including institutional theory, social ontology, and theories of performativity. Consequently, this book argues that collectively accepted generic performativity is an essential component of social institutions. To support this argument, this book analyzes the recent development of Japanese accounting from two types of deductively interpreted generic performativity. In other words, both globalization and financialization have had strong impact on the changes in accounting in Japan. More specifically, the global unification and convergence of accounting standards, as well as the proliferation of active financial markets, have been given the highest priority. Although the trends of globalization and financialization have been strong, some counterperformative actions in Japan have affected institutional details. I hope that the interactions between performativity and counterperformativity presented in this book will resonate across various disciplines.

The idea for this book took shape and progressed during my sabbatical leave from 2022 to 2023, allowing me to visit the Department of Accounting at the London School of Economics and Political Science (LSE). I would like to thank my workplace, College of Business at Rikkyo University, the former Dean Kazunori Yamaguchi, and current Vice President Jun Ishikawa for their support and encouragement. I would also like to express my deepest gratitude to Andrea Mennicken, who graciously accepted me as a visiting scholar in 2021 when COVID-19 was still raging. In addition to Andrea's initiative, I am also grateful to Peter Miller and Michael Power for their support of my research visit. The research environment in the office located in the new Marshall Building was very helpful. During my visit to the LSE, I received support from the faculty and staff of the Department of Accounting. Julia Morley provided the supportive impetus for pursuing this project. Professor Emeritus Richard Macve provided helpful suggestions on how to behave and work during the research visit. Richard also introduced me to Carien van Mourik, who conducted extensive research on accounting in Japan. When I had the opportunity to talk to Carien in a café near the LSE, I realized the importance of in-depth research on the recent developments in Japanese accounting, which resulted in this book.

I am also very grateful to my colleagues at Rikkyo University. In particular, in addition to Professor Emeritus Yasunori Matsui, Nobuya Takezawa, Kazuhiro Bai, Atsushi Chino, and Masahiro Hosoda are wonderful colleagues in the field of accounting and finance at the College of Business, and regular meetings with them have greatly stimulated my research. Professor Emeritus Chitoshi Koga, Katsuhiko Kokubu, Donald MacKenzie, Yasuhiro Shimizu, and Tadanori Yosano are all mentors I have looked up to in my research career. In addition, I would like to mention the names of those who have helped me develop a passion for research through conferences and study group activities. They are Paul Ahn, Garcia Clemans, Xin Fu, Koji Ikeda, Ryuzo Kabata, Masato Kikuya, Shiomi Kondo, Takayuki Nakano, Takashi Oguri, Koji Okino, Fudan Semba, Yoshinori Shimada, Kazuyuki Shimanaga, Kunihiro Shimazu, Noriyuki Tsunogaya, and Jun Yao.

Ellie Duncan, an editor at Palgrave Macmillan, was also dedicated to the completion of this book. She has been attentive and supportive of the rough idea of this book and has patiently stayed by my side to help me complete it. Without her presence, this book would not have been completed. Supraja Yegnaraman, Ulrike Stricker-Komba, and Zeenathaul Raeesa from Springer group dedicatedly supported the book production process. I was fortunate and deeply grateful to have found brilliant editors. Pires Dos Santos, a research assistant at Rikkyo University, worked hard to edit the manuscript and complete the reference list. Finally, special thanks go to my family members, Asako, Akari, and Chiaki, for their support throughout this project in London and Tokyo. My daily conversations with them relieved me of the stress and pressure associated with the project. I would also like to mention my adorable Shetland Sheepdog, Rick, who cheered me up with his innocent affection for my home workspace. It is a great pleasure that this book will help develop any future research.

Tokyo, Japan Noriaki Okamoto

Contents

1	**Introduction**	1
	References	6
Part I	**Conceptual Analysis of Institutions, Norms, and Performativity**	
2	**Institutions as Collectively Accepted Norms**	9
	2.1 Various Perspectives of Institutions and Unresolved Ontology	10
	Scope and Definition of Institutions	10
	Dichotomous Viewpoints of Institutions	12
	Institutions and Shared Mental Models	16
	Institutions Are Both Regulative and Normative	19
	A Comparison of Institutional Theory and Actor-Network Theory	20
	2.2 Institutional Reality and Social Ontology	25
	Searlean Framework of Institutional Reality	25
	Collective Acceptance and Deontic Powers	28
	Desire-Independent Reasons and the Significance of Norms	29
	2.3 Analysis of Collective Norms	31
	Classification of Different Types of Norms	31
	Quadripartite Classification of Collective Norms	32

Observable Social Norms and Operative Members' Actions 36
References 39

3 Performativity of Collective Norms 45
3.1 Collective Norms Are Performative 46
Performativity Includes Normativity 46
Classification of Performativity 50
3.2 Generic Performativity of Observable Social Norms 54
Identification of Generic Performativity 54
Felicitous Conditions for Identification 57
Performative Forces and Institutional Change 60
References 63

4 Identifying Contemporary Observable Social Norms 67
4.1 Linguistic Approach to the Analysis of Performativity 69
Linguistic Approach and the Significance of Texts in Institutionalization 69
Focus on Nominalized Linguistic Representations 70
4.2 Identifying Observable Social Norms 73
Globalization 73
Financialization 77
4.3 Methodological Stance to a Specific Institutional Context 81
Process Tracing and the Focus on Changes in a Limited Context 81
Focus on Accounting Reforms in Japan 84
Performative Norm Diffusion Process: Analysis of Key Actors 87
References 91

Part II Performative and Counterperformative Institutional Dynamics: Globalization and Financialization of Accounting in Japan

5 Global Unification of Accounting Standards 97
5.1 Globalization of the Financial Market and the Accounting Big Bang 98
The Japanese Financial Big Bang After the Bubble Burst 98
Beginning of the Accounting Big Bang in Japan 107
5.2 Global Convergence of Accounting Standards in Japan 111

Diffusion of Global Harmonization of Accounting Standards 111
Foundation of the ASBJ and Steps Toward Convergence 113
Tokyo Agreement and Acceleration of Global Convergence 118
5.3 *Partial Adoption of the IFRS and Counterperformative Actions* 122
Political Analysis of the Decision of Voluntary Adoption 122
Counterperformative Reactions: Space for JMIS 124
5.4 *Summary and Analysis* 125
References 128

6 Diffusion and Penetration of Fair Value Accounting 133
6.1 *The Shift from a Manufacturing-Oriented to Finance-Oriented Economy* 134
Deregulation of Financial Transactions in Japan 134
Diffusion of Financialization and Its Implications for Accounting in Japan 138
Issues of Traditional Historical Cost Accounting in Japan 147
6.2 *Performative Financialization and Fair Value Accounting* 150
Financialization and Market Value Accounting 150
Performative Financialization and Globalized Fair Value Accounting 154
6.3 *Counterperformative Actions from Japan: Securing Local Tradition* 160
Japanese Reactions against the Global Idea 160
Counterperformative Actions to Secure Local Practice in Global Context 164
6.4 *Summary and Analysis* 169
References 171

7 The Pursuit of Better Corporate Governance 177
7.1 *The Development of Corporate Governance in Japan* 179
The Traditional Japanese Corporate Governance Model 179
The Penetration of Corporate Governance in Japan 182
The Establishment of Corporate Governance Code 185
7.2 *The Rise and Fall of the Corporate Cross-Shareholding Practice* 189

The Traditional Cross-Shareholding Practice in Japan 189
Growing Pressure to Reduce Cross-Shareholding 191
7.3 *The Globalization and Financialization of Corporate Governance* 197
The Problematization of Cross-Shareholding 197
The Recent Reduction in Cross-Shareholding: The Introduction of Disclosure Requirements 201
7.4 *Summary and Analysis* 205
References 207

8 Conclusion 211
References 216

Index 217

Abbreviations

ABS	Asset-Backed Securities
ANT	Actor-Network Theory
ASBJ	Accounting Standards Board of Japan
BAC	Business Accounting Council
BOJ	Bank of Japan
CAP	Corporate Accounting Principles
CESR	Committee of European Securities Regulators
CGC	Corporate Governance Code
CME	Coordinated Market Economy
EC	European Commission
EPA	Economic Planning Agency
FASB	Financial Accounting Standards Board
FASF	Financial Accounting Standards Foundation
FIEL	Financial Instruments and Exchange Law
FRB	Federal Reserve Bank
FSA	Financial Services Agency
FSRC	Financial System Research Council
FVA	Fair Value Accounting
FVTOCI	Fair Value Through Other Comprehensive Income
FVTPL	Fair Value Through Profit or Loss
IAS	International Accounting Standards
IASB	International Accounting Standards Board
IASC	International Accounting Standards Committee
IFAD	International Forum on Accountancy Development
IFRS	International Financial Reporting Standards
IOSCO	International Organization for Securities Commissions

JBA	Japanese Bankers Association
JICPA	Japanese Institute of Certified Public Accountants
JWG	Joint Working Group
LDP	Liberal Democratic Party
LME	Liberal Market Economy
MOF	Ministry of Finance
MOJ	Ministry of Justice
OCI	Other Comprehensive Income
OECD	Organisation for Economic Co-operation and Development
ROA	Return on Assets
ROE	Return on Equity
SASB	Sustainability Accounting Standards Board
SEC	Securities and Exchange Commission

List of Figures

Fig. 3.1	Austin's classification of speech acts	47
Fig. 3.2	Classification of performativity in the economic context	51
Fig. 3.3	Overview of norms and performativity	53
Fig. 4.1	The number of financialization articles published each year (1990–2022)	78
Fig. 6.1	Annual stock trading volume (monetary base) in Japan (*Source* Produced using Nikkei Needs Financial QUEST2.0. Both purchasing and selling amounts were simply combined to calculate total trading volume)	138
Fig. 6.2	Share ownership ratios among shareholders (1985–2022) (*Source* Japan Exchange Group's Share Ownership Survey. *Kabusiki Bunpu Chōsa*. https://www.jpx.co.jp/markets/statistics-equities/examination/01.html)	139
Fig. 6.3	Annual stock trading volume of individual and foreign shareholders (*Source* Produced using Nikkei Needs Financial QUEST2.0. Both purchasing and selling amounts were simply combined to calculate total trading volume)	140
Fig. 6.4	Asset composition of large Japanese corporations (non-financial/insurance) (*Note* This figure is based on Table 1 in Shimano [2016])	143

Fig. 7.1 The long-term trend of the average ROE of Japanese firms (*Source* The data were collected from the MOF Policy Research Institute's Financial Statements Statistics of Corporations [*Hōjin kigyō tōkei chōsa*]. The total amount of equity was used to calculate the ROE) 183
Fig. 7.2 The percentage of cross-shareholding in Japan 193
Fig. 7.3 The percentage of foreign shareholdings in the Japanese Market from 1995 to 2022 (*Source* Data were collected from JPX and are based on the shares listed on JPX) 196
Fig. 7.4 Shareholding percentages by various investors in Japan 201

List of Tables

Table 2.1	Two views on institutions	15
Table 2.2	Comparison of the key ontological assumptions of institutional theory and ANT	23
Table 2.3	Quadripartite classification of norms	35
Table 4.1	Actor-centric norm diffusion process	91
Table 5.1	Main policies of Japan's Financial Big Bang (Toya, 2006, p. 120)	108
Table 5.2	Major changes in accounting standards in the Accounting Big Bang	110
Table 6.1	Takeda's classification of economic sector characteristics	146
Table 6.2	Opinions on the comment letters to the Questions 10 and 11 of IASB (2009a)	162

CHAPTER 1

Introduction

One of the most important topics in accounting in the past several decades has been the international unification of accounting standards. Currently, the use of the same set of accounting standards (International Financial Reporting Standards: IFRS) is required or permitted for domestic public corporations in more than 160 jurisdictions (as of December 2023).[1] These many countries have their own unique cultures and histories generally demarcated by national borders. Then, what drove this international unification in accounting? To answer this question, considering the background social dynamics in different nations would be useful. Although the comparative study of accounting standards/practices in different countries is beneficial and significant,[2] it would be extremely difficult to examine and compare the events and situations in many countries in the same time frame. To limit the scope of research, this book analyzes the development of accounting institutions in Japan in relation to its social dynamics.

In the early 1980s, when Japan's booming economy attracted global attention, bank finance was dominant among companies, and the radical

[1] It is based on the information on the following website: https://www.ifrs.org/use-around-the-world/use-of-ifrs-standards-by-jurisdiction.

[2] For instance, Godfrey and Chalmers (2007), Nobes and Parker (2020), and Weetman et al. (2020).

N. Okamoto, *Institutional Change and Performativity*,
https://doi.org/10.1007/978-3-031-53393-8_1

reform of corporate accounting standards was not considered necessary by policymakers and regulators. However, after the collapse of the bubble economy, Japanese economic conditions stagnated for a long time, and traditional Japanese institutions, such as accounting standards, encountered a wave of globalization. Moreover, a departure from the traditional bank finance had to be made to achieve active financial markets to attract foreign investments. This book examines the changes in the accounting institutions in Japan from the perspective of globalization and financialization since the late 1980s.

A salient feature of this book is its interdisciplinary nature. First, it considers various perspectives of institutions. Given that contemporary corporate financial accounting is based on a set of principles and rules, regulatory institutions such as official accounting standards matter. Therefore, theoretical perspectives on how institutions emerge, persist, and change would be helpful in considering the dynamics of accounting regulations.

Second, at a deeper level, to address fundamental questions such as what institutions are and how they exist, this book draws on some insights from social ontology. Although readers may not be very familiar with it, in simple terms, social ontology is an interdisciplinary field in which scholars from different disciplines examine how social constructs can exist. Accounting concepts and theories are all institutions or institutionalized social constructs. Many accounting studies tend to assume that traditional accounting concepts such as income, asset, and liability are given and have not considered or asked why and how they exist. Asking such ontological questions may not be helpful in considering or solving the accounting problems at hand.[3] However, as stated above, the development of accounting is inevitably intertwined with society. Therefore, it is useful to consider the long-term macro dynamics of society in understanding changes in accounting institutions.

According to some analyses in social ontology, the underlying essence of institutions is the collective acceptance of normativity. Simply put, an institution exists because it is collectively accepted by a group of people. Although the degree of collective acceptance cannot be rigorously measured, individuals often rely on existing rules or imitate the customs

[3] There are, however, some exceptional studies that grappled with the ontological matters in accounting. For example, see Mattessich (2014) and Mouck (2004).

of others under uncertainty. In the case of standard-setting under uncertainty, selected members of standard-setting bodies are likely to refer to or follow successful attempts or outcomes in other standard-setting contexts. Therefore, the collective acceptance by others is the core normativity of institutions, and it exerts pressure on individuals to follow others. By classifying and analyzing the layers of different types of norms, this book explores what is collectively accepted in society. However, the notion of collective acceptance alone would not be sufficient to explain why certain norms are followed by much more than others.

Then, as a third interdisciplinary endeavor, this book introduces the concept of performativity. It emphasizes the linguistic aspects of discourses and provides theoretical support for the performance of linguistic expressions that dynamically mobilize individual and organizational behaviors. In other words, collective norms that are accepted by a larger number of groups are considered more performative and more likely to influence individual and organizational behaviors, thus shaping institutions.

Another uniqueness of this book is its focus on Japanese accounting regulation, which has been neither extensively studied nor widely known by people in other countries. Contrary to the rapid growth of the Japanese economy supported by leading manufacturing companies in the 1970s and 1980s, Japan's prolonged economic downturn diverted researchers' attention from Japan. As a result, the recent development of accounting regulation in Japan has not been thoroughly studied. It is often said that Japan is such a country that has been susceptible to foreign external pressure (*gaiatsu*) from outside of the country. In other words, the Japanese government used to take advantage of such *gaiatsu* to reform the economy (Katada, 2020, p. 27). In fact, Japanese accounting regulation has developed by absorbing the American and German developments of accounting theory and practice in the twentieth century.[4] Since the establishment of the Financial Accounting Standards Board (FASB) in the United States in the early 1970s, its standard-setting trend has had a strong influence on Japanese accounting regulation. However, due to the

[4] An official set of commercial laws completed in 1890 (effective in 1893, revised in 1899), which also included some accounting principles, were drafted by a German legal scholar as well as economist, Karl Friedrich Hermann Roesler. Accordingly, the commercial laws were based on the German Commercial Code of the time, and were believed to have influenced subsequent discussions on the accounting system (Sakamoto, 2011, p. 399).

proliferation of global accounting standards in the twenty-first century and the widespread recognition of the International Accounting Standards Board (IASB) as a global accounting standard setter, Japanese accounting standard setters and relevant actors have paid close attention to the standard-setting activities of the IASB. This book examines how Japanese accounting regulation has changed from the 1980s to the present through the uniquely constructed theoretical framework.

The main contribution of this book is twofold. First, from the formulated theoretical perspective and the political analysis of several accounting standard-settings in Japan, it reveals that accounting institutions in Japan have changed to perform globalization and financialization over the past few decades. During the economic downturn following the bursting of the bubble economy in the late 1980s and early 1990s, Japanese regulators made efforts to catch up with the development of global accounting standards while dealing with pressures from domestic interested parties who did not want radical changes from traditional accounting practices. In addition, since the late 1990s, the development of financial markets and the emphasis on financial transactions have shaped the changes in accounting institutions, which will be considered from the perspective of financialization. Although what globalization and financialization mean will be discussed in subsequent chapters, it is worth mentioning here that these nominalized words represent the direction of institutional changes in accounting in Japan over a couple of decades.

Second, the introduction of a social ontology perspective and its synthesis with the performativity theories suggests a fresh viewpoint to analyze long-term institutional changes. Studies on performativity in the social sciences are still limited to specific situations. Thus, the identification and application of comprehensive and generic performativity to a set of institutional changes can establish a link between macro-social dynamics and micro changes in institutions. It can also draw attention to the directions of a set of institutional changes that, in some cases, tend to be ideological or biased. In short, focusing on performativity can highlight (individual and organizational) counterperformative directions. Assuming that society can always change and never be stable, it would be useful to pay attention to any counterperformative actions when considering large-scale performativity. In other words, the identification of performative institutional changes gives us the opportunity to deliberate alternative institutional options.

This book consists of two parts. In Part I, the next chapter considers the essence of institutions. It initially reviews various strands of research on institutions and raises a challenge of the ontology of institutions. The chapter then brings some insights from social ontology to bear on the matter and teases out the significance of the collective acceptance of normativity for the existence of institutions. Finally, it provides a conceptual classification of norms and signifies the identification of collective social norms that should be observed by social scientists. Chapter 3 introduces the concept of performativity to explicate the effects of norms. It argues that some collective social norms are generically performative and shape relevant institutions. After explaining how they are identified with felicitous conditions from a linguistic perspective, Chapter 4 identifies two pervasive collective social norms in contemporary society: globalization and financialization. It also mentions the methodological approach and stance of the book and justifies the scope of the analysis in Part II.

Part II begins with a detailed analysis of the international unification of accounting standards in Japan. Chapter 5 highlights the radical financial reforms in the late 1980s as the turning point for the modern development of accounting and finance in Japan. Since then, rapid accounting changes have been made to perform globalization and financialization in Japan. Despite the overwhelming recent global convergence of accounting standards in Japan, there have been counterperformative attempts to establish a set of institutions that are expected to show Japanese identity. Chapter 6 focuses on accounting standards for financial instruments, which had a significant impact on the introduction of market value accounting in Japan. The global diffusion of market value accounting was strong, and Japanese standard setters could not resist the strong wave of financialization. Consequently, Japan has adopted most of the market value-based accounting standards. Interestingly, however, as will be discussed in the same chapter, Japanese interested parties were able to persuade the IASB members to make a small concession on a special accounting treatment for cross-held shares. This incident can be seen as a successful counterperformative action against financialization. Chapter 7 examines more recent corporate governance reforms in Japan. It particularly focuses on the traditional unique corporate practice of cross-shareholdings. From the perspective of performative globalization and financialization, the practice of corporate cross-shareholdings seems to be inappropriate. Due to the performative forces of globalization and financialization, through the introduction and modification of the corporate governance code, the reduction of cross-shareholdings was intended by regulators. In particular, the chapter interprets that globalization and financialization seem to have a strong performative effect. In other words, there have been few counterperformative actions to increase cross-shareholdings. Overall, Part II describes mostly performative forces of globalization and financialization on Japanese accounting standards but also alludes to counterperformative actions from Japan. Finally, Chapter 8 presents conclusions and tasks that this book leaves for future studies.

References

Godfrey, J. M., & Chalmers, K. (Eds.). (2007). *Globalisation of accounting standards*. Edward Elgar.

Katada, N. S. (2020). *Japan's new regional reality: Geoeconomic strategy in the Asia-Pacific*. Columbia University Press.

Mattessich, R. (2014). *Reality and accounting: Ontological explorations in the economic and social sciences*. Routledge.

Mouck, T. (2004). Institutional reality, financial reporting and the rules of the game. *Accounting, Organizations and Society, 29*(5–6), 525–541.

Nobes, C., & Parker, R. (Eds.). (2020). *Comparative international accounting 14th edition*. Pearson.

Weetman, P., Tsalavoutas, I., & Gordon, P. (Eds.). (2020). *International corporate reporting: Global and diverse 5th edition*. Routledge.

In Japanese

Sakamoto, T. (2011). *Kaikei Seido no Kaimei*. Chuo Keizai Publishing.

PART I

Conceptual Analysis of Institutions, Norms, and Performativity

CHAPTER 2

Institutions as Collectively Accepted Norms

As an innumerable number of institutions exist in many spheres of society, it is quite natural that their origin and impact have been central subjects in academic research. However, despite the development of institutional theory over the past seven decades, the definition of the term "institution" remains obscure. Institutions have attracted scholars' attention for a long time because the power of institutions[1] matters to us (MacIntyre, 2002). Although institutions do not have physical substances as material things, they always restrain or enable our actions and decision-making. In fact, social scientific studies have consistently analyzed institutions from various perspectives. This chapter provides a conceptual analysis of institutions from the perspective of social ontology, which is generally concerned about how social constructs such as institutions exist. Social ontology has become an influential field that has drawn the attention of scholars not only in philosophy but also in other disciplines. A synthesis of the social ontology perspective with institutional analysis gives rise to a unique understanding of the essence of institutions, namely, the collective acceptance of normativity.

[1] The concentration of power and its differences capture the various institutional configurations (MacIntyre, 2002, p. 34).

N. Okamoto, *Institutional Change and Performativity*,
https://doi.org/10.1007/978-3-031-53393-8_2

The first section of this chapter discusses different institutional theories and their development. It contrasts institutional theory with actor-network theory and raises an unresolved issue of ontology of institutions. To address this issue, Sect. 2.2 draws on some insight from social ontology and argues that the essence of institutions is the collective acceptance of normativity. In particular, the section relies on John Searle's theory of institutional reality. However, as Searle has not sufficiently explained what the normativity of an institution is,[2] Sect. 2.3 considers what kind of norms constitute social institutions and proposes characteristics of different types of collective norms that explain the dynamics of social institutions.

2.1 Various Perspectives of Institutions and Unresolved Ontology

Scope and Definition of Institutions

Our daily life is rife with a myriad of institutions (e.g., traffic rules, tax laws, or dress codes). Various individuals and organizations (groups of people) have created, maintained, changed, and/or abolished institutions on various occasions. Most of us generally acknowledge that institutions often restrain our behaviors. One may think of immigration laws and corporate accounting standards, both of which typically regulate our individual and organizational behaviors. Institutions in contemporary society always affect our daily decisions and behaviors both explicitly and implicitly.[3] Accordingly, one of the central tasks of social science is to understand and explain the mechanism of institutional phenomena in society and provide unequivocal answers to the following fundamental questions: what are institutions and how do they change? The aim of this section is to consider and compare a few major perspectives on institutions and identify an unresolved matter in those relevant studies of

[2] As will be discussed in later chapters, Searle called it "deontic power."

[3] There is a tacit substratum of knowledge that cannot be fully articulated as *we can know more than we can tell* (Polanyi, 2009). Polanyi suggested scientists' tacit knowledge that accounts for: (1) a valid knowledge of a problem, (2) the scientists' capacity to pursue it, guided by their sense of approaching its solution, and (3) the valid anticipation of the yet indeterminate implications of the discovery arrived at in the end (Polanyi, 2009, p. 24). Like implicit moral norms, there are types of rules that are rarely explicit but identifiable. Section 2.3 of the present book analyzes such informal rules in depth.

institutions. However, an exhaustive review that covers a whole range of applications of institutional theories is beyond the scope of this section. Rather, it examines how various perspectives have theorized institutions differently and points out a fundamental issue that remains unanswered in the literature on institutions (e.g., Hodgson, 2006; Scott, 2013).

Institutions are certainly everywhere, but they are not everything (Ocasio & Gai, 2020).[4] There are an enormous number of studies on institutions in many disciplines (Hodgson, 2006),[5] and a range of different perspectives as well.[6] Various social scientific studies of institutions have relied on a specific institutional perspective and applied it to the changes in (or the stability of) a selected institution in a specific domain.[7] Many of those studies by and large apply what is called institutional theory, and the application spans several disciplines, such as economics, management, politics, and sociology. Although institutions are a crucial object of study among social scientists, defining an institution is undeniably an arduous task.

Accordingly, there have been endless disputes over the appropriate explanation of the term "institution" (Glynn & D'aunno, 2023; Hodgson, 2006).[8] It is particularly difficult to set a boundary for institutions as there are often dichotomies between the formal and informal.

[4] Ocasio and Gai (2020) suggest researchers to specify which institutions are being studied, distinguish between institutions and cultures, and identify the relationship between institutions and organizations.

[5] According to Hodgson (2006, p. 1), the term "institution" has a long history of usage in the social sciences, dating back at least to Giambattista Vico (Italian philosopher, rhetorician, historian) in his *Scienza Nuova* of 1725.

[6] To understand different applications of various institutional perspectives, for instance, see Greenwood et al. (2017) and Morgan et al. (2010).

[7] Some studies have distinguished organizational institutional theory from other institutional theories (we can see it as the distinction between new and neo-institutionalism) (Meyer, 2017). For instance, Meyer and Rowan (1977) and Zucker (1987) are oft-cited seminal studies of organizational institutionalism. This book takes a broader view of institutional theory and does not treat the organizational institutional theory as independent. Specifically, new-institutionalism differs from neo-institutionalism. The former departs from a moral framing in terms of norms and values and draws attention to the taken-for-granted scripts, rules, and classifications as the basis of institutions (Phillips & Malhotra, 2017, p. 396). The latter neo-institutionalism's distinctive feature is its emphasis on culture as acritical dimension of institutions (Thornton et al., 2012, p. 150).

[8] The long-lasting issue concerning the definition of institution is comprehensively analyzed in Glynn and D'aunno (2023).

For instance, whether institutions should include informal norms or culture remains contentious. On the one hand, institutions can encompass complex and often coherent mixtures of cultural and organizational material (Meyer, 2017, p. 835). On the other hand, it may be useful to assume that institutions are well identified and isolated from cultural influences (including trust, family ties, individualism, and generalized morality) (Alesina & Giuliano, 2015, p. 899).[9] For the sake of simplicity, it is useful to refer to one of the most prevalent definitions. Douglass North, who received the Nobel Memorial Prize in Economic Sciences in 1993, broadly defined an "institution" as "rules of the game" or "humanly devised constraints that shape human interaction" (North, 1990, p. 3). Although this definition comprehensively includes formal and informal institutions, the meaning of the metaphorical term "game" remains obscure. Assuming that any human interaction is a game, as the status of the "game" is not clear, we cannot decide if a specific rule is within or beyond the scope of a specific game. Referring to another comprehensive definition, Hodgson (2006, p. 2) considered institutions as "the systems of established and prevalent social rules that structure social interactions."[10] However, it seems difficult to specify what kind of social rules structure social interactions.

As this brief analysis shows, there is no single, agreed-upon definition of institution. Therefore, "which definition of an institution to adopt is not an issue of right or wrong; it depends on the purpose of the analysis" (Aoki, 2001, p. 10). From this standpoint, we can categorize various institutional perspectives for different analytical purposes.

Dichotomous Viewpoints of Institutions

Among many attempts to analyze institutions, a simple dichotomous perspective is useful to show how scholars' understandings of institutions have diverged. For instance, in relation to their basic objectives, institutions can enable and constrain individual and organizational behaviors

[9] Alesina and Giuliano (2015) argue that culture and institutions interact and evolve in a complementary manner, with mutual feedback effects.

[10] Following this definition, some social structures may not be codified in discourse; demographic structures in animal species or human societies before any understanding of demography are not part of institutions (Hodgson, 2006, p. 3).

(Hodgson, 2006, p. 2). While institutions enable individual choices and actions, they simultaneously impose constraints and sanctions on both.

This two-dimensional analysis provides us with different pictures of institutions. If we presume that institutions give enabling reasons for an actor's understanding of reality and behavior, it facilitates and constitutes individual actions. On the contrary, if we emphasize the constraints imposed by institutions, they restrain or restrict individual actions driven by one's desire. In the absence of such regulative institutions, conflicts and negotiations among different individuals and groups are likely to occur everywhere. To avoid these adversarial or inefficient outcomes, explicit institutions such as traffic rules and corporate laws exist. Although one of the most widely read books on institutions applies a tripartite view (regulative, normative, and cultural-cognitive) to classify different types of institutions (Scott, 2013),[11] the present book persists with the assumptions presented in the above dichotomous viewpoints,[12] through which different understandings of institutions can stand out.[13]

A constitutive view of institutions has an affinity with sociological perspectives. It originated from Weber's study of bureaucracy and was influenced by the intellectual tradition of phenomenological sociology (Kohno, 2002, p. 35).[14] Notably, Berger and Luckmann's (1967) *The Construction of Social Reality* has been a landmark in the research stream.[15] They considered institutions the acceptance of habitualized behaviors by members of society: "Institutionalization occurs whenever

[11] Phillips and Malhotra (2017, p. 411) doubted the usefulness of this tripartite mechanism by arguing that there is no clear way to differentiate actors' behaviors between regulative and normative institutions.

[12] This classification is indebted to a thoughtful analysis by Kohno (2002) that classified institutional viewpoints into sociological and economic ones.

[13] In her organizational institutional analysis, Zucker (1987, p. 444) similarly applied dichotomous viewpoints of institutions. They are (a) a rule-like, social fact quality of an organized pattern of action (exterior) and (b) an embedding in formal structures, such as formal aspects of organizations, that are not tied to particular actors or situations (nonpersonal/objective).

[14] Glynn and D'aunno (2023) also assure that sociology is the founding discipline of institutional theory.

[15] It is difficult to overstate the importance of this work because it carefully specified the mechanisms driving institutionalism; such specification is core to any institutional theory (Glynn & D'aunno, 2023, p. 305). It is said that Berger and Luckmann's (1967) analyses were influenced by the founder of phenomenological sociology, Alfred Schutz (Overgaard & Zahavi, 2009).

there is a reciprocal typification of habitualized actions by types of actors. Put differently, any such typification is an institution. What must be stressed is the reciprocity of institutional typification and the typicality of not only the actions but also the actors in institutions" (Berger & Luckmann, 1967, p. 72). In a nutshell, taking a constitutive view of institutions enables us to understand that individuals recognize and accept institutions that comprise certain practices of patterned and habituated behaviors.

In contrast, a regulative view of institutions takes constraints seriously and is often used in the fields of transaction cost economics and game theory. It conceives of institutions as the consequences of games among individual actors under given constraints. For example, Aoki (2001, p. 10) characterized institutions as a "self-sustaining system of shared beliefs about a salient way in which the game is repeatedly played." From the viewpoint of game theory, the content of shared beliefs is a summary representation (compressed information) of an equilibrium of the game (out of the many that are theoretically possible) (Aoki, 2001, p. 10). This viewpoint considers institutions' stable conditions following interactions among individual actors. One advantage of the regulative view of institutions is that it allows the possibility of endogenously considering the origin and effectiveness of a specific institution (Aoki, 2001, p. 14). However, there is a shortcoming in the approach: It cannot explain why a specific institution survives and remains among various plausible alternatives. Addressing such a question cannot help but assume the existence of multiple equilibria.

The general characteristics of these dichotomous views of institutions are summarized in Table 2.1. On the one hand, a constitutive view of institutions assumes the existence of institutions prior to individual belief and preference. On the other hand, a regulative view of institutions emphasizes the existence of an "individual." An individual has a belief or preference that is a priori, and institutions exist in tandem with the actions of independent individual actors and exert influences on their behaviors (Kohno, 2002, p. 14). One advantage of the regulative view of institutions is its analytical viewpoint on the origin of and changes in institutions. It enables us to analyze institutions and their functions comparatively and historically by positing them as the result of human interaction. For example, based on the regulative view of institutions, it is possible to understand that people of old created traffic rules for car drivers and pedestrians to avoid crashes and achieve one's purpose (such as getting to the destination efficiently). However, to repeat, this view

Table 2.1 Two views on institutions

	A constitutive view of institutions	*A regulative view of institutions*
Ontological postulate	Institutions	Individuals
Advantages	Explains practices and rituals that cannot be analyzed in terms of utility and functions	Explains the origin and changes in institutions by considering equilibria
Disadvantages	Cannot explain why and how some institutions originated and created	Cannot explain how and why a specific institution survives and remains among other alternatives

cannot fully explain how and why a specific institution survives among multiple alternatives. More specifically, under the regulative view of institutions, it would be challenging to provide an obvious reason as to why some countries adopt the traffic rules of driving on the left side of the road while other countries do the opposite.

By contrast, a constitutive view of institutions considers inefficient institutions to be habitualized patterned behavior. However, it cannot sufficiently explain why a specific institution exists. It can probably argue that a specific institution exists because it is regularized, ritualized, or embedded. This being the case, a regulative view of institutions seems to be useful to pay particular attention to the changes in institutions whereas a constitutive view of institutions seems helpful to explain their continuity and persistence (Kohno, 2002, p. 17).

To reiterate, which view is more suitable depends on the researcher's interest in institutions (Aoki, 2001). In other words, it is not yet clear how to integrate these two divergent views to understand the mechanism of institutions. The difference between these dualistic views of institutions may be profound because it seems to be attributed to the differences in the intellectual tradition and assumptions of economics and sociology. But these disciplines have different assumptions of actors in relation to institutions: *homo economicus*[16] and *homo sociologicus*[17] (Mantzavinos, 2001, 2021).[18] However, to consistently understand the dynamism of institutions, a more overarching theoretical perspective that integrates divergent perspectives and provides fresh, fruitful insight into institutions is necessary. The next two subsections consider some attempts to integrate different institutional viewpoints to establish an overarching institutional viewpoint.

Institutions and Shared Mental Models

To summarize the analysis of various institutional theories in the previous subsections, a regulative (or relatively economic) view of institutions places emphasis on the individual choices and actions that are restricted by various constraints. A constitutive (or relatively sociological) view of institutions assumes that institutions themselves are given and that they affect individual behaviors. As it is intuitively difficult to deny the fact that we recognize many institutions in our daily life, the logic that institutions precede individual behaviors sounds plausible. However, given the chasm between these two divergent viewpoints of institutions, whether we should emphasize individual human actors and see institutions as secondary social constructs or acknowledge that institutions come first and mobilize individual behaviors ultimately depends on one's value judgment. Nevertheless, there have been some attempts to bridge the gap between such different viewpoints.

A notable attempt by Denzau and North (1994) introduced the shared mental model, which is defined as the internal representations that individual cognitive systems create to interpret the environment (Denzau & North, 1994, p. 4). Based on this model, institutions are the external (to the mind) mechanisms that individuals create to structure and order the

[16] According to the Oxford Dictionary of Philosophy (2nd edition), *homo (o)economicus* is defined as economic man, or the rational agent depicted in economic models. Such an agent has consistent and stable preferences. The agent is intentional, entirely forward-looking, and pursues only his/her own self-interest (Mantzavinos, 2001, p. 55).

[17] *Homo sociologicus* is pushed from behind by quasi-internal forces (Elster, 1989, p. 99) and follows norms or rules blindly (Mantzavinos, 2001, p. 55).

[18] According to Elster (1989), Ott and Ivens (2009, p. 580) stated the distinction between *homo economicus* and *homo sociologicus*: While the behavior of the former is guided by instrumental rationality to attain the maximization of the return, the behavior of the latter is dictated by socially accepted conventions (norms).

environment (Denzau & North, 1994, p. 4). As the external world is too complex for a single individual to learn how it works, the individual mental model derives from the experiences of each individual specific to the local, socio-cultural, and linguistic environment (Denzau & North, 1994, p. 14). The creation of mental models is possible because an individual interacts with a distinct individual through the communication channel of language and encodes/decodes ideas in each shared mental model environment (Denzau & North, 1994, p. 20).

Therefore, under the condition of uncertainty, individuals construct and share their mental models to make sense of the world around them and specifically institutions that order interpersonal relationships. The connection between mental models and institutions[19] crucially depends on the product and process of representational redescription (Denzau & North, 1994). Denzau and North (1994) did not clearly explain representational redescriptions in detail that would play a significant role in understanding the mechanism of shared mental models. Rather, they stated that understanding representational redescriptions would require the knowledge of how the progression in human cognition unfolds (Denzau & North, 1994, p. 21).[20] The redescriptions may be expressions of specific categorizations or conceptualizations, but whose categorizations or conceptualizations and how they can be selected are still ambiguous.[21] Moreover, how representational redescriptions differ from theories or discourses is also a matter of concern.

Mantzavinos (2001) constructed a simple systematic account of institutions by relying on the theory of shared mental models. His account starts with a situation in which an individual faces a new problem. The

[19] In addition to institutions, Denzau and North (1994) used the term "ideologies," which are shared frameworks of mental models of groups of individuals who provide an interpretation of the environment and a prescription of how that environment should be structured (Denzau & North, 1994, p. 4). This study assumes that we can comprehensively include such ideologies in the notion of institutions in most cases.

[20] From a thorough reading of Denzau and North (1994), it can be inferred that representational redescriptions include at least punctuated equilibrium dynamic that typically denotes a theory or model that captures evolutionary changes in individual behaviors.

[21] They only state that at the individual level, the representational redescription is a reorganization of the categories and concepts, and is distinct from the parameter update that takes place in the "normal learning" phase. Once we gain a useful set of categories and concepts, the normal learning period is long relative to the oft-sudden shifts in viewpoint that accompany representational redescriptions (Denzau & North, 1994, p. 14).

individual utilizes readymade solutions from the environment instead of creating new alternatives *ex nihilo* each time (Mantzavinos, 2001, p. 68). The readymade solution is generally built into one's cognitive system through communication. Acts of communication lead to shared rules for individuals and thus give rise to correspondence to shared mental models. Mantzavinos (2001) proposed a coherent view through which individuals interact with others, share mental models, and bring about evolutionary institutional change. For instance, "culture" is a perturbing notion for both constitutive and regulative views of institutions, as it typically constitutes cultural constructs while it also restrains individual behaviors in following cultural practices that appear inefficient or dysfunctional in some cases. These unique individual and organizational behaviors in conformity with cultures can be explained via our learning process[22] and shared mental models of individuals. Therefore, "cultural heritage provides a means of reducing the divergence in the mental models that people in a society have and also constitutes a means for the intergenerational transfer of unifying perceptions" (Denzau & North, 1994, p. 15). From this perspective, beliefs and values are acquired by the members of a society in a process of cultural evolution (transmission of knowledge) (Mantzavinos, 2001, p. 72). It is a continuous "collective learning" to solve various problems. Overall, the viewpoint of institutions proposed by Mantzavinos (2001) focuses on individual actors who share cognitive mental models that affect their decision-making.

Similarly, Petracca and Gallagher (2020) suggested cognitive institutionalism that is also based on the theory of shared mental models. From their perspective, a cognitive institution is an institution that operates as a problem-solving entity when properly coupled with cognitive characteristics (socially extended mind/cognition) (Petracca & Gallagher, 2020, p. 765). The socially extended mind/cognition comprises cognitive processes that are enabled or constituted by practices involving social institutions and are characterized by varying degrees of functional integration and task dependency (Petracca & Gallagher, 2020, p. 762). This

[22] Under conditions of uncertainty, individuals' interpretation of their environment will reflect their learning (Denzau & North, 1994, p. 3). Individuals with different learning experiences (cultural or environmental) will have different theories (or models or ideologies) to interpret their environment (Denzau & North, 1994, p. 4). According to Denzau and North (1994), there are distinct levels of learning. The first level is to develop a structure with which to make sense of the varied signals received. The second is to acquire and develop ideas regarding the details and applicability of the existing knowledge.

idea originates from an externalist approach to institutions that assumes they are legitimate candidates for mind extension,[23] which is closely interconnected with one's cognition (Petracca & Gallagher, 2020, p. 753).

To summarize, Denzau and North's (1994) theory of shared mental models and its development can explain both interactions between individuals and the acquisition of institutional knowledge by sharing each mental model. However, the manner in which representational redescriptions enable sharing knowledge through mental models remains unclear. It is still ambiguous as to what kind of shared knowledge can be represented and considered an institution. Such representations may be equivalent to widely agreed common sense or social norms. Although Mantzavinos (2001, pp. 73–75) explained that the shared mental model of individuals allows them to share a common problem and that a shared collective solution with both formal and informal institutions[24] can solve the problem efficiently, the relationship between mental models and formal/informal institutions is not well understood. In other words, while Mantzavinos (2001, p. 73) argues that two different types of knowledge (theoretical and practical) are transmitted through formal or natural languages and imitation, the mechanism of the transmission and the distinction between knowledge and institution are still vague.

Institutions Are Both Regulative and Normative

From a different angle, Guala (2016) offered a coherent picture of institutions (fundamental architecture of modern societies) by integrating different viewpoints in different disciplines. His analysis is based on the notion of "token institution," which denotes social institutions situated in space and time, and there are more general and comprehensive higher-level type of institutions (Guala, 2016, p. xx). He emphasized the functions of those token institutions because they can abstract away from innumerable ways in which the same goal may be achieved in different

[23] Mind extension is a hypothesis about the nature of cognition introduced by Clark and Chalmers (1998) according to which cognitive processes do not necessarily take place in the head/brain but can also be realized through external resources. A high degree of functional integration and a low degree of task dependency characterize it (Petracca & Gallagher, 2020, p. 765).

[24] In addition to formal institutions, Mantzavinos (2001) admits three types of informal institutions (conventions, moral rules, and social norms).

contexts (Guala, 2016, p. xxii). By this, Guala (2016) integrated two divergent perspectives of institutions; one can cognitively recognize token institutions as regulative rules that are also regarded as the equilibria of strategic games among individuals.

Guala (2016, p. 73) argued that institutions involve the creation and implementation of rules that make us better-off, compared to alternative outcomes. Notably, he stated that most rules are, to some extent, regulative, and advocated the "normativity" of institutions on actors. Norms provide reasons for acting that are independent of some desires (Guala, 2016, p. 73). His strategy lies in the conception of plural "desires." Such desires mainly comprise self-interest, but not all of them do. One individual can have other conflicting desires, and another may have a desire to abide by a rule. Accordingly, Guala's stance is clear: Instead of asking what (ambiguous) normativity is, what it does or how it functions is more important (Guala, 2016, p. 78). However, the problem of multiple desires remains; how desire-independent actions among others are prioritized is not clear in many cases. Why do some people follow cultural rules that are not clearly beneficial or meaningful? It may be the result of their self-realization, or it may be for the sake of their fellows. What matters is that different individuals have different combinations of multiple desires. Thus, to single out one's desire for one specific action is not easy; it would not be so productive to look only at one's action and claim that it was triggered by the strongest desire. To address this issue, Guala (2016) used the notions of mind-reading, interactions, and reflection (reflexivity). Through these processes, which are equivalent to the notion of "communication" that Mantzavinos (2001) proposed, desire-independent actions can take over desire-dependent ones.

Despite his consistent regulative viewpoint of institutions and emphasis on individual actions, Guala (2016, p. 77) himself admitted that his thesis remains neutral on the nature of normativity or where it comes from. Thus, it is necessary to consider in detail what constitutes normativity and how it exists.

A Comparison of Institutional Theory and Actor-Network Theory

A review of some attempts to integrate different perspectives of institutions reveals that a simple question concerning institutions remains unanswered: How do institutions (or their normativity) exist? Without considering the ontological status of components of institutions, such as the representative redescription or shared knowledge in shared mental models (Denzau & North, 1994; Mantzavinos, 2001) and the normativity of regulative institutions (token institutions) (Guala, 2016), we will not have a clear picture of institutions. In short, ontology matters to institutional theory.

Before considering the ontological status of institutions, it is useful to unpack the meaning of ontology. Cambridge Dictionary (https://dictionary.cambridge.org) defines ontology as "the part of philosophy that studies what it means to exist." As discussed, previous studies have investigated the classifications of institutions but have not thoroughly grappled with their ontological status. In the context of natural science, to present an example of experiments in a laboratory, scientists generally know what they are studying or have at least a basic idea of the observable components that construct the research object. It is the unity of scientific experimentation that provides an accepted general ontology of experiments and that (natural) scientists suppose both possible and desirable (Soldatova & King, 2006). Such ontological status would promote the sharing of results within and between subjects, reducing both the duplication and loss of knowledge (Soldatova & King, 2006, p. 803). Assuming that social scientific research aims to be scientific (Bartholomew, 2006), it is not entirely out of line to consider the ontological characteristics of institutions as research objects, rather than regarding them as given social constructs.

Fundamentally, institutions have no physical, material substance. They are linguistic expressions that exist as concepts. But they can be both formal and informal.[25] We can often verbalize or even name informal implicit rules as etiquette or moral rules. However, we also acknowledge that institutions are something more than linguistic representations. In this regard, the problem of ontology among institutional theorists remains undecided (Smith, 2001, p. 167),[26] and many studies rely on

[25] Therefore, I do not consider institutions that can never be linguistically represented (either directly or indirectly). In that sense, my stance is sympathetic to the argument that truth emerges out of social and discursive practices and in turn constitutes the reality of things by endowing it with salience and significance (Barnett, 2017, p. 148). It is a constructive view of truth in which language plays a central role in constituting social realities (Barnett, 2017, p. 149).

[26] Smith (2001, p. 166) argued that institutions can exist only in people's activities and yet cannot be reduced to them.

institutional theories as though institutions were objects of scientific investigation (Willmott, 2015, p. 109).[27] As such, there is a dilemma in which researchers are compelled to conceptualize in the cognitive spaces of social science, a social reality whose metaphysics and ontology cannot be grasped within these cognitive spaces (a Kantian dilemma, if one wishes) (Spencer, 1982, p. 139).

If we take a broad look at the recent development of social scientific studies, there is an appreciated theoretical perspective whose ontological assumption of institutions differs starkly from a number of other institutional theories. It does not have a particular focus on institutions, nor does it prioritize human actors. This is the actor-network theory (ANT) developed by Bruno Latour and Michel Callon.[28] From an ontological viewpoint, Modell et al. (2017) undertook a comparative study between institutional theory and ANT. Although Modell et al. (2017) limited their focus to institutional theory based on new (or neo-) -institutional sociology,[29] their analysis is still insightful here. Table 2.2 summarizes and contrasts the key ontological assumptions of both theories (Modell et al., 2017).

One of the unique characteristics of ANT is its focus on material objects in the network of human and non-human actors[30] in a specific context. From the perspective of ANT, both human and non-human entities (actants) interact continuously, and through this interaction, reality emerges in a relational and constructed manner (Modell et al., 2017).

[27] Willmott (2015, p. 109) criticized that institutional theory does not consider the domination, oppression, and resistance vis-à-vis power during the institutionalization process.

[28] Bruno Latour, Michelle Callon, and John Law (e.g., Callon, 1986; Latour, 1987, 2005) developed ANT. It has been quite influential within and beyond social scientific research over the last couple of decades (Sismondo, 2010).

[29] It emphasizes the influence of broader social structures, but takes a more cultural view of institutions, highlighting their role in providing models or scripts for action (Powell & Bromley, 2015, p. 764).

[30] What non-human actors refer to is polemical. Although it is an umbrella term that encompasses a wide range of things, Sayes (2014, p. 136) tried to pin down the scope of non-human: The term is used to denote entities as diverse as animals (such as scallops—Callon, 1984), natural phenomena (such as reefs—Law, 1987), tools and technical artifacts (such as mass spectrometers—Latour & Woolgar, 1979), material structures (such as sewerage networks—Latour & Hermant, 2006), transportation devices (such as planes—Law & Callon, 1992), texts (such as scientific accounts—Callon et al., 1986), and economic goods (such as commodities—Callon, 1999).

Table 2.2 Comparison of the key ontological assumptions of institutional theory and ANT

	Institutional theory	*Actor-network theory*
Over-riding conception of reality	The real is socially constructed, but the realist dimension also recognized as social structures become objectified over time (depth ontology)	While the real emerges in a relational and constructed manner, objects are fully real at any given moment, as in naïve realism. An actor does not exist outside its relations to others. All actors are on the same level (flat ontology)
Conception of social structures (institutions)	Structures exist as socially real entities that condition, but are ontologically distinct from, human agency	Structures are not immutable, pre-existing entities that condition agency. They can emerge and stabilize temporarily only at the end of a translation process
Conception of agency	Human agency is institutionally embedded and conditioned by historically contingent structures. More attention is paid to collective agency	Agency is not embedded. Human and non-human entities (actants) continuously interact and both have the capacity to exercise agency
Conception of change and stability	Change is a relatively exceptional and episodic state and is always conditioned by extant institutions	Change is ubiquitous and intertwined with the ongoing transformation of actor-networks. Stability is seen as a temporary and fragile state

Note This is based on Table 1 in Modell et al. (2017)

In this regard, ANT takes the strategy of flat ontology, which assumes that an actor does not exist outside of its relations to others. Accordingly, although the ontology of structures and actors does not matter under ANT, its research findings tend to be ad hoc, which makes the analysis indeterminate or difficult to generalize. The primary focus of ANT is on empirical work and it insists on seeing each event as the outcome of a convergence of multiple interacting influences including those of material objects, all to be taken equally seriously by the investigator (Elder-Vass, 2015, p. 101).

In contrast, the ontological stance of institutional theory is far from the flat ontology that ANT espouses.[31] Within the scope of Modell et al. (2017), the ontology that underpins institutional theory has combined a social constructivist view with a realist dimension. The situation represents a form of depth ontology according to which social realities are hierarchically structured and partly independent of individual actors (Modell et al., 2017, p. 64).

More specifically, after the 1980s, there was a transition in the institutional theories' ontological position that placed greater emphasis on the agency implicated in affecting structural change while simultaneously accepting the significant influence of pre-existing structures on such changes (Modell et al., 2017, p. 64). Individual actors' human agency is not a free-floating and relatively unconstrained phenomenon; however, most institutional theorists now subscribe to a conception of agency as institutionally embedded and often implicated in a complex interplay with historically contingent structures (Modell et al., 2017, p. 64). With regard to agencies embedded in structures, different ontological assumptions underpin the distinct strands of research on institutions. For example, some institutional studies have maintained much of the structuralist emphasis, which characterized the early advances in institutional theory, whereas others have followed a range of approaches that are united by a more actor-centric ontology (Modell et al., 2017, p. 64). Given this difference, important questions often come down to "What are structures?" and "How can institutionally embedded actors exist?," both of which are ultimately ontological matters. When one thinks through the institution, the question of ontology is unavoidable.

In conclusion, this section brought the significance of the ontological status of institutions to light. To understand the consistent dynamism of institutions, the ontology of institutions would be a fundamental Achilles' heel. The ontological status of social structures, shared mental models (knowledge), cognitive institutions, and normativity, all of which constitute a significant part of institutions, have not yet been well researched.

[31] Nevertheless, if ANT relies on bracketing terms such as assemblage (Latour, 2005) and socio-technical (Callon, 2007) and market *agencements* (Çalışkan & Callon, 2010; Callon, 2016), its analytical power would be undermined by their unclear boundaries of translation (Beunza & Ferraro, 2019, p. 518).

Apart from the field of institutional theory, there is an emerging interdisciplinary area of social ontology in which the construction of social institutions has been extensively discussed. John Searle's seminal work on institutional reality (Searle, 1995) was groundbreaking and has been quite influential in the field. One of his theses is that social institutions are not ontologically objective but epistemologically objective (i.e., ontologically subjective). To examine this difference more closely, the next section starts by considering the essences of Searle's institutional reality and social ontology.

2.2 Institutional Reality and Social Ontology

Searlean Framework of Institutional Reality

John Searle's theory of institutional reality (Searle, 1995) shed new light on how we conceive institutions, as it highlighted the ontological foundations of institutions. Searle initially distinguished institutional facts from brute facts. Institutional facts are so called because they require a human institution for their existence (Searle, 1995, p. 2). For instance, sentences such as "There are some trees over there" and "I am holding some round-shaped metals" are types of brute facts. Examples of institutional facts include "Those trees are fir trees and are used as Christmas trees" and "I am grabbing some coins to donate." These statements do not make sense without the institutions of Christmas or the monetary/currency system. According to the early Searlean account, institutional facts require three elements for their existence: the assignment of functions, collective intentionality, and constitutive rules (Searle, 1995, p. 13).

First, we assign functions to many kinds of objects and events. Such functions are never intrinsic to the physics of any phenomenon, but are externally assigned by conscious observers and users (Searle, 1995, p. 14). For example, we assign the function of transportation to a river or the function of timber to natural trees. Referring to the above-mentioned examples, as celebrating Christmas in December is collectively accepted in many countries, people give the fir tree the function of a Christmas tree as the symbol of the event. Although we grab coins less frequently nowadays given the wide-ranging use of debit and credit cards, the governments of many countries still grant specific types of round-shaped metals the function of money as coins via laws. Such a function is never intrinsic to the physics of any phenomenon, but is assigned from outside by conscious observers and users (Searle, 1995, p. 14).

Second, we have the capacity for collective intentionality that is not the aggregation of individuals' intention. This enables us to assign functions to objects and events for the creation and maintenance of institutional facts. Collective intentionality means that we engage in cooperative behavior and share intentional states such as beliefs, desires, and intentions (Searle, 1995, p. 23).[32] A crucial element in collective intentionality is a sense of doing something together, and the individual intentionality that each person has is derived from the collective intentionality that they share. Playing basketball as a team is a simple example. As a team member, a specific player dribbles, passes, and shoots in a game, but the player's movements generally depend on the team's strategy to win the game. According to Searle, collective intentionality cannot be reduced to individual intentionality.[33]

Third, constitutive rules in the form of "X counts as Y in C" mean that the Y-term must assign some new status function that the entities named by the X-term do not have, and this new status function must be such that human agreement, acceptance, and collective intentionality are necessary and sufficient for its creation in context C. In addition to these three elements, we must consider the factors that work in the background when we unconsciously follow rules. Intentional states function only given the set of background capacities[34] that do not themselves consist in intentional phenomena (Searle, 1995, p. 129).

According to Searle (1995), these three conditions are necessary for ontologically subjective social constructs to be epistemologically objective institutional facts. Although Searle (1995) did not clearly mention

[32] There are various kinds of "collective" concepts in this field: collective intentionality, acceptance, commitment, goals, and rationality. Strictly speaking, these collective concepts are different from the perspectives of social ontologists. However, how their essential collectivity mobilizes institutional reality is a central concern of this book, and the remaining part of this book relies on "collective acceptance."

[33] Intentionality does not imply a special connection with intentions in the ordinary sense; rather, it is a general notion that has to do with the directedness of the mind (Searle, 2005, p. 6).

[34] For instance, small infants neither have collective intentionality nor recognize rules and others' belief or desires in the absence of mature cognitive capacities. Whereas Searle's concept of background seems prepared to supplement his theoretical framework, there would be the danger of overreliance on the concept to explain various social phenomena.

how we can identify collective intentionality, his conception at least distinguishes it from individual intentionality or its simple aggregation.[35] Nevertheless, we can assume that an individual has both individual and collective intentionality at the same time and that there are interactions between both types of intentionality in one's mind in the decision-making process.

This theorization of institutional reality gained wide recognition, but it also provoked some critical analyses.[36] Two types of critics deserve to be mentioning here. Raimo Tuomela, a leading scholar in social ontology, pointed out several insufficiencies in the theoretical framework (Tuomela, 2002b, p. 293). According to Tuomela, first, Searle's theory is too narrow because it leaves out a central class of social institutions. This class is based on expectation-based social norms or, "proper social norms" (Tuomela, 1995). In particular, Tuomela pointed out that Searle relied heavily on constitutive rules and missed conventions that more or less tightly correspond to proper social norms (Tuomela, 2002b, p. 295). Second, Searle's emphasis on both status functions and collective intentionality seems to be too demanding. While the emphasis may work well for some cases (e.g., money), it neither applies to other institutional cases where a new "conceptual and social status" is involved, nor is it applicable to institutional cases that only involve norm-governed social practices (Tuomela, 2002b).[37]

In sum, Tuomela's criticism boils down to the claim that Searle's argument does not include the normativity that institutions entail. After these criticisms, Searle shifted the core of his theoretical framework to the collective acceptance of status functions in more recent works.

[35] Thus, Searlean framework is classified as a non-reductive approach because collective intentionality cannot be reduced to each individual intentionality.

[36] For instance, as of August 2023, Searle (2005) is the most cited article in the *Journal of Institutional Economics* which is a multi-disciplinary journal that is of interest to all academics working on the analysis of institutions.

[37] In addition, Tuomela (2002b, p. 296) criticized Searle's concentration on "we-intentions" that bolster the concept of collective intentionality by arguing that there are different kinds of we-intentions ranging from what is called weak we-intentions to strong agreement-based we-intentions (2002a, p. 260).

Collective Acceptance and Deontic Powers

In Searle's later works, the notions of status function and collective acceptance play a significant role by serving as a basis for institutional reality. What connects these two notions is the deontic power that carries rights, duties, obligations, requirements, permissions, authorizations, entitlements, and so on (Searle, 2010, p. 9). What is the essence of these deontic powers? Searle explains it in relation to institutional contexts in the following way:

> There is no single purpose served by all human institutions, and indeed, institutional reality is almost as various as human reality itself. But, I have argued, there is a common element that runs through all (or nearly all) institutions, and that is that they are enabling structures that increase human power in many different ways. Think what life would be like if we did not have money, schools, property rights, and above all, language. Some social theorists have seen institutional facts as essentially constraining. That is a very big mistake. There is indeed an element of constraint in social institutions. For example, you cannot be president unless you get elected, you cannot spend money you do not have, and in baseball, you cannot have four strikes. But the very institutions of money and baseball increase our powers. (Searle, 2010, pp. 105–106)

Admitting that some rules are constraints-based, Searle still places an emphasis on the enabling or constitutive aspects of institutional reality. In short, the institutions of language (such as English and Japanese) or baseball games that consist of a myriad of rules can exist, as their status (of language or sport) is collectively accepted by a group of individuals (English/Japanese speakers and baseball players/fans). When an individual is involved in a specific institution, the individual should know or follow many rules. In other words, an individual can choose not to engage with a specific institution. For instance, some people are barely interested in baseball and therefore do not know any of its rules.

Therefore, in addition to highlighting constitutive aspects of institutions, Searle illustrated the situation in which participants of a specific institution are constrained by various rules. For instance, a baseball player should know not only the basic three-strike rule, but also many other detailed rules such as the two-strike bunt or tugging up rules. Moreover, to constitute a fair game of baseball, abusing each other and aggression toward opponents during a game is not allowed because it is inappropriate and goes against sportsmanship. It is taken for granted but is not conceptually clear why individuals who participate in a specific institution have to follow such belief-based rules. To take a more ordinary example, suppose you would like to have dinner with your partner at a popular restaurant on a cold winter day. If there is a long queue in front of the restaurant, you (or your partner) would not cut the queue. You would probably stay at the end of the queue because of the deontic power of the social rules that holds us together. If you cut to get to the front of the queue, somebody might try to tell you not to do so. If you do not listen, there may be a quarrel. However, many people do not cut the queue not for fear of retaliation. If the only people in line were small children, would we cut in? No, we would not.

Then, we finally encounter a crucial question: Why do we stand at the end of the queue outside of a restaurant on a cold winter evening? Of course, you may really want to eat something specific at the restaurant. Simultaneously, you may sincerely hope to get inside of the warm restaurant as soon as possible. That is your desire. Thus, these questions are interconnected with reasons that are independent of human desire, which arise from the declaration of status functions (Searle, 2018, p. 308). Then, why do we give status functions to follow (or prioritize) desire-independent reasons in many cases? Answering this question helps us to consider the normativity of deontic powers.

Desire-Independent Reasons and the Significance of Norms

While Searle emphasized the constitutive aspect of institutional reality, his recent reliance on deontic powers does in itself not sufficiently explain why individuals follow rules in a specific institutional context. Understanding one's decision process requires considering human behaviors and rationality, which involves the analysis of one's reasoning (Searle, 2014, pp. 19–20). The following Searlean statement is not apparently circular, as he emphasizes desire-independent reasons that exist in the creation and maintenance of institutional reality: "Institutional facts are the glue that holds human civilization together because they provide us with reasons for action that are independent of our inclination" (Searle, 2014, p. 20).

Simultaneously, it raises crucial questions: "What is the normativity of individuals to follow desire-independent reasons?" and "Where does it come from?" To answer these questions, we need to tackle a crucial question: "What are norms?" It is a profound question that many scholars have grappled with for a long time.[38] The concept of social norms is one of the most fundamental notions of social ontology (Detel, 2008, p. 469). According to Hacking (1990, p. 3), the notion of "normality"[39] is in large part a modern artifact of the exponential growth of mathematics as a cultural discourse and a way of understanding the world (Jenkins, 2014, p. 199). Even though norms can be assumed to be social constructs, our central concern regarding norms is why individuals follow them for their desire-independent reasons.

The important shift from desire-dependent reason to desire-independent reason can be restated as the process of how "the way things are done" becomes "the way things should be done" (Jenkins, 2014, p. 162), the latter of which corresponds to the constitutive existence of normativity. This may be the case partly because strong sanctions are associated with the deviance from institutionalized practice. However, there are many institutions that do not accompany direct explicit sanctions.[40] To consider further what norms (and their normativity) are, various approaches are possible (Brennan et al., 2013). Among them, behavioral approaches such as psychological investigation are typical and have a long history (e.g., Bicchieri, 2005, 2016). However, the main concern of this book lies in the ontological and conceptual underpinnings of norms and institutions. Thus, the next section considers how different types of norms become collective and interact with each other.

[38] As Bicchieri (2016, pp. 204–206) stated, changing social norms is particularly complex because they are embedded in a thick web of beliefs, values, and other norms.

[39] Although normativity may differ from normality, normativity incorporates something as normal as a norm always has content.

[40] If you do not want to follow specific rules in a community, you can leave it. Alternatively, individuals can choose Hirschman's (1970) exit strategy. Nevertheless, there are many situations in which individuals follow reasons independent of desire, such as the one that moral principle dictates.

2.3 Analysis of Collective Norms

Classification of Different Types of Norms

As is often the case with institutions, norms are often classified differently.[41] There is a common controversial dichotomy between formal and informal norms. Although we often pay attention to explicit formal norms (institutions) in our daily life, we have to admit crucial influences of informal norms that allow formal institutions to operate efficiently (Jütting et al., 2007). Informal norms are frequently self-enforcing through mechanisms of obligation, which leads individuals to avoid unnecessary conflicts and arguments.[42]

However, the distinction between formal and informal norms is not a simple matter and should be considered from different angles. First, there is a great deal of overlap between formal and informal norms (Brennan et al., 2013, p. 40). As norms dynamically change as the external situation changes, there is always some gray area around the boundary between formal and informal norms. Second, writing down a norm may alter its character in some ways (Brennan et al., 2013, p. 41), as it makes informal norms formal. This also characterizes the interpretative aspects of informal norms; as informal norms are often tacit and unfathomable, different people interpret them differently.

Christina Bicchieri synthesized the behavioral aspects of human beings with her conceptual analyses of norms (Bicchieri, 2005, 2016) and proposed a unique classification of norms that is not just a simple formal and informal dichotomy: descriptive and injunctive norms. A descriptive norm is a pattern of behavior such that individuals prefer to conform to it on the condition that they believe that most people in their reference network conform to it (Bicchieri, 2016, p. 19). In contrast, an injunctive norm, which constitutes most of the social norms, is what we collectively believe ought to be done or what is socially approved or disapproved of (Bicchieri, 2016, pp. 30–31).

[41] For instance, Ott and Ivens (2009) proposed seven different uses of the concept of norm in various disciplines (in sociology, political science, anthropology, psychology, economics, legal theory, and marketing).

[42] That is because following such informal norms is in the best interests of individuals who may find themselves in situations where everyone is better-off through cooperation (Jütting et al., 2007, p. 31).

However, Bicchieri's classification still includes some ambiguity. Based on the criterion of social expectation, Bicchieri asserted that collective shared moral or religious codes differ from both descriptive and social (injunctive) norms, as those codes of conduct are frequently independent of what one observes others doing (Bicchieri, 2016, p. 59). While I admit that there are some people who sincerely believe in religious codes or moral norms such as justice irrespective of what others do, it is likely that some people more or less follow them because of social expectations or peer pressure from others. For instance, it is evident that the frequency of worshipping Gods such as Buddha is decreasing among young and middle-aged people in Japan (Kobayashi, 2019). Kobayashi (2019) concluded that this is because these people have become more realistic and less spiritual, and do not see religious events or organizations as a community where they can get to know each other and make friends. This result implies that a religious code can be less binding with fewer expectations and less pressure from others. There is also ample evidence that people nowadays have become less religious (Inglehart, 2020).[43] What matters here is whenever we consider the essence of norms, we cannot ignore sociality or what others do. Although Bicchieri (2016) used the notion of one's preference to separate collective customs and shared moral rules from norms (including descriptive and injunctive norms), it is doubtful if the former is independent of others' social expectations.[44]

Quadripartite Classification of Collective Norms

Raimo Tuomela similarly conducted a systematic classification of norms founded on his theory of collective acceptance, which overlaps with the late Searlean argument and is quite useful for considering the ontological status of the normativity of institutions. From Tuomela's perspective, institutions presuppose relevant members' collective acceptance in a specific group, community, or society. Therefore, institutionalization

[43] According to Inglehart's analysis from 2007 to 2019, the overwhelming majority of the countries studied—43 out of 49—became less religious. The decline in belief was not confined to high-income countries and appeared across most of the world (Inglehart, 2020, p. 110).

[44] As Bicchieri (2016) targets at identifying, measuring, and changing real norms, her focus is limited to conditional social norms by which pluralistic ignorance largely matters.

amounts to the creation, by group members via their collective acceptance, of specific repeatable ways of acting relative to group tasks and functions, given that the group is internally controlled by its members (Tuomela, 2002a, p. 137).

Institutions generally offer cooperative and public good-friendly solutions to collective problems, especially problems in which individual interests or preferences conflict with collective ones (Tuomela, 2002a, p. 158). While there are various types of institutions, every "standard" kind of social institution requires for its maintenance the presence of some we-mode we-attitudes and activities based on them (Tuomela, 2002a, p. 162). In other words, institutions need we-mode collective intentionality rather than mere I-mode individual intentionality (Tuomela, 2002a, p. 175). In this regard, Tuomela has something in common with Searle since Tuomela proposed the non-reductive individualistic idea through the concept of collective intentionality.

Tuomela's central thesis is that social institutions have two types of normative characteristics (Tuomela, 2002a, 2003): (1) formal or informal rule-norms (r-norms), based directly or indirectly on group-authorized agreement, and (2) proper social norms (s-norms).[45] Whereas the first type is based directly or indirectly on group-authorized agreements, the latter s-norms are either society-wide or group-specific norms that are based on collective expectations and mutual beliefs. These two types of norms (r-norms and s-norms) constitute the systems of social institutions that lend normative force.

R-norms are usually stated explicitly, as in the paradigmatic cases of corporate accounting standards, and they can exist in a weak sense even if people pay little attention to them, although they ought to be known in many cases (Tuomela, 2002a, p. 165). In practice, operative members of society generally act on behalf of non-operative members, and non-operative members only need to tacitly accept what the operative members have decided.

S-norms are based on shared normative expectations within the collective in question, and they may be transmitted as habits; individuals just

[45] Tuomela applied his norm-classification framework to r-institutions based on r-norms and s-institutions based on s-norms (mixed cases can also occur) (Tuomela, 1997, p. 437). More specifically, he indicated that the institutions of money and property rights are examples of r-institutions, whereas language seems to represent a mixed case. Mutual gift-giving is an example of an s-institution (Tuomela, 1997, p. 437).

learn to obey s-norms during their socialization (Tuomela, 2002a, p. 165). S-norms are often based on strong subconscious or tacit beliefs that are approved or disapproved by one's peers, such as dress codes or table manners. Based on this classification, many moral rules and cultural beliefs are informal s-norms. They may be traditional and transmitted in connection with habits: People just learn to obey the norms during socialization (Tuomela, 2003, p. 138). There may be tension and explicit conflicts between both types of norms. When there is a conflict between an r-norm and an s-norm, the s-norm tends to override the r-norm (Tuomela, 2002a, p. 262). Nevertheless, both types of norms with the same content can coexist temporarily.[46]

This categorization of norms that constitutes social institutions offers a systematic perspective on the normativity of institutions, possibly allowing for the formation of a micro–macro conceptual link through the introduction of operative and non-operative members. Notably, Tuomela's theory of social institutions distinguishes between agreement-based formal and informal r-norms from belief-based informal s-norms. This carefully framed distinction is more profound than a simple dichotomy posited as formal and informal institutions. Furthermore, Tuomela noted that implicit s-norms can be verbalized or formulated by social scientists (Tuomela, 1995, p. 26). In our daily life, formal r-norms matter a great deal because both individual and organizational behaviors are often regulated by formal rules with explicit sanctions. As most collectively accepted s-norms are implicit and informal, we rarely consciously recognize them.[47] Therefore, an exploration of the mechanism of the construction of social institutions through s-norms would be worth investigating.

What Tuomela argued is that r-norms are agreement-based whereas s-norms are mainly based on mutual beliefs, and there are both formal and informal r-norms. However, he did not clearly mention how formal r-norms differ from informal ones. Table 2.3 clarifies his classification of norms and develops it further within 2×2 matrix.

[46] According to Tuomela (1995, 2003), sanctions are either "official" authority-imposed sanctions (r-sanctions) or social sanctions (s-sanctions consisting of social approval and disapproval).

[47] The idea of s-norms is similar to Granovetter's (1985) embeddedness approach that he intended to be moderate between an under-socialized atomic individualistic approach and over-socialized normative structural approach (Granovetter, 1985).

Table 2.3 Quadripartite classification of norms

	Agreement-based (r-norms)	*Belief-based (s-norms)*
Explicit	**Formal rules** (Authoritative agreement-based rules) Examples: laws, accounting standards, university curriculums	**Explicable social norms** (Widely accepted beliefs) Examples: conventional moral rules, etiquettes, manners
Implicit	**Informal rules** (Agreement-based principles) Examples: abstract professional guidelines, principles-based regulations	**Observable social norms** (Observer-relative context-dependent beliefs) Examples: fairness, reciprocity, equality

The first criterion (vertical one in the table) determines whether norms are explicit or implicit. It is equivalent to the difference between rules and principles-based regulation. The more explicit the rules, the more detailed they are. Agreement-based formal rules (the top left cell on the table) are relatively detailed and clear, whereas informal rules (the bottom left in the table) are more abstract and principles-based. The right side of the matrix classifies belief-based s-norms into explicit and implicit ones, as some belief-based norms can be easily verbalized or explicable (the top right cell in the table). In other words, if a specific belief is widely recognized as legitimate (or illegitimate), it can be generally made explicit. Otherwise, belief-based norms are not easily transmitted or habitualized. Then, those implicit belief-based norms are tacit, interpretative and, relying on a Searlean term, observer-relative (the bottom right cell on the table). Such abstract observable social norms are context-specific and subject to different interpretations. For instance, the norm of mutual gift-giving or reciprocity is observer-relative, and the content of it depends on a specific context in which actions of individual/organizations are observed.

This hypothetical classification of different types of norms is not clear-cut. For instance, the distinction between informal rules and explicable social norms is equivocal because the classification between them can be made according to whether a specific norm is based on either agreement or belief. For example, you may wonder if the norm “You should not cut in queue” is an informal rule or an explicable social norm. I would say it is an explicable social norm as it is not an agreed-upon rule but depends on individual belief-based moral judgment. Furthermore, it is relatively more explicit than other informal belief-based norms. In contrast, a comprehensive norm of fairness (e.g., you should be fair) is a type of an observable s-norm because its application is context-specific and observer-relative.[48] Therefore, explicable social norms and observable social norms overlap to some extent.

Moreover, in terms of sanctions attached to different types of norms, r-norms normally entail formal sanctions (r-sanctions) whereas s-norms often accompany informal s-sanctions (Tuomela, 2002a). Noncompliance with formal rules is easily detectable and it often accompanies explicit sanctions. Sanctions for nonconformity with informal rules are judgmental, and there would be both formal and informal sanctions. As for sanctions on social norms, there are often indirect social sanctions (s-sanctions). For example, if you do not keep your word at work occasionally, you may be disrespected and lose the trust of others. It is notable that there would be no direct sanctions on not following observable social norms (in this case, keeping promises) because each norm is context-specific and exposed to different levels of interpretations (Tuomela, 2002a, p. 188). You may feel anxious if you do not follow or imitate a context-specific observable norm. Or you occasionally feel some pressure from others to follow it under uncertainty to some extent. For instance, widely accepted observable social norms such as fairness and reciprocity are often invoked in our daily life, while relatively less diffused emerging ones such as diversity in organizations are not pursued on some occasions. This difference in normativity will be analyzed from the perspective of performativity in the next chapter.

Observable Social Norms and Operative Members' Actions

As mentioned above, there are sometimes tensions and conflicts between r-norms and s-norms. For instance, corporate sustainable development goals (SDGs) and sustainability have been recently standardized by global organizations such as the Sustainability Accounting Standards Board (SASB). This is a real case that demonstrates how a belief-based observable social norm becomes agreement-based rules. Although Tuomela (1995, pp. 20–21) mentioned that an s-norm ceases to be in force when it becomes articulated and more public, it is not the case all the time.

[48] Many pro-social norms, such as fairness, reciprocity, and cooperation, are subject to multiple interpretations (Bicchieri, 2016, p. 79).

For instance, in Japan, the norm of recycling home appliances was legalized in 2001, and since then, their dumping has been deemed illegal and punished with a fine of up to 200,000 yen. According to the assessment of the effect of the institution, the legalization has tremendously improved citizens' overall awareness of the significance of recycling not only home appliances but other items. Public awareness of the need to use things with care was also raised by this regulation (Subcommittee on Waste & Recycling in the Central Environment Council, 2008). This case illustrates that an s-norm expands and comprehensively mobilizes derivative r-norms and continues to exist as the s-norm of recycling.

Therefore, both formal and informal norms can be combined as a set of rules. The relationship between the two matters. Informal rules can interact with formal ones in four ways: complementary, accommodating, competing, and substantive (Jütting et al., 2007).[49] For instance, legal structures in many countries are understood as being at least complementary and accommodating with the combination of agreement and belief-based norms because they comprise abstract constitutions and a myriad of detailed rules. Generally, while principles-based regulation requires actors' careful and professional judgments, there would be conflicts of subjective judgments among actors in some cases. Under the rules (agreement)-based regulation, actors do not need to exercise their judgment frequently, whereas rule-makers' efforts are necessary to stipulate appropriate rules.

Then, what are the relationships between belief- and agreement-based norms? As mentioned above, some belief-based norms are made explicit and become agreement-based formal and informal rules. However, many belief-based norms remain implicit and just direct or mobilize other rules. For instance, typical observable social norms such as fairness or justice have consistently impacted the content of agreement-based rules. I shall analyze this point in terms of performativity in the next chapter. But, let me refer to a specific case study to mention how observable social norms are significant in a specific context.

De Soto (2001) revealed the elusiveness and mysterious aspects of "capital" by analyzing sluggish economic development in Peru. His basic research question is: Why does capitalism thrive only in the West even though reforms directed at creating capitalist systems have been tried in

[49] Their argument is based on Helmke and Levitsky (2004).

Peru at least four times since independence from Spain in the 1820s? In conclusion, he implied the importance of the collective agreement in society by insisting that "the philosopher John Searle has noted that by human agreement we can assign 'a new status to some phenomenon, where the status has an accompanying function that cannot be performed solely in virtue of the intrinsic physical features of the phenomenon in question'" (De Soto, 2001, p. 234). De Soto argued that legal properties cannot perform their functions to generate capital without the collectively accepted status of legal property rights. Grounded in a Searlean perspective, De Soto (2001) shed light on the significance of belief-based norms. In short, standard setters and bureaucrats in a developing country who had knowledge of how capitalism worked well in developed countries thought that imitating an effective policy taken in developed countries would be a shortcut to achieve quick economic development and tried to introduce similar rules directly. However, as ordinary citizens' collective acceptance of the significance of private property rights was absent or insufficient, the prediction of the standard setter became a castle in the sky. Those bureaucrats should have considered the measures to change ordinary citizens' collective belief.

In this regard, Tuomela's distinction between operative and non-operative members is helpful. Operative members are leaders who are internally authorized by delegation to give orders and directives concerning group-relevant (basically, ethos-relevant) matters. The other members need only tacitly accept what (e.g., intentions or views) the operative members have jointly accepted for the group and have directed them to do (Tuomela, 2013, p. 117). With regard to setting agreement-based norms, operative members often have authoritative power. Nevertheless, those operative members usually have responsibility to consider the ideas of broader non-operative members who would benefit from or suffer because of the operative members' decisions. However, they are generally selected representatives who tend to have similar knowledge or skills, which would make them reach similar decisions. Of course, members of standard setters are neither inherently villainous nor selfish; they are more or less determined to serve the public (or other non-operative members). However, reaching a final agreement on a controversial matter is not an easy task under uncertainty because there are different interested parties who have their own vested interests in the existing standards and oppose to alternative options.

References

Alesina, A., & Giuliano, P. (2015). Culture and institutions. *Journal of Economic Literature, 53*(4), 898–944.

Aoki, M. (2001). *Toward a comparative institutional analysis*. The MIT Press.

Barnett, S. (2017). *Rhetorical realism-rhetoric, ethics, and the ontology of things*. Routledge.

Bartholomew, D. J. (Ed.). (2006). *Measurement—SAGE benchmarks in social research methods*. Sage.

Berger, P. L., & Luckmann, T. (1967). *The social construction of reality: A treatise in the sociology of knowledge*. Penguin.

Beunza, D., & Ferraro, F. (2019). Performative work: Bridging performativity and institutional theory in the responsible investment field. *Organization Studies, 40*(4), 515–543.

Bicchieri, C. (2005). *The grammar of society: The nature and dynamics of social norms*. Cambridge University Press.

Bicchieri, C. (2016). *Norms in the wild: How to diagnose, measure, and change social norms*. Oxford University Press.

Brennan, G., Eriksson, L., Goodin, R. E., & Southwood, N. (2013). *Explaining norms*. Oxford University Press.

Çalışkan, K., & Callon, M. (2010). Economization, part 2: A research programme for the study of markets. *Economy and Society, 39*(1), 1–32.

Callon, M. (1984). Some elements of a sociology of translation: Domestication of the scallops and the fishermen of St Brieuc Bay. *The Sociological Review, 32*(1-supplemental), 196–233.

Callon, M. (1986). The sociology of an actor-network: The case of the electric vehicle. In M. Callon, J. Law, & A. Rip (Eds.), *Mapping the dynamics of science and technology* (pp. 19–34). The Macmillan.

Callon, M. (1999). Actor-network theory—The market test. In J. Law & J. Hassard (Eds.), *Actor network theory and after* (pp. 181–195). Blackwell Publishers.

Callon, M. (2007). What does it mean to say that economics is performative? In D. A. MacKenzie, F. Muniesa, & L. Siu (Eds.), *Do economists make markets?* (pp. 311–357). Princeton University Press.
Callon, M. (2016). Revisiting marketization: From interface-markets to market-agencements. *Consumption Markets & Culture, 19*(1), 17–37.
Callon, M., Law, J., & Rip, A. (Eds.). (1986). *Mapping the dynamics of science and technology. Sociology of science in the real world.* Palgrave Macmillan.
Clark, A., & Chalmers, D. (1998). The extended mind. *Analysis, 58*(1), 7–19.
Denzau, A. T., & North, D. C. (1994). Shared mental models: Ideologies and institutions. *Kyklos, 47*(1), 3–31.
De Soto, H. (2001). *The mystery of capital.* The Black Swan Books.
Detel, W. (2008). On the concept of basic social norms. *Analyse & Kritik, 30*, 469–482.
Elder-Vass, D. (2015). Disassembling actor-network theory. *Philosophy of the Social Sciences, 45*(1), 100–121.
Elster, J. (1989). Social norms and economic theory. *Journal of Economic Perspectives, 3*(4), 99–117.
Glynn, M. A., & D'aunno, T. (2023). An intellectual history of institutional theory: Looking back to move forward. *Academy of Management Annals, 17*(1), 301–330.
Granovetter, M. (1985). Economic action and social structure: The problem of embeddedness. *American Journal of Sociology, 91*(3), 481–510.
Greenwood, R., Oliver, C., Lawrence, T. B., & Meyer, R. E. (Eds.). (2017). *The SAGE handbook of organizational institutionalism* (2nd ed.). Sage.
Guala, F. (2016). *Understanding institutions.* Princeton University Press.
Hacking, I. (1990). *The taming of chance.* Cambridge University Press.
Helmke, G., & Levitsky, S. (2004). Informal institutions and comparative politics: A research agenda. *Perspectives on Politics, 2*(4), 725–740.
Hirschman, A. O. (1970). *Exit, voice, and loyalty: Responses to decline in firms, organizations, and states.* Harvard University Press.
Hodgson, G. M. (2006). What are institutions? *Journal of Economic Issues, 40*(1), 1–25.
Inglehart, R. F. (2020). Giving up on God: The global decline of religion. *Foreign Affairs, 99*(5), 110–118.
Jenkins, R. (2014). *Social identity* (4th ed.). Routledge.
Jütting, J., Drechsler, D., Bartsch, S., & Soysa, I. (Eds.). (2007). *Informal institutions: How social norms help or hinder development.* Development Centre of the Organization for Economic Co-operation and Development (OECD).
Latour, B. (1987). *Science in action: How to follow scientists and engineers through society.* Harvard University Press.
Latour, B. (2005). *Reassembling the social: An introduction to actor-network-theory.* Oxford University Press.

Latour, B., & Hermant, E. (2006). *Paris: Invisible City* (L. Carey-Libbrecht, Trans.). http://www.bruno-latour.fr/sites/default/files/downloads/viii_paris-city-gb.pdf

Latour, B., & Woolgar, S. (1979). *Laboratory life: The construction of scientific facts*. Sage.

Law, J. (1987). Technology and heterogeneous engineering: The case of Portuguese expansion. In W. E. Bijker, T. P. Hughes, & T. J. Pinch (Eds.), *The social construction of technological systems: New directions in the sociology and history of technology* (pp. 111–134). MIT Press.

Law, J., & Callon, M. (1992). The life and death of an aircraft: A network analysis of technical change. In E. Bijker & J. Law (Eds.), *Shaping technology/building society: Studies in sociotechnical change* (pp. 21–52). MIT Press.

MacIntyre, A. (2002). *The power of institutions: Political architecture and governance*. Cornell University Press.

Mantzavinos, C. (2001). *Individuals, institutions, and markets*. Cambridge University Press.

Mantzavinos, C. (2021). *A dialogue of institutions*. Springer.

Meyer, J. W. (2017). Reflections on institutional theories of organizations. In R. Greenwood, C. Oliver, T. B. Lawrence, & R. E. Meyer (Eds.), *The SAGE handbook of organizational institutionalism* (pp. 831–852). Sage.

Meyer, J. W., & Rowan, B. (1977). Institutionalized organizations: Formal structure as myth and ceremony. *American Journal of Sociology, 83*(2), 340–363.

Modell, S., Vinnari, E., & Lukka, K. (2017). On the virtues and vices of combining theories: The case of institutional and actor-network theories in accounting research. *Accounting, Organizations and Society, 60*, 62–78.

Morgan, G., Campbell, J., Crouch, C., Pedersen, O. K., & Whitley, R. (Eds.). (2010). *The Oxford handbook of comparative institutional analysis*. Oxford University Press.

North, D. C. (1990). *Institutions, institutional change and economic performance*. Cambridge University Press.

Ocasio, W., & Gai, S. L. (2020). Institutions: Everywhere but not everything. *Journal of Management Inquiry, 29*(3), 262–271.

Ott, C. M., & Ivens, B. S. (2009). Revisiting the norm concept in relational governance. *Industrial Marketing Management, 38*(6), 577–583.

Overgaard, S., & Zahavi, D. (2009). Phenomenological sociology: The subjectivity of everyday life. In M. H. Jacobsen (Ed.), *Encountering the everyday: An introduction to the sociologies of the unnoticed* (pp. 1–41). Palgrave Macmillan.

Petracca, E., & Gallagher, S. (2020). Economic cognitive institutions. *Journal of Institutional Economics, 16*(6), 747–765.

Phillips, N., & Malhotra, N. (2017). Language, cognition and institutions: Studying institutionalization using linguistic methods. In R. Greenwood, C.

Oliver, B. Thomas, T. B. Lawrence, & R. E. Meyer (Eds.), *The SAGE handbook of organizational institutionalism* (2nd ed., pp. 392–417). Sage.
Polanyi, K. (2009). *The Tacit Dimension, with a new foreword by Amartya Sen.* The University of Chicago Press.
Powell, W. W., & Bromley, P. (2015). New institutionalism in the analysis of complex organizations. *International Encyclopedia of the Social & Behavioral Sciences Second Edition, 16*, 764–769.
Sayes, E. (2014). Actor-Network theory and methodology: Just what does it mean to say that nonhumans have agency? *Social Studies of Science, 44*(1), 134–149.
Scott, W. R. (2013). *Institutions and organizations: Ideas, interests, and identities* (4th ed.). Sage.
Searle, J. R. (1995). *The construction of social reality*. The Free Press.
Searle, J. R. (2005). What is an institution? *Journal of Institutional Economics, 1*(1), 1–22.
Searle, J. R. (2010). *Making the social world: The structure of human civilization.* Oxford University Press.
Searle, J. R. (2014). Are there social objects? In M. Gallotti & J. Michael (Eds.), *Perspectives on social ontology and social cognition* (Studies in the philosophy of sociality, Vol. 4, pp. 17–26). Springer.
Searle, J. R. (2018). Status functions. In M. Jankovic & K. Ludwig (Eds.), *The Routledge handbook of collective intentionality* (pp. 300–309). Routledge.
Sismondo, S. (2010). *An introduction to science and technology studies* (2nd ed.). Wiley.
Smith, D. E. (2001). Texts and the ontology of organizations and institutions. *Studies in Cultures, Organizations and Societies, 7*(2), 159–198.
Soldatova, L. N., & King, R. D. (2006). An ontology of scientific experiments. *Journal of the Royal Society Interface, 3*(11), 795–803.
Spencer, M. E. (1982). The ontologies of social science. *Philosophy of the Social Sciences, 12*, 121–141.
Thornton, P. H., Ocasio, W., & Lounsbury, M. (2012). *The institutional logics perspective: A new approach to culture, structure, and process*. Oxford University Press.
Tuomela, R. (1995). *The importance of us: A philosophical study of basic social notions*. Stanford University Press.
Tuomela, R. (1997). Searle on social institutions. *Philosophy and Phenomenological Research, 57*(2), 435–441.
Tuomela, R. (2002a). *The philosophy of social practices: A collective acceptance view*. Cambridge University Press.
Tuomela, R. (2002b). Searle, collective intentionality, and social institutions. In G. Grewendorf & G. Meggle (Eds.), *Speech acts, mind, and social reality: Discussions with John R. Searle* (pp. 293–307). Kluwer Academic Publishers.

Tuomela, R. (2003). Collective acceptance, social institutions, and social reality. *The American Journal of Economics and Sociology, 62*(1), 123–165.
Tuomela, R. (2013). *Social ontology: Collective intentionality and group agents*. Harvard University Press.
Willmott, H. (2015). Why institutional theory cannot be critical. *Journal of Management Inquiry, 24*(1), 105–111.
Zucker, L. G. (1987). Institutional theories of organization. *Annual Review of Sociology, 13*, 443–464.

In Japanese

Kobayashi, T. (2019). Nihonjin no syūkyō teki ishiki ya kōdō ha dou kawattaka. *Housou Kenkyū to Chyousa, 49*, 52–72.
Kohno, M. (2002). *Seido: Shyakai-Kagaku no Riron to Moderu*. The University of Tokyo Press.
Subcommittee on Waste and Recycling in the Central Environment Council. (2008). *Kaden Risaikuru Seido no Shikkō Jyōkyō no Hyōka/Kentō ni Tsuite* (Report on the Evaluation and Review of the Enforcement Status of the Home Appliance Recycling System).

CHAPTER 3

Performativity of Collective Norms

The previous chapter revealed that the ontological analysis of institutions has not been conducted thoroughly in past studies. Furthermore, relying on the works of John Searle and Raimo Tuomela and considering the characteristics of institutions that mobilize individual and organizational behavior, the essence of institutions was decomposed into four types of collectively accepted norms[1] (formal and informal rules, and explicable and observable social norms). Among them, the significance of observable social norms has been overlooked in the literature. Such an informal norm that a group of individuals unconsciously or tacitly follow at times is generally identified by observers such as social scientists. If those who follow a specific collective norm are operative members in a powerful organization, the norm crucially mobilizes those members' actions and standard-setting activities. This chapter expands on this account through the lens of performativity. The performativity perspective emphasizes the linguistic representations that shape institutional reality. As performativity is a sense of force that influences individual and organizational behaviors (Nealon, 2021), the perspective explicates the normativity of collective norms that shapes institutional change.

[1] From now on, for the sake of simplicity, "collectively accepted norms" will be described as "collective norms."

N. Okamoto, *Institutional Change and Performativity*,
https://doi.org/10.1007/978-3-031-53393-8_3

The first section of this chapter examines the nature of performativity by reviewing several studies from different fields, ranging from linguistics to sociology and politics. In considering the linguistic aspect of performativity, the section draws in particular on Donald MacKenzie's classification of types of performativity, arguing that the identification of observable social norms is equivalent to exploring the generic performativity of discourses. Section 3.2 looks at how generic performativity is interpretively identified and considers how it shapes institutional change through its performative forces.

3.1 Collective Norms Are Performative

Performativity Includes Normativity

The concept of performativity was originally proposed by a philosopher of language, J. L. Austin, who identified two types of utterance: constative and performative. Constative utterances are descriptive statements, whereas performative utterances (1) do not describe, report, or constate anything and, hence, are neither true nor false; and (2) are, or form a part of the doing of an action that would not normally be described as saying something or as "just" saying something (Austin, 1975, pp. 5–7). Thus, the concept of performative utterances implies that when we articulate words, we are doing something rather than reporting something (Austin, 1975, p. 13). Furthermore, Austin distinguished illocutionary acts from perlocutionary ones (Fig. 3.1). Both acts are performative; illocutionary acts entail the performance of an act *in* saying something as opposed to the performance of an act *of* saying something (Austin, 1975, pp. 99–100, emphasis in original). Perlocutionary acts may entail either the achievement of a perlocutionary object (e.g., text or symbols) or the production of a perlocutionary sequel (e.g., actions or behaviors) (Austin, 1975, p. 118). For instance, assume you have a conversation with your colleagues and tell them "I would like to get promoted as I have worked so hard lately"; this is an illocutionary act as it communicates your feelings with your colleagues. The next day, suppose you tell your boss this, and if your boss decides to have a one-to-one meeting concerning your performance and finally agrees to raise your rank and salary, it is a perlocutionary act because your speech created the promotion and pay raise.

Aside from this abstruse classification of utterances, some sociologists have paid attention to the perspective of performativity. For example,

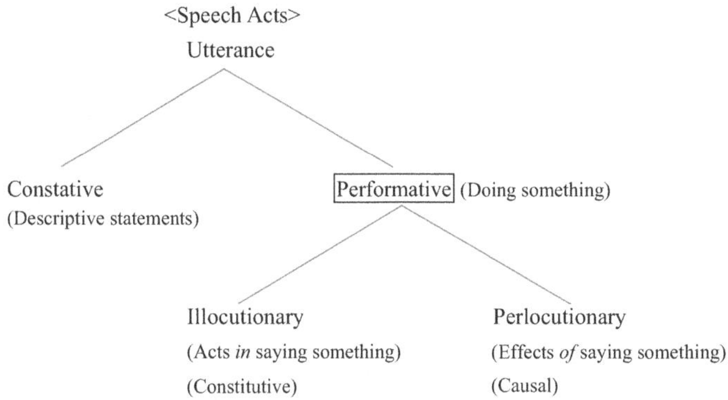

Fig. 3.1 Austin's classification of speech acts

Bloor (1997, p. 134) argued that as we are dealing with a social institution in the form of a self-referring system, it can be analyzed in terms of its self-referring or performative character. Furthermore, following MacKenzie's (2006) seminal analysis of option-trader behaviors in financial markets, in which he highlighted the performativity of financial models, the concept of performativity has captured the attention of social scientists who have especially applied the insights in the areas of finance and economics (e.g., Callon et al., 2007; MacKenzie et al., 2007). For example, Svetlova (2018) argues for performativity through the diffusion of theoretical financial models into the realm of markets (from science/ academia to markets) without directly acknowledging that the context of model application changes from epistemic to non-epistemic during the move.[2]

However, Mäki (2013, pp. 447–448) criticized such sociologists' use of performativity (e.g., MacKenzie, 2006; MacKenzie et al., 2007), arguing that it obscures the authentic meanings of performativity in

[2] A perspective of non-knowledge can be useful in understanding the actions within the chains of finance where various judgment devices—for instance, brands, rankings and ratings, as fabricated by diverse intermediaries such as rating agencies, audit companies, and marketing agencies—cannot be understood solely as aids for producing knowledge in the face of radical uncertainty (Svetlova, 2018, p. 146). According to her analysis, those judgment devices in financial markets can be analyzed through the notion of illusions of knowledge or pseudo-knowledge that consist of non-knowledge as knowledge (Svetlova, 2018, p. 146).

Austin's analysis of speech acts. According to Mäki (2013), the uniqueness of Austinian performativity lies in its constitutive property; if an economic model is to be performative, it is imperative to show that it constitutes the economic object to which it refers (Peled, 2020, p. 53). Mäki (2013) found that the definition of the illocutionary act should rest on a constitutive relation, whereas the perlocutionary act relies on a causal relation.

Although I agree with the idea that performative (speech) acts have different types of effects, I do not agree with Mäki's (2013) argument that an illocutionary act is purely constitutive. For example, if a new economic model emerges by modifying the previous version, it does not entirely constitute a new phenomenon; it is slightly different from the old one because of its new status function. According to Searle (2018, p. 305), the creation of status functions iterates upward indefinitely and spreads out laterally. This kind of iterative process could reinforce its normative nature. Similarly, Guala did not consider the illocutionary act to be strongly constitutive, noting that "it is customary to interpret the illocutionary aspect of an act as being essentially communicative, and the perlocutionary one as [being] causal or pragmatic" (Guala, 2016, p. 36).

For the causal characteristics of perlocution, from a different angle, Brisset (2019, p. 139) expressed skepticism about the distinction between illocution and perlocution: what is at stake is no more the distinction between causal and constitutive effects, but the split between necessary effects and contingent effects. Svetlova (2016, p. 185) eloquently summarized the dual effects of performative acts: "Illocution refers to the production of reality by means of conventional speech, and perlocution draws attention to processes of beliefs' formation by means of theatrical persuasion and conviction (performance)."[3] Thus, synthesizing the arguments of Brisset (2019) and Svetlova (2016) on performativity, conventional speech acts necessarily produce social reality that persuades and convinces individuals and organizations.

Although the distinction between illocutionary and perlocutionary performative acts tends to be ambiguous and controversial, we rarely

[3] Similar attempts that have applied the concept of performativity include Czarniawska (2016) and Gergen and Gergen (2011).

consider the difference between these types of speech acts in daily conversations.[4] Rather, as perlocution and illocution are two sides of the same coin (Svetlova, 2016), different performative effects need to be noted. On the one hand, considering the illocutionary aspects of performativity, we need to focus on how a specific speech act (e.g., a discourse or a theory) is used in explicit and conventional practices. On the other hand, the perlocutionary aspects of performative acts need to be considered in order to identify the contingent effects of the speech act (illocution) that changes people's beliefs through persuasion and, consequently, brings about behavioral and institutional changes (perlocution).

Therefore, the performativity of a particular discourse or theory is considered appropriate for explaining and understanding contingent changes. The key is the theatrical elements of language that contribute to bringing about shared (collective) beliefs when they are staged, with actors behaving as if "the staged reality" is real (Svetlova, 2016, p. 193). This understanding of performativity that it comes from shared (collective) beliefs (illocution) corresponds to the normativity of belief-based (explicable and observable) social norms that shape individual actors' behaviors (perlocutionary effects). As mentioned in the previous chapter, there are different stages in the belief-based social norms. Some of them are explicitly verbalized whereas others are implicit and context-dependent. Social scientists are well placed to interpret and identify observable social norms by examining and considering their consequential effects retrospectively. Some norms perform more than alternative ones and such situations are carefully compared and analyzed by observers.

In other words, the normativity of performativity arises from the power of language to bring about change in the world (Cavanaugh, 2015). Such a normative force exists because "performativity constitutes a set of practices that look axiomatically at force before meaning" (Nealon, 2021, 194). It comprises four interrelated processes of naturalization of ideas, namely, reiteration, codification, entanglement, and cementation (Nyberg & Wright, 2016).[5] If a particular discourse is collectively

[4] Searle (1976), for instance, argued that it would be difficult and arbitrary to distinguish an illocutionary act from a perlocutionary one.

[5] As a specific example, according to their extensive analysis of actors involved in the climate change risks, the idea of "climate change is a risk" is repeated in various circumstances (reiteration), then climate change becomes calculable, comparable, and exchangeable as a commodity (codification); commodified climate change is brought into

accepted in a specific community, most individuals in the community take it for granted, and it can be performative, as well. The more the norm is collectively accepted, the stronger its performative force is.[6] Hence, the analysis of the performativity of a speech act (a discourse or a theory) can be understood as an attempt to study the interactions among collective belief-based (as well as agreement-based) norms that mobilize various social institutions.

Classification of Performativity

As Austin's original linguistic distinction between illocutionary and perlocutionary acts (performative utterance) seems to be too profound to analyze actual social phenomena, it is useful to consider the effects of performative forces. To embrace the multifaceted aspects of performativity, Donald MacKenzie's classification is useful in that it identifies multiple ways in which social knowledge may "perform." For instance, the influence of a particular theory, doctrine, or procedure can perform, and therefore actors' persuasion, beliefs, and state of mind matter (MacKenzie et al., 2007, p. 6). According to his theoretical analysis, there are different levels of performativity (MacKenzie, 2006, p. 17; MacKenzie et al., 2007, p. 55).[7] Figure 3.2 develops the original classification of performativity in the context of economics (MacKenzie, 2006).

Generic performativity means that social knowledge (theories, models, concepts, procedures, etc.) is used in individual and organizational activities, such as different types of regulation. Actors are not always aware of the broad and macro generic performativity. However, observers and researchers interpret and identify them. In short, the identification of generic performativity is observer-relative. Of course, widely accepted discourses can be candidates for more persuasive performative knowledge.

the market, which provides solutions to climate change (entanglement), and enables public or political interventions such as regulations (cementation) (Nyberg & Wright, 2016).

[6] Accordingly, the collective acceptance of a particular discourse is thought to provide the discourse with normative power (Okamoto, 2020).

[7] To consider performativity in the context of economics, the scope of economics matters. For instance, "In the economic reality, there is a continuum between 'laboratory,' with its clear boundaries between 'interior,' and 'exterior,' and 'in vivo experiments,' which occur directly in the outer reality, with different 'platforms' in between, which are more or less flexible and open to the contribution of external persons" (Esposito, 2013, p. 113).

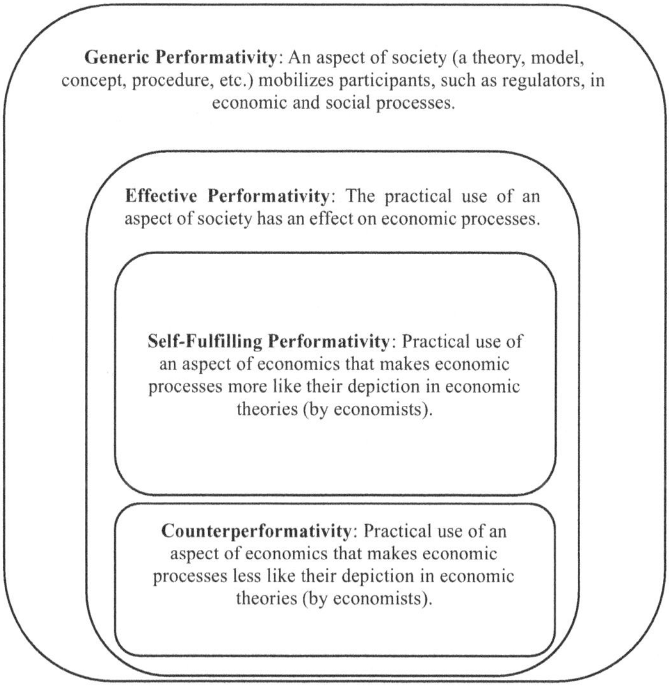

Fig. 3.2 Classification of performativity in the economic context

As will be discussed in the next chapter, terms such as "globalization" and "financialization" are nowadays recognized as discourses that are heavily used in society because of the efforts of observers and researchers. For example, there are very few people with a certain level of knowledge of the economy and politics who deny outright that the phenomenon of globalization has taken place in the past few decades.

Within comprehensive generic performativity, there are more specific types of effective performativity, meaning that, in the context of economics, the practical application of economic knowledge has an impact on actual economic activity. Effective performativity can be classified into two specific types: self-fulfilling performativity[8] and counterperformativity. Self-fulfilling performativity is the practical application or use of economic knowledge that makes economic activity closer to its depiction by economists, whereas counterperformativity is the practical application or use of economic knowledge that makes economic activity less like its depiction by economists. Accounting knowledge can be a typical example. As the ratio of return on equity (ROE: corporate net income divided by the amount of shareholders' equity) is understood to reflect corporate profitability, a story about a specific company's ROE increase giving rise to an additional investment from outside investors is a typical case of self-fulfilling performativity. The counterperformative movement, by contrast, corresponds to a collective, skeptical attitude toward the precedence of ROE over other profitability metrics such as the return on assets (ROA) or the return on invested capital (ROIC).

Based on this classification of performativity, the case of effective performativity (self-fulfilling performativity or counterperformativity) in a specific context can be pursued by identifying typical or anomalous results within the specific context, which provides alternative interpretations or presents new explananda. Such attempts generally need a pragmatic and detailed investigation of the context. For instance, Beunza and Ferraro (2019, pp. 515–516) emphasized the gist of analyzing effective performativity: "At the core of performativity lies the hypothesis that statements by economists or other social scientists are not 'outside the world(s) to which they refer' but 'actively engaged in the constitution of the reality that they describe' (Callon, 2007, p. 318)." Besides, taking counterperformativity into account in a specific context is useful in analyzing unexpected anomalies, which also facilitates inferences and explanations through an attitude of ontological skepticism that leads to doubting specific methods or treatments in a specific domain.

Therefore, based on the analysis of performativity perspectives, the normativity of observable social norms is equivalent to generic performativity. The way generic and effective performativity interact remains under-researched. It may be possible to assume that the accumulation

[8] MacKenzie referred to sociologist Barry Barnes's self-validating feedback loops (Barnes, 1983) in social life (MacKenzie, 2006, p. 19) as "Barnesian performativity," but also cited "Mertonian performativity" in a footnote, drawing on Robert K. Merton (MacKenzie, 2006, p. 306). I call the phenomenon "self-fulfilling performativity," by drawing from Merton's famous "self-fulfilling prophecy."

of different types of effective performativity (self-fulfilling performativity and counterperformativity) may affect generic performativity. Although MacKenzie (2006) pointed out the self-fulfilling performativity of a theory in financial economics, understanding such a theory (a body of knowledge) requires an understanding of basic concepts (e.g., money and interest rates) and a working knowledge of mathematics. Therefore, it is possible to think of these concepts as being performed separately from financial economics. Put another way, if we take a broad view of the performative forces of linguistic representations, there are numerous layers of performativity. Figure 3.3 summarizes the overview of performativity, which represents a spectrum of different levels of performativity. The vertical axis of the figure represents the comprehensiveness of the norms/discourses; the higher up the axis is, the broader and more abstract the norm/discourse is, while the lower down the axis is, the more specific the norm/discourse is. The horizontal axis simply represents the number of norms/discourses. There are a large number of various context-specific norms/discourses with effective performativity, while there are fewer candidate norms/discourses with pervasive generic performativity.

Although MacKenzie (2006) mentioned the possibility of generic counterperformativity, he did not fully discuss how it works in a specific

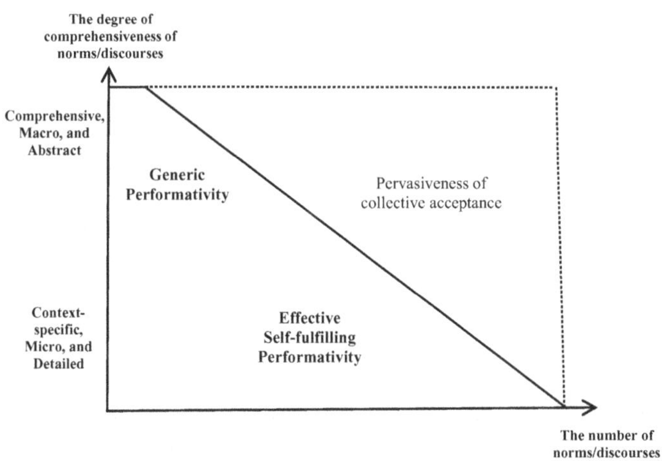

Fig. 3.3 Overview of norms and performativity

context. However, given that it at least covers broader macro situations, a consideration of generic counterperformativity can be useful for understanding dynamic institutional change. Yet, as the identification of generic performativity is interpretive, different interpretations may provoke some tensions (Bamford & MacKenzie, 2018, p. 121) at the macro level. Nevertheless, the powerful forces and mechanisms that drive individual and organizational behavior and institutional change should not be ignored. How to explore and identify generic performativity is discussed in the next section.

3.2 Generic Performativity of Observable Social Norms

Identification of Generic Performativity

Although one of the challenges that social scientists face is how to describe, theorize, and analyze social phenomena, the level of social scientists' interest in the ontological status of social constructs such as institutions varies. We are surrounded by so many social institutions and most of us tend to take them for granted. It is certain that all social constructs (notions, theories, assumptions, hypotheses, etc.) were originally emergent and came to be collectively accepted with time. In other words, some of the many social constructs can survive and achieve collective acceptance.

Think about ordinary social constructs we see or hear almost every day, namely inflation, GDP, currency exchange rates, stock prices, corporate net income, and so on. Textbooks in the social sciences such as economics and accounting explain what these social constructs are (definitions) and how they work systematically (mechanisms). By contrast, social scientists do not often ask how those social constructs came to exist in the first place because ontology does not matter in addressing social issues. It is understandable as we tend to emphasize material ontology, and the Searlean idea of epistemological objectivity is useful to fathom that aspect.

In short, from another angle, linguistic representations can be given greater priority. It is supported by the idea of rhetorical ontology that highlights the means by which things come into relation and have effects on other things in ways that resonate strongly with existing and emerging understandings of rhetoric (Barnett & Boyle, 2016, p. 9). According to this view, reality consists of relations among things that are connected by rhetoric. More specifically, rhetorical expressions can stage and dramatize configurations and interrelations between human and non-human agency (Barnett & Boyle, 2016, p. 10).

How can we identify a performative discourse among various rhetorical expressions as a specific collective norm in society? It at least involves considering many contingent social factors surrounding discourses and is by all means, interpretive. As I have emphasized, the observer-relativeness in the identification process is inevitable. Different interpretations of performativity can coexist and they are compared to see which one is more persuasive. Furthermore, there are derivative byproducts of performativity, such as counterperformativity (Bamford & MacKenzie, 2018) and the failure of performativity (Brisset, 2019). Studies in social science have typically sought to identify various causal relationships between social phenomena and social constructs in a specific setting, and those causal relationships have been accepted or rejected by rigorous methods within each research community. From that standpoint, the identification of generic performativity sounds too subjective and arbitrary. However, a social science study can never be completely objective because interpretation is an integral part of the different processes of research, such as understanding the phenomenon, reviewing the literature, building hypotheses, and collecting, interpreting, and analyzing data.

This aspect of social science was articulated by George Soros, who characterized the social by proposing two propositions. The first tells us that "the participants' views of the world never perfectly correspond to the actual state of affairs in situations where thinking participants exist. People can gain knowledge of individual facts, but when it comes to formulating theories or forming an overall view, their perspective is bound to be either biased or inconsistent or both" (Soros, 2013, p. 310). Soros (2013) called this the principle of fallibility. Second, "these imperfect views can influence the situation to which they relate through the actions of the participants" (Soros, 2013, p. 310). This is the principle of reflexivity. For example, if investors believe that markets are efficient, this belief will change the way they invest, which will change the nature of the markets in which they participate (though not necessarily by making them more efficient) (Soros, 2013, p. 310). Soros then stated that the combination of reflexivity and fallibility forms the human uncertainty principle. The human uncertainty principle "is much more specific and stringent than the subjective skepticism that pervades Cartesian philosophy. It gives us objective reasons to believe that the theories held by the participants, as distinct from statements of specific facts, are liable to be biased, incomplete, or both" (Soros, 2013, p. 315). According to this viewpoint, social science is crucially different from natural science: Humans are fallible and reflexively participate in and change institutional reality.

Therefore, according to Soros (2013), human beings often make mistakes, and those mistakes change social reality. Thus, social scientists need to adapt to changes in social reality by considering different interpretations or alternative understandings of widely accepted theories and discourses. Yet, it does not mean that a specific performative force cannot persist for a long time. We often see specific cases in which self-fulfilling performativity prevails for extended periods of time. Assuming that generic performativity consists of myriad interactions between specific self-fulfilling performativity and counterperformativity, the interpretations and identifications of generic performativity should change as well.

However, to identify the generic performativity of a specific observable social norm that shapes social institutions, we should at least pay attention to its linguistic representations in texts and discourses. Observable social norms mobilize operative members to confer status functions on institutions through declarations, which can be performed through repeated representations that have the effect of changing reality so that it matches the representation (Searle, 2018, p. 308). Therefore, it is necessary to focus on the frequent appearance and use of discourses (in different types of texts) in society, with the aim of tangibly identifying observable social norms. The frequency of their use can be measured in different ways, and the observers' subjective judgment is essential. To cope with this, this book relies on Austin's felicitous conditions that support the collective acceptance of a specific discourse in society.

The time base needs to be considered as well. Collective norms affect individual and organizational behaviors and give rise to institutional change performatively. The extent of the perlocutionary effects of those norms is located historically, which changes over time (Brisset, 2017, p. 443). Put differently, words can be actions if there is a time lag between them (Svetlova, 2016, p. 192); speech acts "are purposefully produced or reproduced by people, and they are named in accordance with history, either psychological or social, rather than shape" (Millikan, 2014, p. 37). Following these arguments, this book takes a stance that a specific performative discourse (speech act) is retrospectively examined by analyzing what operative members thought and shared to bring about consequential institutional change. Instead of taking a fully inductive approach, this book takes a deductive approach, as it initially identifies observable social norms that are generically performative and possibly mobilize changes in relevant institutions.

Felicitous Conditions for Identification

Based on the above discussion, it can be seen that observable social norms that are generically performative can be identified via observers' interpretations. This subsection explores how it can be done with some possible conditions. There are at least two essential characteristics of generic performativity. First, it represents macro comprehensive social dynamism and affects individual and organizational behaviors. It may also shape social institutions through regulators or standard setters' (operative members') rule-making activities. Second, generic performativity is explored and identified by observers and researchers. Thus, the identification is likely to be retrospective and must, to some extent, be accepted by the audience as persuasive and plausible. However, to repeat, the identification process is necessarily interpretive in nature, as it is inherently observer-relative in the Searlean sense. This does not mean that such identification is useless in social science because it can provide certain space where social scientists can discuss a set of institutional changes and the accompanying behaviors from a consistent performative lens. Beunza and Ferraro (2019, p. 537) argued that the concept of performative work[9] contributes to the literature on institutional work by extending the concept of normative network and regulatory network to the realm of performativity and material artifacts. A performativity perspective can be useful to closely consider the normative and regulatory aspects of institutional change. This is what Part II of this book tries to achieve by arguing that regulatory bodies' (or operative members') decisions are performatively mobilized by collective social norms. Furthermore, the identification of generic performativity can provide an opportunity to highlight a counterperformative movement by drawing our attention to reactions against unidirectional regulatory measures.

[9] They define performative work as the institutional work to enable translation and the subsequent adoption of a performative device. It emphasizes the gains from jointly considering the emphasis on materiality that characterizes the performativity literature with attention to norms, roles, and resources that are found in institutional theory (Beunza & Ferraro, 2019, p. 535).

A major concern we should acknowledge in identifying observable social norms, or their generic performativity, is the subjective aspect of one's interpretation. For instance, the doctrine of objectivism or realism tells us to eliminate all subjective elements, such as our own feelings and desires in our pictures of the external world, from our views about reality (Bunge, 1993, pp. 209–210). However, we cannot avert our gaze from the forces of collective belief-based norms. The force of them is such that if a person believes that fact X is real, he will behave as if X were real even if X is actually nothing but a figment of his imagination (Bunge, 1993, p. 226; Merton, 1957, pp. 421ff).[10] In fact, social scientists are inclined to be interested in the way subjective factors, such as beliefs, valuations, and attitudes, influence objective ones such as actions and, in turn, how the actions of other people influence our subjective experiences (Bunge, 1993, p. 226).

Therefore, the key condition on this matter is whether one's identification of generic performativity is reasonable or satisfactory to the audience (readers). As mentioned earlier, there are many candidates for generic performativity in society. To make an identification of a specific performative discourse persuasive, the idea of felicitous conditions can be helpful. According to Austin's speech act theory, a performative utterance is neither true nor false; rather, it is deemed "felicitous" or "infelicitous" according to a set of conditions. Austin (1975) mainly focused on infelicitous conditions rather than felicitous ones that could be determined by posing the following three questions: (1) To what types of "acts" does the notion of infelicitous apply?; (2) How complete is this classification of infelicity?; and (3) Are these classes mutually exclusive? Austin (1975) did not clearly indicate who should answer these esoteric questions. However, given his focus on infelicitous rather than felicitous conditions, the conditions of generic performativity require a broad analysis of specific discourses (or theories), whether true or false, that many of us in society do not negate. As MacKenzie (2007, p. 78) observed from a Bourdieuan perspective, "we cannot identify performativity purely as a linguistic process since we need to consider the social, cultural, and political nature of the 'conditions of felicity' of the process."

[10] Merton (1957, p. 400) implied that the man of letters succeeds better than rigorous scientists in depicting, in unmistakable and vivid colors, the social situation which those scientists have abstractly analyzed.

To consider the essential felicitous conditions for the identification of generic performativity, it is useful to review other scholars' thoughts. First, referring to both Austin's and Searle's analyses and to her own conceptualization of performativity, Svetlova (2016) expressed her concerns about potential institutional regress within performative studies, contending that the central condition of the felicity of a performative utterance depends on pre-existing shared rules and conventions (Svetlova, 2016, p. 190). This assertion points out the significance of reviewing what has been shared retrospectively.

Second, another criticism of performativity studies made by Brisset (2019) concerns their inadequate consideration to failures in performativity. Brisset focused on sociological performativity studies, insisting that those studies foreground the positive progressive performances of a specific theory or discourse, which means insufficient attention to counterperformativity. He criticized their excessive emphasis on materials assembled to reflect performativity:

> If performativist sociology builds its social ontology around the technical devices containing the economic theories and producing individual behaviours in conformity with them, it will be required to concentrate on a necessary precondition to this process, knowing that the uses of these devices become conventions, shared practices based on collective beliefs. (Brisset, 2019, p. 6)

Third, recent performativity studies ignore or neglect macro social status dimensions, such as social norms (Brisset, 2019). Although previous sociological studies of markets and finance (e.g., Callon et al., 2007) with the essence of ANT have applied the performativity perspective and placed an emphasis on human and non-human material actors, social factors that affect human behaviors should be taken into account.[11] That is what I will argue narratively in Part II that observable belief-based social norms performatively drive individual (or organizational) behaviors and shape a specific set of institutions.

The above-mentioned analyses signify several conditions that need to be considered when one argues that something is performative. First, it

[11] As will be discussed in the next chapter, it is debatable whether linguistic expressions are physically material. If a linguistic expression appears in any texts, it is at least partially material. And if it is communicated as speech in any conversations, it is material as a set of sounds.

should be based on a broad analysis to find the performances of different discourses that many of us recognize and whose existence cannot be denied. Second, it should take the human tendency to follow existing rules and conventions, or social norms, into account (Svetlova, 2016). Third, it should be neutral to consider the failure of performativity or counterperformativity (Brisset, 2019). This book attempts to deal with all these conditions. The second condition can be understood as the human tendency of the imitation and diffusion of specific discourses and theories, and will be considered in the case studies in Part II. It also involves considerations to the collective norms existing in society that the previous chapter has already discussed vis-à-vis performative forces. As for the third condition, the possibility of counterperformativity is also discussed in those case studies. Thus, only the first condition needs to be elaborated upon. To analyze the broad performative forces of observable social norms, it would be necessary to describe a set of institutional changes that are particularly caused by such forces. The challenging task, however, is to explain the relationship between performativity and institutional change. Even if the task is interpretive in nature, a detailed analysis of operative members' decision-making process and the reasons for the decisions is at least necessary.

Performative Forces and Institutional Change

This subsection discusses how performative forces of observable social norms shape formal institutions.[12] Like Hermann-Pillath and Hederer (2023), this book proposes that operative members with specific types of cognitive frameworks rely on the same observable social norms and establish formal institutions to perform them. First, as discussed with reference to Tuomela (2002, 2003), macro formal institutions are generally set democratically by a group of selected people. In many cases, operative members are representatives who decide to create, change, or sustain institutions for non-operative members.

These operative members are generally selected based on others' consensus in terms of their attributes, such as skills and experiences. Some

[12] Performativity can contribute to our understanding of how institutions are created, maintained, and disrupted (Beunza & Ferraro, 2019, p. 516).

roles of operative members[13] are shaped by the process of self-selection and education (Hermann-Pillath & Hederer, 2023, p. 221). For example, in a company, not everyone aspires to become a CEO, and not everyone enrolls in an MBA program; only a limited subset of individuals selects the development track and eventually ends up as a certain type of agent, which is publicly visible by having an MBA, belonging to a golf club, and wearing business attire (Hermann-Pillath & Hederer, 2023, p. 221). Obviously, the most powerful operating member in a corporation is a CEO who has the authority to change the institutions and strategies of the corporation. The point is that, those who become CEOs or other directors in companies above a certain size, or those who desire to be in those positions, have a similar behavioral style and cognitive framework.

What then is the mechanism of performative institutionalization? I have already mentioned some necessary theoretical tools. Basically, uncertainty always exists and operative members are frequently confronted with difficult decisions. Modern society has become complicated and many things are now connected with other things,[14] which amplify the complexity of society. Uncertainty is the basic resource of economic behavior and offers room to obtain profits (Esposito, 2013, p. 110). The economy could not function or exist for long without uncertainty because it can be a source of continuous creativity and innovation (Esposito, 2013, p. 110). Operative members' decisions must be difficult, because, in addition to high levels of uncertainty, they must take human fallible principles (Soros, 2013) into account. The selected operative members are responsible for the consequences of their decisions and have an incentive to avoid mistakes and failures for other non-operative members. The theory of sharing mental models becomes important in this context. Operative members try to collect necessary and reliable data by exchanging relevant information with others. It may be, for instance, future predictions based

[13] Instead of operative members, Hermann-Pillath and Hederer (2023) used "agents" who perform institutions.

[14] "With advances in communications technology, the world is moving toward a connected society. Changes in network speed, improvements in accessibility, and the pervasiveness of online connections mean that people can access information and services around the clock. This enables new approaches in education, health care, transportation, energy, and entertainment. In this series, we address the policy, legal, and regulatory aspects of the connected society" (https://www.brookings.edu/series/connected-society-internet-of-things-innovation/).

on context-independent cost-benefit calculations (Hermann-Pillath & Hederer, 2023, p. 224).

However, similar people have similar networks, and therefore operative members in a specific context are likely to have similar cognitive frameworks or mental models. When operative members have to decide on whose mental models are reliable, they should rely on their own knowledge and experiences. Operative members not only rely on their own experiences but also try to consider the impacts of their decisions on society by reaching out to others (Hermann-Pillath & Hederer, 2023, p. 224). The decisions of operative members sometimes reach a deadlock because there may be many preferences and consequences.

In such cases, what operative members do is to refer to collective norms. There are at least two options for them. The first is to rely on collectively accepted existing rules and stay with the status quo. This is called path dependency that explains the stability of institutions. It happens when operative members are not sure if the benefit of radically changing institutions would exceed the cost of changing existing practices.

The second option for the operative members to take is to search for applicable successful cases in a similar context. Such successful models can be found in the results of a different group, organization, cooperation, country, or supranational organization. Extensive radical institutional change tends to occur through this mechanism. The target of the search for successful models may range from formal institutions to informal principles or norms depending on the context. It even includes observable social norms such as SDGs and gender-free movements. In that case, operative members cannot clearly tell if the norms of SDGs are successful. They follow those norms because successful individuals and organizations seem to follow them. This often happens because imitation is a basic mechanism for operative members (Hermann-Pillath & Hederer, 2023, p. 167). "Imitation is an important means to overcome the uncertainty over one's own preference and to express one's social identity; in other words, imitation is an essential form of performative mechanism of choice" (Hermann-Pillath & Hederer, 2023, p. 167). The imitation is, according to Esposito (2013, p. 116), called "second performativity," which implies not only the ability of the theory to transform the world, but also the way in which observers observe each other, and observers (unlike the world) have a certain freedom with regard to this observation. They can follow others and act like them, or they can choose to deviate and act differently because they know what others are doing and observing. The latter may give rise to counterperformative consequences.

Therefore, for a group of operative members, imitating collective norms in different contexts such as in a different country, can be a viable option. However, it should be noted that imitating or following a specific institution in a different country is not always welcomed by other non-operative members because some of them believe that if a country is different, many aspects, including culture, must also be different.

Accordingly, it is necessary to closely observe the institutional changes made by the operative members and interpret a belief-based social norm shared by them. In other words, based on the infelicitous conditions discussed above, paying attention to the kind of beliefs or discourses collectively accepted by operative members is significant. Observable social norms are typically "symbolic expressions" that are occasionally inscribed in different forms of texts (Phillips & Malhotra, 2017, p. 401). Such symbolic expressions need to reflect the dynamism of society so that operative members deserve imitating or following as a viable option under uncertainty. However, as I have repeatedly mentioned, those observable norms are identified and analyzed by social scientists. To put it more clearly, my aim in this book is not to shed light on an emerging new collective norm, but rather to consider how widely accepted collective norms have performatively mobilized some institutional changes and if there is any counterperformative action in a specific context. The next chapter will identify belief-based observable norms that are generically performative in contemporary society.

References

Austin, J. L. (1975). *How to do things with words* (2nd ed.). Harvard University Press.

Bamford, A., & MacKenzie, D. (2018). Counterperformativity. *New Left Review, 113*, 97–121.

Barnes, B. (1983). Social life as bootstrapped induction. *Sociology, 17*(4), 524–545.

Barnett, S., & Boyle, C. A. (Eds.). (2016). *Rhetoric, through everyday things*. The University of Alabama Press.

Beunza, D., & Ferraro, F. (2019). Performative work: Bridging performativity and institutional theory in the responsible investment field. *Organization Studies, 40*(4), 515–543.

Bloor, D. (1997). *Wittgenstein, rules and institutions*. Routledge.

Brisset, N. (2017). The future of performativity. *Œconomia, 7*(3), 439–452.
Brisset, N. (2019). *Economics and performativity: Exploring limits, theories and cases* (M. Webb, Trans.). Routledge.
Bunge, M. (1993). Realism and antirealism in social science. *Theory and Decision, 35*(1), 207–235.
Callon, M. (2007). What does it mean to say that economics is performative? In D. A. MacKenzie, F. Muniesa, & L. Siu (Eds.), *Do economists make markets?* (pp. 311–357). Princeton University Press.
Callon, M., Millo, Y., & Muniesa, F. (Eds.). (2007). *Market devices*. Blackwell.
Cavanaugh, J. R. (2015). Performativity. In J. L. Jackson Jr. (Ed.), *Oxford bibliographies in anthropology*. Oxford University Press.
Czarniawska, B. (2016). Performativity of social sciences as seen by an organization scholar. *European Management Journal, 34*(4), 315–318.
Esposito, E. (2013). The structures of uncertainty: Performativity and unpredictability in economic operations. *Economy and Society, 42*(1), 102–129.
Gergen, M. M., & Gergen, K. J. (2011). Performative social science and psychology. *Historical Social Research, 36*(4), 291–299.
Guala, F. (2016). Performativity rationalized. In I. Boldyrev & E. Svetlova (Eds.), *Enacting dismal science: New perspectives on the performativity of economics* (pp. 29–52). Palgrave Macmillan.
Herrmann-Pillath, C., & Hederer, C. (2023). *The new principles of economics: The science of markets*. Routledge.
MacKenzie, D. (2006). *An engine, not a camera: How financial models shape markets*. MIT Press.
MacKenzie, D. (2007). Is economics performative? In D. MacKenzie, F. Muniesa, & L. Siu (Eds.), *Do economists make markets? On the performativity of economics* (pp. 54–86). Princeton University Press.
MacKenzie, D., Muniesa, F., & Siu, L. (Eds.). (2007). *Do Economists make markets? On the performativity of economics*. Princeton University Press.
Mäki, U. (2013). Performativity: Saving Austin from MacKenzie. In V. Karakostas & D. Dieks (Eds.), *EPSA11 perspectives and foundational problems in philosophy of science* (pp. 443–453). Springer.
Merton, R. K. (1957). *Social theory and social structure* (Rev. ed.). Free Press.
Millikan, R. G. (2014). Deflating socially constructed objects: What thoughts do to the world. In M. Gallotti & J. Michael (Eds.), *Perspectives on social ontology and social cognition* (pp. 27–39). Springer.
Nealon, J. T. (2021). *Fates of the performative: From the linguistic turn to the new materialism*. University of Minnesota press.
Nyberg, D., & Wright, C. (2016). Performative and political: Corporate constructions of climate change risk. *Organization, 23*(5), 617–638.

Okamoto, N. (2020). Collectively accepted social norms and performativity: The pursuit of normativity of globalization in economic institutions. *Journal of Economic Methodology, 27*(3), 226–239.

Peled, M. (2020). Restoring constitution: Saving performativity from Mäki's critique. *Journal of Economic Methodology, 27*(1), 51–65.

Phillips, N., & Malhotra, N. (2017). Language, cognition and institutions: Studying institutionalization using linguistic methods. In R. Greenwood, C. Oliver, B. Thomas, T. B. Lawrence, & R. E. Meyer (Eds.), *The SAGE handbook of organizational institutionalism* (2nd ed., pp. 392–417). Sage.

Searle, J. R. (1976). A classification of illocutionary acts. *Language in Society, 5*(1), 1–23.

Searle, J. R. (2018). Status functions. In M. Jankovic & K. Ludwig (Eds.), *The Routledge handbook of collective intentionality* (pp. 300–309). Routledge.

Soros, G. (2013). Fallibility, reflexivity, and the human uncertainty principle. *Journal of Economic Methodology, 20*(4), 309–329.

Svetlova, E. (2016). Performativity and emergence of institutions. In I. Boldyrev & E. Svetlova (Eds.), *Enacting dismal science: New perspectives on the performativity of economics* (pp. 183–200). Palgrave Macmillan.

Svetlova, E. (2018). *Financial models and society: Villains or scapegoats?* Edward Elgar.

Tuomela, R. (2002). *The philosophy of social practices: A collective acceptance view.* Cambridge University Press.

Tuomela, R. (2003). Collective acceptance, social institutions, and social reality. *The American Journal of Economics and Sociology, 62*(1), 123–165.

CHAPTER 4

Identifying Contemporary Observable Social Norms

Part I of this book has introduced and synthesized interdisciplinary perspectives of institutional theories, social ontology, and performativity. It has been completely outside the field of accounting, but its interdisciplinary nature is the strength of this book. In an article based on his plenary address at the 2006 annual meeting of the American Accounting Association, Anthony Hopwood, founder of the European Accounting Association and founding editor of one of the leading accounting journals, *Accounting, Organizations and Society*, cautioned that accounting is left with a research community whose members are too conservative, too intellectually constrained, too conformist, and insufficiently excited and involved with the changing practice or regulation of the craft (Hopwood, 2007, p. 1372). This book takes the warning seriously and seeks to engage with interdisciplinary perspectives to provide fresh insights into changes in accounting. Although accounting is practical and technical, the numbers it generates are connected to society through disclosures in corporate financial statements and other communication channels. In other words, accounting institutions are inherently intertwined with society.

In order to take the social dynamics into account, this chapter explores generically performative collective norms in contemporary society. It is a challenging interpretation because it is similar to searching for and comparing the degree of collective acceptance of various discourses.

N. Okamoto, *Institutional Change and Performativity*, https://doi.org/10.1007/978-3-031-53393-8_4

Some may criticize the selection of collective social norms as biased or arbitrary. To address such criticism, this book adopts a linguistic approach and considers the process of nominalization as a reflection of the collective acceptance of a certain discourse. In particular, among several nominalized discourses, this book limits its focus to a specific type of nominalization with the suffix "-ation," which often represents the fixation of collective belief (Walsh, 2004) and the dynamism of society. This approach significantly limits the scope of subjectivity in identifying collectively observable norms (Okamoto, 2020).

However, there are still many nominalized words with the suffix "-ation" that reflect social dynamics. In this respect, the present book does not aim to discover a collective norm that has not yet received significant attention. Instead, it relies on widely accepted discourses to analyze retrospectively whether they have performatively shaped relevant institutions. Using some data that reliably support widespread social acceptance, this chapter highlights two types of observable social norms.

Furthermore, the pervasiveness of their performativity needs to be clarified. In this regard, the collective acceptance of norms does not require unanimous acceptance by the members of a particular group, organization, or society. Only selected operative members represent other non-operative members and influence the maintenance and change of institutions, while non-operative members tacitly accept the decisions of operative members. As the degree of adherence to collective norms may vary among operative members, Part II will examine the minutes and documents from the standard-setting process and carefully analyze the shared discourses.

The crux of the matter lies in determining whether the decisions made by the operative members and the institutional changes are performative. In fact, the process of institutionalization is complicated, and it is difficult to identify a single direct cause of a particular institutional change (or stability). Therefore, the relationship between generic performativity and institutional change tends to be interpretive and descriptive. Nevertheless, this book focuses only on specific instances of Japanese accounting regulation and aims to ensure that the interpretation is plausible.

Moreover, the focus on a limited time frame in a specific country allows for the analysis of detailed institutional changes. As noted earlier, the effects of macro generic performativity can be seen in a particular time and space. The review of several case studies on the global diffusion of norms in this chapter shows that it is useful to highlight and examine relevant actors' reliance on collective norms or discourses in a limited historical time frame. In particular, their ideas and decisions are examined through the analysis of symbolic expressions from different types of texts, including minutes of meetings, official reasons for standard-setting, and comments in articles or interviews. Overall, this chapter justifies the scope of the case analyses in Part II, focusing specifically on recent Japanese accounting regulation.

4.1 Linguistic Approach to the Analysis of Performativity

Linguistic Approach and the Significance of Texts in Institutionalization

To capture the performative nature of the institutionalization process, a linguistic perspective is useful because it allows us to understand the black box aspects of the institutionalization process when studying institutional reality (Phillips & Malhotra, 2017, p. 401). From that perspective, four analytical methods (discourse analysis, rhetorical analysis, narrative analysis, and semiotic analysis) can be used to study institutional dynamics. Although these methods differ in detail, what they have in common is the analysis of texts that can take different forms, such as written documents, spoken words, artworks, images, videos, blogs, tweets, buildings, and songs (Phillips & Malhotra, 2017, p. 401).

Regardless of the forms of texts, a crucial question is how commonly a particular discourse is shared. For example, to analyze linguistic representations or discourses, the characteristics of a rhetorical expression are sometimes considered by the Aristotelian classifications of logos, pathos, and ethos. However, there are no meta-criteria for prioritizing the effectiveness of these different streams of rhetorical legitimacy. Moreover, the classification of rhetorical types tends to be complicated and arbitrary. Indeed, rhetoric certainly plays a significant role in the standard-setting process, as different actors, including the standard setter, aim to persuade others of the viability, credibility, and plausibility of their positions, beliefs, problems, solutions, and perspectives (Young, 2003, p. 623). Therefore, the persuasiveness of key rhetorical expressions is significant during the standard-setting process. For instance, if a regulator enthusiastically prioritizes achieving a "free, fair, and global" financial market at the expense of traditional local standards, it is likely to resonate with multiple values of operative members. In this instance, if a series of institutional changes are undertaken to achieve a "free, fair, and global" financial market, its performative nature can be analyzed. What is essential here is how an observer understands, interprets, and expresses the generic nature of performativity through the careful analysis of the context.

To identify the generic performativity of a specific discourse, one way to analyze the performative forces that arise from it is to focus on the interrelations between texts, changes in texts, and new textual forms that constitute discourses over time (Phillips & Malhotra, 2017, p. 403). The essence of semiotic analysis, characterized as the phenomenon of representation—how things stand for or substitute for other things (Phillips & Malhotra, 2017, p. 408)—is useful in understanding the relationship between texts and institutions. In a semiotic analysis, complex texts are thought to generate sets of cultural understandings that underpin our social conventions. For instance, "ideas such as patriotism, ethnic identity, and religious belief are often associated with complex signs—flags, religious symbols, styles of dress—that come to represent these important cultural myths" (Phillips & Malhotra, 2017, p. 409). In addition to these material things, this book emphasizes the communicative aspects of rhetorical representations/discourses that manifest in various types of texts and reflect performative collective social norms. Communication through discourse is an interaction between actors through text. Conversation between speakers and listeners and education through textbooks are also material interactions that produce communication through discourse.

Focus on Nominalized Linguistic Representations

Therefore, this book particularly identifies both operative and non-operative members' acceptance of a specific discourse via the structures and frequent use of words within society, which is in line with the essence of Austin's emphasis on infelicitous aspects of speech acts. Based on the insights from discourse studies, the form and process of nominalization matter in the representation of collective norms. Nominalization is a concise way of linguistically expressing the conceptualization of a process or state of affairs in a nominal form (Bello, 2016). According to Billig (2008, p. 786), "By turning verbs into nouns, speakers/writers can convey that the entities, denoted by nominalization, have a real and necessary existence." Moreover, "these linguistically created things have a privileged discursive status because of their presumed existence" (Billig, 2008, p. 786).[1] Bello (2016) observed that "when compared with verbs, nominalizations can be more ambiguous due to valency reduction, but they also provide valuable opportunities to organize discourse and express abstract relations among processes in a more efficient way" (Bello, 2016, p. 19).

Nominalization thus serves as a functional guide that helps organize information in the mind of the receiver. It appears in written genres because it can establish abstractions and objectify and stratify the processes to which it refers (Bello, 2016, p. 3). Owing to the augmentation of abstraction in the modern sciences, the abundance of nominalization is conspicuous (Bello, 2016, p. 3). It is useful in the transmission and extension of scientific knowledge because language becomes more compact and direct from the point of view of specialists. Through nominalization, scientific activity is conceptualized and perceived as an object (Bello, 2016, p. 4) that reinforces the unquestionability of the concepts introduced, facilitating their assimilation by the reader. Nominalization accordingly enables realities, facts, and statements to be presented as unalterable or, at least, indisputable (Bello, 2016, p. 4). Therefore, the purpose of identifying observable social norms is to pursue possible nominalized linguistic representations that capture the dynamism of society. Nominalization refers to the process of producing a noun from different parts of speech, such as a verb, adjective, or adverb. The process typically involves adding a suffix (and slightly changing its form) to the word. There are different types of suffixes for nominalization. For example, the verb "move" can be nominalized to "movement" by adding the suffix "-ment." Similarly, the adjective "creative" can be nominalized to "creativity" by adding the suffix "-ity."

[1] Martin (2008) analyzed the nominalization from a functional perspective (systematic functional linguistic), according to which "we can treat nominalization at the level of grammar (syntax if you will) as a grammatical resource for deriving nouns from other word classes–for example, nouns from verbs (*transform/transformation*) or nouns from adjectives (*free/freedom*). As a second step, we can ask how this resource may or may not evolve to affect the relationship between discourse semantics and lexicogrammar. For example, if we derive runner from run, we have a nominalization that refers to a participant which operates as a human entity in semantic figures of various kinds (*the runner won, the runner said…, the runner was tired*); a *runner* is someone who runs, not a process. The grammar and semantics match because we have a semantic entity realized by a noun" (Martin, 2008, p. 802).

Nominalized words represent the fixation of collective belief (Walsh, 2004). Under uncertainty, people must form some beliefs about situations in which they find themselves before they can decide what actions are in their interest. Often, "groups form beliefs routinely, such as, for instance, when central bankers must decide what the rate of inflation is before setting interest rates, or when environment managers must decide what the air quality is in a particular region before recommending regulation" (Walsh, 2004, p. 9). The mechanisms of nominalization can be used to establish common understandings (at least temporarily) to repair uncertainty, and to direct inquiry (by fixing its direction) (Walsh, 2004, p. 9). In short, the fixation of collective belief should be reflected in the changes in linguistic representations. The process of nominalization represents such a change.

Accordingly, the frequent use of the term with the suffix "-ation" and individuals' exposure to it resonates in their cognitive frameworks. Referring to insights from behavioral studies, a distinction can be drawn between declarative (explicit) and nondeclarative[2] (implicit) memory (Corballis & Suddendorf, 2010, p. 367). Declarative memory can be subdivided into two categories: semantic memory, namely memory for recalling more or less enduring facts about the world, and episodic memory, which involves the recall of specific events. "Roughly, semantic memory can be linked to a combined dictionary and encyclopedia, and provides our basic concepts about the world, while episodic memory can be linked to a personal diary and provides us with our sense of [a] personal past" (Corballis & Suddendorf, 2010, pp. 367–368).

Given that, for instance, frequent exposure to the word "globalization" through various media outlets leads us to store globalization as a semantic memory, whereas the actual experiences of global mobilization of economic or human resources, such as global migration (e.g., an increase in foreign workers in the same workplace) and cross-border corporate activities (e.g., an acquisition of foreign subsidiaries) remain in our episodic memory. The collective acceptance of globalization by both operative and non-operative members proceeds through this dialectic process. The accumulation of individuals' episodic memories leads to epistemologically objective large-scale collective memory (Michaelian &

[2] The non-declarative component comprises procedural memory, which typically represents know-how and skills that are not generally articulated (Michaelian & Sutton, 2018, p. 141).

Sutton, 2018). However, individual and collective memory may conflict and the aggregation of individual memory to elevate to collective memory may be problematic (Olick, 1999).[3] With regard to this matter, Michaelian and Sutton (2018, pp. 148–149) proposed the right solution to the issue of consolidation of individual and collective memory: one must take a long-term perspective to consider broadly various forms of material artifacts, ranging from museum collections and textbooks to articles in news media and scientific journals. This suggestion is in line with the approach of this book in that it takes a long-term perspective and focuses on symbolic linguistic expressions in various forms of texts.

4.2 Identifying Observable Social Norms

Globalization

As discussed above, the judgment of collective acceptance of a specific norm is not rigorous but rather subjective and interpretive. This book takes a broad scope to capture a collective norm/discourse that is generically performative. Thus, the focus is not limited to a specific community or organization. For instance, members of a specific religious organization are likely to share belief-based norms that shape the organization's principles and rules. A specific country has its own cultural norms that have been traditionally accepted by its citizens for a long time. This section pays attention to transnational norms that tend to have more influence on people in various jurisdictions in contemporary society.

The previous section suggested that a linguistic process of nominalization transforms a word that is not a noun (e.g., a verb, an adjective, or an adverb) into a noun by adding a suffix to the word. Applying this perspective assumes that the addition of the suffix "-ation" represents the process of depicting social dynamism. There are an infinite number of such nominalized words—not only globalization, but Westernization, capitalization, digitalization, etc. Of course, there are other suffixes that are added in

[3] Olick (1999, p. 346) recommended not sticking to the issue of aggregation of individual memories and instead, striving to develop social memory studies comprehensively.

the process of nominalization.[4] This book especially focuses on the transformation of the word from an adjective (global) to a verb (globalize) to a noun (globalization). Given that nominalization enables realities, facts, or statements to be presented as unalterable and indisputable (Bello, 2016, p. 4), this three-step nominalization reflects a strong foundation of collective acceptance. Words that end with "-ation" at least commonly depict organizational or social phenomena (changes). In that sense, they are collective as well as performative and likely to have normativity to a greater or lesser extent. Among those words nominalized with "-ation," globalization reflects not only the ongoing phenomena such as cross-border trading or international convergence of various standards, but it can also be a collective belief-based norm that performatively changes institutional reality. Although there are numerous types of theoretical or discursive "-ations," the pervasiveness and penetration of "globalization" in society attest to its widespread usage as a collective norm that represents a long-term social movement.

To understand how globalization is a widespread phenomenon, the etymology and genealogy of globalization, or considering the trajectory of the word of "globalization," are useful. James and Steger (2014) conducted a genealogical analysis of globalization as they considered it "one of the most important concepts for understanding the passage of human society into the third millennium" (James & Steger, 2014, p. 418). Based on their analysis, during the 1930s to 1970s, "there was no first genius who coined 'globalization'—a term which then, slowly or quickly, became part of the common sense of an age" (James & Steger, 2014, p. 425), even "across the middle of the twentieth century, 'globalization' remained an idiosyncratic and rarely used term, deployed with a surprising variety of meanings" (James & Steger, 2014, p. 428). The concept of globalization gained traction after 1980. It "was in the air in the late 1980s and provided oxygen across a number of fields that, through the medium of writing and publishing, are mutually supportive" (James & Steger, 2014, p. 431).

Although the level of collective acceptance of globalization cannot be measured rigorously, some reliable data are given below. The status

[4] As mentioned earlier, the suffix "-ment" is used to nominalize a word; the word "improvement" is a nominalized word of the verb "improve." However, this nominalization is not as frequently seen as the suffix "-ation" to represent a social phenomenon.

of this nominalized term of "globalization" as a collective norm was found out through a search conducted in February 2023, using the Google search engine, for four nominalized words with the "-ation" suffix, namely globalization, Westernization, financialization, and marketization. The numbers of hits were 257,000,000, 14,500,000, 2,670,000, and 2,170,000 for globalization, Westernization, financialization, and marketization, respectively. Although these nominalized words are more or less collectively accepted by looking at the number of hits on Google search, the wide diffusion of "globalization" is tremendous. By ensuring frequent exposure to the nominalized term, "globalization," the concerned actors performatively organize the minds of their audiences, inducing an assumption that globalization is real.

Almost two decades ago, economists expected favorable economic impacts (status functions) of globalization from the following changes: increasing links through trade flows between high- and low-income countries; integration of national economies through trade, finance, production, and a growing web of treaties and institutions; a sharp rise in foreign direct investments; and increased harmonization of economic institutions (Sachs, 1998, pp. 98–99). To capture the economic implications of globalization further, Sachs (1998) posed the following essential questions: (1) Will globalization promote faster economic growth?; (2) Will globalization promote or undermine macroeconomic stability?; (3) Will globalization promote growing income equality?; and (4) How should governmental institutions at all levels adjust their powers and responsibilities in view of the emerging global market? Twenty years later, we were able to reflect whether decisive answers to these general questions were provided by economics (or economists). On this point, Sachs (2017) affirms that (only) global poverty levels have fallen sharply since 1950 thanks to globalization and convergent growth (Sachs, 2017, p. 248).

Many economists have provided many partially optimized results of globalization in their specific fields; however, on the whole, clear answers to those questions have not been provided. For example, current views on financial globalization in economics are, at best, ambivalent (Rodrik, 2018, p. 20). This stems from the elusiveness of the concept of globalization. Nevertheless, despite this elusiveness, the term "globalization" has acquired the collective acceptance of the majority of people through its promotion via education and socialization processes. Over the past decades, students of international relations have tried to come to grips with the myriad international economic and political changes that seem to characterize globalization, and have found that there are perhaps as many meanings as there are analysts (Sjolander, 1996, p. 603).

The depth of penetration of this term is apparent in its genealogy: "for all the intensifying processes of globalization, the concept draws most of its power from a condensation of associations across all four levels of the formation of social meaning" (James & Steger, 2014, p. 431). First, at the level of ideas, the increased use of a concept creates momentum. The concept can gain certain limited purchase, as it is actively used by critical agents—authors, editors, and journalists—who are all attempting to explain changing fields of understanding or conditions of practice. Second, at the level of ideologies, the burgeoning of globalization is evident as various political groups place it within a conceptual framework that provides ammunition for concrete political programs and agendas. Third, within the imaginary layer of meaning formation, as globalization has gained expressive consonance with a newly emerging social imaginary, it has simultaneously named this largely pre-reflexive "global" imaginary, acquiring further condensing force. Fourth, at the ontological level, the concept has tapped into a core of social meanings about contemporary shifts in time, space, and other dimensions of social relations. Consequently, the belief in globalization can serve as the basis for actions to ensure that globalization is productive, fair, and sustainable. It can also serve as the basis for engagements of the business sector, universities, politicians, civil society, religious leaders, and other key groups in society (Sachs, 2017, p. 250). Meanwhile, operative members (standard setters) who establish or maintain economic institutions for most non-operative members are often in a situation in which considerations to the net economic benefit of introducing a specific institution are necessary. In this context, following and accepting the elusive, but totalized and homogenized concept of globalization constitutes a viable choice given its collective acceptance.

The purpose of this book is not to provide various data to compare or affirm the pervasiveness of the norm of globalization, but to highlight how globalization has become common and rooted (embedded) in our daily life by referring to the claims of intellectuals. Considering this discussion, globalization is collectively accepted and internalized in our institutions and cognitive frameworks. How globalization performatively shapes operative members' standard-setting activities and institutions will be investigated in a specific context later in Part II.

Financialization

This book also proposes financialization as another case of generic performativity that has shaped contemporary social institutions. Compared to globalization, financialization seems less widespread in terms of its popularity and the level of collective acceptance. There is a viewpoint that financialization is one of the comprehensive processes of ongoing globalization. However, as this subsection argues, financialization differs from globalization in some ways, and it is useful to treat it as a separate case of generic performativity.

What is financialization? On the one hand, it has been defined broadly in the literature. For instance, it is summarized as "the increasing role of financial motives, financial markets, financial actors and financial institutions in the operation of domestic and international economies" (Epstein, 2005, p. 3). The impact of financialization is not limited to the realm of the international economy: "financialization refers to the web of interrelated processes—economic, political, social, technological, cultural, etc.—through which finance has extended its influence beyond the marketplace and into other realms of social life" (Van der Zwan, 2014, p. 101). An important aspect of financialization could be cultural, manifesting as the expansion and creep of financial ideas, metaphors, processes, and structures into everyday life and social institutions (Haiven, 2014, p. 38). From these broad analyses, there would be no major disagreement that financialization represents a macro-social dynamism.

On the other hand, some studies have introduced a slightly more limited scope in defining the concept of financialization. For example, regarding "accumulation" in the economy, financialization is defined as "a pattern of accumulation in which profit-making occurs increasingly through financial channels rather than through trade and commodity production" (Krippner, 2005, p. 181). It is also argued to be "both a macroeconomic structural phenomenon and a socio-political process that requires reconfiguration of social and economic institutions that support accumulation" (Gunnoe & Gellert, 2011, p. 270).

In addition, financialization has been defined further in relation to the widely known political concept of neoliberalism and (financial) capitalism (Bieling, 2013): "Neoliberalism meant, in short, the financialization of everything and the relocation of the power center of capital accumulation to owners and their financial institutions at the expense of other fractions of capital" (Harvey, 2006, p. 24). These varied perspectives reveal that different authors have interpreted financialization differently. However, they also indicate that financialization is now a social phenomenon recognized by various scholars even though the recognition broadly encompasses different interpretations.[5]

Particularly after the collapse of Lehman Brothers and the subsequent global financial crisis, many countries, corporations, and individuals suffered from sluggish economic recovery, and excessive financialization of the economy and society was often viewed as the prime factor. Since then, the number of studies on financialization from various perspectives has grown rapidly.[6] Nevertheless, there are various viewpoints on the elusive concept of financialization and its meaning remains expansive.

As indicated above, the use of the word "financialization" is far less frequent than the use of globalization. However, particularly after the financial crisis, the expression has rapidly drawn the attention of observers, such as academic researchers. Figure 4.1 shows the number of articles that include the keyword "financializ[s]ation" on Google Scholar. It is evident that the volume of articles on financialization has grown rapidly since 2008, which shows that financialization has penetrated into society to some extent.

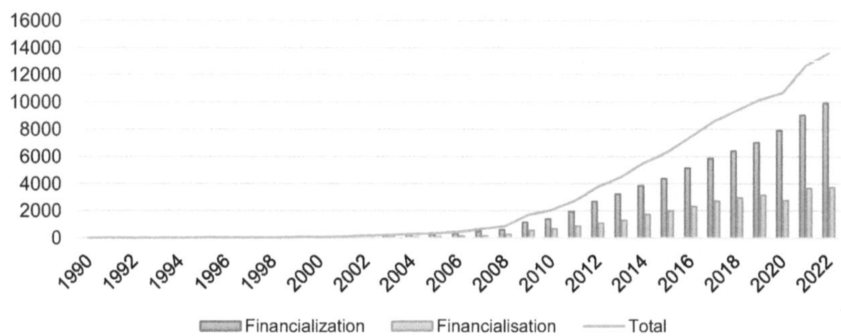

Fig. 4.1 The number of financialization articles published each year (1990–2022)

[5] The situation is expressed as "a danger that financialization will become a chaotic concept, a blanket term which is stretched too far to cover a range of related, but fundamentally different, projects" (French et al., 2011, p. 801).

[6] For instance, the work of Mader et al. (2020) is a large volume encompassing a wide range of studies on financialization.

Corporate financial activities and transactions have at least amplified over a couple of decades.[7] The fact has been triggered by the shift in corporate behaviors to seek financial returns in financial markets. Thus, "financialization is another name for the growing role played by investment activities as an autonomous profit centre in the corporate structure" (Preda, 2009, p. 5). It is also characterized by the transformation of future income streams into marketable securities (Lucarrelli, 2012, p. 431), which represents a "profound shift away from direct investment in productive capacity, towards the open financial markets in which profitability can be temporarily boosted through speculative operations in the stock markets" (Zhang & Andrew, 2014, p. 19).

Moreover, one of the most conspicuous characteristics of financialization is its global nature. It would be difficult to understand the processes of financialization without properly considering the networks of international finance in which corporate profit-seeking activities take place. On this point, French et al., (2011, p. 810) suggested recognizing a more holistic integration of international and domestic financial systems and paying close attention to the local context. Although financial markets around the world have essentially become borderless, it is still important to consider geographical differences, because each country maintains its own local financial regulations and practices. Davis and Kim (2015, p. 216) pointed out that financialization takes on different characteristics based on local circumstances. Therefore, it is useful to analyze Japan, a non-Western country, as a site of global financialization. The significance of extending the research agenda on financialization to an Asian context was also highlighted by Jackson (2016, p. 5).

If we look at the specific institutional context of accounting regulation, financialization has been conspicuous. For example, Collison et al. (2014) examined changes in company laws in the UK in the context of financialization. They saw formal company laws as a set of institutions that reflect the social dynamism in the context of financialization. Following interviews with those involved in the company law review process, they emphasized directors' responsibility for maximizing shareholder value as an aspect of financialization. Zhang and Andrew (2014) explored the connection between accounting regulations and financialization by discussing some of the key changes to the conceptual framework project

[7] This is obvious given the growth in corporate derivatives and securitization transactions during the period (Lavoie, 2012).

being developed jointly by the International Accounting Standards Board (IASB) and US Financial Accounting Standards Board (FASB). They argued that the movement toward neoliberalism and the financialization of the global economy have been eased and legitimized in part by the adoption of global accounting regulations through the development of the conceptual framework for accounting. This involved defining the concept of users narrowly in financial reporting, which represents a shift in the purpose of financial reporting and reflects an emphasis on faithful representation instead of reliability, which highlights the use of investors/shareholders' accounting information to make investment decisions (Zhang & Andrew, 2014, p. 20). These studies have argued that financialization has shaped the reforms of corporate laws and accounting standards (including the conceptual framework) through explicit formal institutions. Moreover, they have argued that the principle of shareholder value maximization and supremacy of the shareholder value can be considered informal belief-based norms.

Compared to globalization, financialization is not comprehensive and widespread a phenomenon. However, as mentioned above, considering the penetration of financial transactions in our daily life, there seem to be so many non-operative members who tacitly accept financialization. To put it differently, operative members who are involved in financial regulation have collectively acknowledged and accepted financialization because they tend to have similar "financial cognition," which denotes the processes of interactive knowledge production and cognitive schemas—in combination with technical instruments, financial models, specific room layouts and group interactions, among other things, which play a central role in the formation and execution of investment and trading strategies (Vollmer et al., 2009, p. 621).[8]

Part II examines how these two observable collective norms, or their generic performativity, have mobilized the accounting regulations in Japan. Before that, the methodological stance of the case studies in Japan within the proposed theoretical framework is discussed in the next section.

[8] In addition to financial cognition, there is also a "market cognition" (Zaki et al., 2021). Although not all market participants must have market cognition (market reasoning) in order to participate in the transactions, these cognitive frameworks as well as the representations anchored to financial documents are necessary components of the financial institutions and their functioning.

4.3 Methodological Stance to a Specific Institutional Context

Process Tracing and the Focus on Changes in a Limited Context

To analyze performative institutional changes, the following chapters in Part II trace the detailed standard-setting process in Japan. Process tracing is a fundamental tool for qualitative analysis that involves a systematic examination of diagnostic evidence selected and analyzed in relation to research questions and hypotheses formulated by the investigator (Collier, 2011, p. 823).[9] Diagnostic evidence provides the basis for descriptive and causal inference (Collier, 2011, pp. 823–824). Such diagnostic evidence is usually understood as part of a temporal sequence of events with probative value in supporting or overturning descriptive and explanatory hypotheses (Mahoney, 2012, p. 571). In brief, process tracing is intricately linked to a specific theoretical perspective, as identifying the bits of diagnostic evidence depends centrally on prior knowledge (Collier, 2011, p. 824). These statements support this book's focus on the symbolic linguistic representations that connect performative forces with institutional changes.

In the process of theory development, researchers can utilize collected diagnostic data in an inductive manner, wherein they meticulously analyze hypotheses in relation to a constructed or widely accepted theory. More specifically, the process tracing method investigates empirical case(s) to determine if the theoretically elaborated causal mechanisms effectively explain the relationship between X and Y (Trampusch & Palier, 2016, p. 439).[10] Although the process tracing method can be inductive in an explorative manner, aiming at theory or hypothesis building (that is, uncovering and specifying causal mechanisms) (Collier, 2011, p. 824), this book employs a deductive approach. This is because it attempts to

[9] Process tracing has become increasingly popular in case studies, in political science, and political economy in recent years (Trampusch & Palier, 2016, p. 437). Although there are various objectives for applying the process tracing method, it is at least helpful in identifying novel political and social phenomena and systematically describing them, evaluating prior explanatory hypotheses, discovering new hypotheses, and assessing these new causal claims (Collier, 2011, p. 824).

[10] See also George and Bennett (2005).

demonstrate, within the context of recent Japanese accounting regulation, how collective norms' generic performativity has shaped institutional changes.

To summarize the essence of the process tracing method, it is used to establish that (1) an initial event or process occurred, (2) a subsequent event or process also occurred, and (3) the former was a cause of the latter (Mahoney, 2012, p. 571). Regarding the first point, we can assume enough that "globalization" and "financialization" have actually occurred and become to affect individual and organizational behaviors. The following chapters will look into institutional changes in Japanese accounting regulation, particularly emphasizing the second and third points, to reveal these collective norms performatively shape formal institutions.

For the causal inference, process tracing focuses on unfolding events or situations over time, which is impossible if one cannot adequately describe an event or situation at one point (Collier, 2011, p. 824). Hence, the descriptive component of process tracing does not begin with observing change or sequence but rather with capturing accurate snapshots at a series of specific moments. To characterize a process, we should be able to characterize key steps in the process, which in turn permits good analysis of change and sequence (Collier, 2011, p. 824). In this regard, one's interpretation matters because the links between globalization or financialization and those institutional changes are not explicitly visible. Therefore, referring to the essential ideas of globalization and financialization, it is necessary to highlight operative members' key ideas and mementous decisions by relying on the data from primary sources, such as official documents, and secondary literature that objectively recorded the specific outcome (Trampusch & Palier, 2016, p. 442). By referring to the previous actions, interactions, and events represented in texts such as newspaper articles, this book shows the key factors for the final decisions of accounting standard setters and regulators.

In so doing, if a specific final decision made by standard setters or regulators is obviously influenced by global standards or suggestions from outside the country rather than maintaining or prioritizing domestic standards, the consequence (institutional change) is interpreted as performative "globalization." In other words, while a specific regulator may sustain domestic practices or standards instead of introducing global rules, there are instances where it may opt for global rules due to future uncertainty or the lack of clear advantages (or disadvantages) of sustaining existing rules. Regarding financialization, if the decision of standard setters or regulators is obviously made to achieve the development of financial markets or more active financial transactions, this book considers it as a component of financialization.

Therefore, the methodology of Part II is rather descriptive than purely causal because it does not rigorously test a specific hypothesis. Mahoney (2012, p. 579) asserts that for a hypothesis to be valid, it is necessary to have a given piece of evidence—a specific causal-process observation—. "While X being necessary for Y is in doubt, the status of M being sufficient for Y and X being necessary for M may be more readily established. These established or obtainable findings can be used to infer whether X is necessary for Y logically" (Mahoney, 2012, p. 579). Within this analytical framework, X refers to globalization or financialization, the mechanism M is considered a performative norm diffusion process, and Y represents institutional changes. This tripartite viewpoint is applicable to the consequential aspects of performative globalization and financialization that this book aims to argue.

Moreover, process tracing can yield robust results even when the test is formulated post hoc in response to the serendipitous discovery of data (Mahoney, 2012, p. 587). Like detectives, qualitative and case-oriented researchers commence their investigations with an outcome to be explained and multiple theories. During the investigation, they discover unanticipated and perhaps unforeseeable causal-process observations that have a tremendous bearing on their conclusions. Considering these discoveries, they formulate new hypotheses and conduct process tracing tests (Mahoney, 2012, p. 587).

In short, the deductive process tracing method does not rigidly test the hypothesis nor identify a definitive causal relationship between two variables. In this book project, it is applied to describe and understand the consequences of globalization and financialization within the context of Japanese accounting regulation. As a tool of causal inference, process tracing focuses on the unfolding of events or situations over time. Understanding this unfolding is unattainable unless one can adequately describe an event or situation at a specific moment. Hence, the descriptive component of process tracing entails observing change or sequence by capturing accurate snapshots at various specific instances. The process tracing method is appropriate to analyze changes by focusing either on recurring events or a single event (Collier, 2011, p. 825).

As noted above, analyzing the actions of operative members, such as regulators, is crucial to understanding performative institutional change. However, not all operative members explicitly recognize the generic performativity of observable social norms at all times; those norms often tacitly influence operative members' decisions in uncertain situations. Even more cumbersome is that observers, such as social scientists, cannot completely capture the thoughts of operative members, which necessitates the need for interpretations to understand the motivations and reasons behind those operative members' decisions.

To address this issue, one can narratively analyze how selected operative members in charge of setting institutions are affected by such performative forces. On this point, Kay (2006, p. 18), who analyzed policymaking dynamics, distinguishes between the "conditions of causality" and the "conditions of understandability." He emphasizes the importance of the latter. On the one hand, the former is a statement about the causal or generative relationship between two facts. On the other hand, the latter focuses on increasing the understandability of the process by presenting and explaining the mechanism through which that causal relationship occurred. The understandability indicated here is enhanced by inferring the underlying mechanism of the event and elucidating its origins (Kay, 2006, p. 18). Kay (2006) states that the "structured narrative" is crucial for understandability. The structure comprises various social elements, such as networks with other agents, institutions, and norms (Kay, 2006, p. 64). Accordingly, the case analyses in Part II are limited in time and space in order to narratively explain how collectively accepted norms performatively shape accounting institutions. The next subsection considers the limited setting of this book that covers radical changes, which is appropriate to apply the performativity perspective.

Focus on Accounting Reforms in Japan

As mentioned earlier, to understand a set of institutional changes as performative, it would be appropriate to focus on radical institutional changes rather than institutional stability because a performativity perspective sheds light on a dynamic process rather than a path-dependent situation.[11] This subsection briefly

[11] However, it would also be interesting to investigate a case of long-term institutional stability in terms of long-lasting strong performativity.

describes the unique research context of Japan in Part II, which focuses specifically on the significant institutional changes in a limited period of time.

As an island country, Japan is separated from the rest of the other Asian countries, which has enabled it to develop a unique culture. The development of accounting has followed a unique path. The historical development of accounting in Japan has undergone three revolutionary phases (Kikuya, 2019). The first revolution occurred during the late nineteenth century with the introduction of Western double-entry book-keeping in the Meiji era (1868–1912). Before that phase, or in the Edo era (1603–1867), single-entry bookkeeping, *Daifukucho* style, was employed to record commercial transactions and certain stocks. During the Meiji era, textbooks on double-entry bookkeeping were translated into Japanese and gradually studied by practitioners. Simultaneously, commercial laws were enacted in 1890, which required business organizations to prepare an inventory of their assets (*Zaisan mokuroku*) and a balance sheet. The fundamental concept of the inventory of properties originated from Germany. Before the prosperity and popularization of accounting in the United States, which gained influence in the 1970s, particularly after the establishment of the FASB, many accounting researchers in Japan studied and learned much about German accounting traditions (Sakamoto, 2011).

Following World War II, Japan experienced the second accounting revolution, which involved the development of a set of accounting principles. The General Headquarters (GHQ: Office of the Supreme Commander of the Allied Powers) led the development. In particular, Japanese generally accepted accounting principles, Corporate Accounting Principles (CAP), were officially promulgated in 1949.[12] In July 1949, the Investigation Committee on Business Accounting Systems (ICBAS) (*Kigyō kaikei seido taisaku chōsa-kai*) of the Economic Stabilization Board, predecessor of the Business Accounting Standards (Deliberation) Council (BAC) (*Kigyō kaikei kijyun shingi-kai*), published the CAP to achieve uniformity in financial accounting standards. The principles were based on "A Statement of Accounting Principles" authored by Thomas Henry Sanders, Henry Rand Hatfield,

[12] Japanese accounting standards, at least until the Accounting Big Bang at the turn of the century, were based on a system that culminated in the "Corporate Accounting Principles" (Obinata, 2023, p. 19).

and William Underhill Moore in the United States in 1938 (Sanders et al., 1938). The CAP was recommended as a practical guideline for adoption whenever existing laws are changed or new laws are promulgated, even if the new regulations are compulsory (Cooke & Kikuya, 1992, p. 4). Independent auditors were obligated to express an opinion on whether a company had fairly prepared the financial statements in conformity with the CAP under the provisions of the Securities and Exchange Law and the Certified Public Accountants Law. The Securities and Exchange Law, which was based on the U.S. Securities Act of 1933 and the Securities Exchange Act of 1934, was promulgated in a phased manner in 1947 and 1948. The Certified Public Accountants Law became effective in 1948. The Business Accounting Council (BAC) served as both an accounting standard-setting body and an advisory body to the Ministry of Finance (*Ōkurashō*). The council's members, post-1952,[13] included academic scholars, government officials, and representatives from business and industry.

The CAP, functioning as a single comprehensive standard, was subsequently amended in 1954, 1963, 1974, and 1982 to effectively address economic, social, or legal changes. Furthermore, the BAC had published various opinions to reconcile the provisions of the Commercial Code and the Corporation Tax Law, as well as to supplement the initial provisions contained in the CAP. These opinions were not the individual and independent accounting standards. However, they provided a perspective on the reconciliation of the CAP and the related laws (domestic harmonization) and the interpretation of significant items in the CAP. Since May 1968, the BAC issued specific opinions concerning foreign currency translation and allowances for severance payments (Kikuya, 2001, pp. 355–356). The CAP was based on the accrual basis of accounting and historical cost accounting. Under this framework, revenue should be recognized based on realization principles, while expenses are accrued to match the revenue. In other words, the amount of expenses was assessed by the historical cost of resources under the realization principle (Yamaji, 1999, p. 36). The CAP relied heavily on the United States while also adopting Japanese accounting practices to remain distinct (Yamaji, 1999, p. 35). Indeed, it was believed to model Sanders et al. (1938) "A Statement of Accounting Principles" in the United States at that time (Kikuya, 2019,

[13] Its predecessor organization, the Business Accounting Standards Council was taken over by the BAC in 1952.

p. 9). According to Obinata (2023, pp. 97–99), the BAC did not prioritize the principle of decision-usefulness or the protection of investors. Instead, it highlighted the calculation and disclosure of "true income" based on the academic literature, which did not result in flexible or pragmatic accounting standard-settings at that time.

These accounting revolutions in Japan rendered the development of Japanese accounting a unique research subject because two different accounting traditions in Germany and the United States influenced it. According to a global comparative classificatory method, Japan has been classified as a country with code-law-type accounting regulation (e.g., Ball et al., 2000) because the traditional development of Japanese accounting had a German origin.

However, particularly after World War II, the influence of the United States on Japanese accounting regulation became much stronger. The global IFRS has recently become widely recognized and influential in Japan. This intriguing matter can be regarded as the third revolution in developing Japanese accounting regulation since the late 1980s, when the rapid reform of accounting took place. Part II of the book will particularly grapple with the struggles of Japanese actors in dilemmas between traditional Japanese accounting regulation with some Germans origin and the dominance of Anglo-Saxon market-oriented accounting. Therefore, the accounting changes in Japan discussed in Part II are interesting research objects, and the time period covered is limited to from the late 1980 onward, when the generic performativity of observable social norms can be analyzed accordingly.

Performative Norm Diffusion Process: Analysis of Key Actors

Before examining the performative forces of globalization and financialization in Japan, it is useful to consider how normativity spreads and becomes powerful. One strand of research is informative because it provides how norms emerge, diffuse, spread, and persist. Such norm-centered studies assume that norms diffuse from person to person through various interactions. The diffusion of norms extends beyond the interpersonal situation to a broader situation in which groups of people embrace collective norms. Since this book aims to consider the generic performative forces of collective norms, the scope should not be limited to domestic or local norms, which typically pertain to a single country or community. Therefore, insights from studies of the dynamics of norms in international politics are considered. One seminal study defined norms as standards of appropriate behavior for actors with a given identity (Finnemore & Sikkink, 1998, p. 891). Thus, an international norm comprises a set of standards that dictate the appropriate behavior of states.[14]

A fundamental question here is whether a state adopts a norm in the same way as an individual citizen. Since the "state" is one of the collectively accepted institutions, individual actions at the micro-level and their accumulation constitute state actions. Put differently, these individual actions are restricted by institutions such as laws, which are set by operative members, including regulatory governmental bodies, bureaucrats, and politicians. From this perspective, it is not strange to assume that operative members in different countries share the same international norms. Typically, such international norms include democracy, anti-slavery, and reciprocity, all of which are widely accepted and observable. Therefore, international norms are collective because they are shared by many people who hold similar beliefs about proper behavior; however, they are also social because they have an intersubjective quality that goes beyond the mere aggregation of these beliefs (Raymond, 1997, p. 215).

Many international norms originate as domestic ones and subsequently become international through the efforts of various norm entrepreneurs. In addition, international norms always have influences through the filter of domestic structures and norms, which can produce important variations in compliance with and interpretation of these norms (Finnemore & Sikkink, 1998, p. 893). Occasionally, international norms may conflict with domestic norms; thus, domestic norms in a specific country are often entwined with the workings of international norms.

Regarding the mechanism of international norms, there are three distinct stages in the life cycle of norms: "norm emergence," "norm acceptance (or norm cascade)," and "norm internalization" (Finnemore & Sikkink, 1998). During the "norm emergence" stage,

[14] At the ontological level, sovereignty matters as each country is respected all over the world. Even though some may see state "actors" as an illegitimate reification or anthropomorphization of what are, in fact, structures or institutions, it might be possible to see states as agents or purposive actors because decision-makers routinely speak in terms of national "interests," "needs," "responsibilities," "rationality," and so on. Through such talk, states constitute themselves and each other agents (Wendt, 1999, p. 10).

norm entrepreneurs attempt to convince or persuade a critical mass of states (norm leaders) to embrace various norms.[15] Agents with firm convictions about appropriate or desirable behavior in their community actively construct such norms (Finnemore & Sikkink, 1998). In the norm acceptance stage, a specific norm attains legitimacy through its reputation and esteem. Finally, during the norm internalization stage, it becomes natural for actors to follow a specific norm.

Among these stages, a critical threshold, called the "tipping point," exists between the first stage, norm emergence, and subsequent stages. This is where a critical mass of relevant state actors adopts emerging norms. Many emergent norms fail to reach the tipping point, and not all norms progress beyond it (Finnemore & Sikkink, 1998, p. 895). For norm acceptance and internalization, linguistic expressions are crucial. Norm entrepreneurs call attention to issues or even "create" issues using language that names, interprets, and dramatizes them (Finnemore & Sikkink, 1998). To achieve this, constructing cognitive frames is essential to the norm entrepreneurs' political strategy. This is because successful new cognitive frames resonate with broad public understanding and can be adapted to provide new ways of discussing and understanding issues (Payne, 2001). For norm acceptance, as Cornelissen et al. (2012) argue, analogical and metaphorical arguments that are associated with past traditions and practices can be effective in shaping normative orders. In light of these arguments, it is reasonable to understand that comprehensive but abstract globalization and financialization can diffuse among individuals, organizations, and countries as collective social norms.

Furthermore, norm entrepreneurs require an organizational platform to promote particular norms (Finnemore & Sikkink, 1998). International organizations may have advantages regarding resources and leverage over states they seek to convert to their normative convictions in the international political arena. Norm entrepreneurs can leverage such an international platform to communicate with global organizations. Operative members, who are involved directly or indirectly in the standard-setting process, play a significant role in this process. For a more detailed analysis of how different actors engage in the norm diffusion process, it may be

[15] Instead of norm entrepreneur, Bicchieri (2016) uses the term "trendsetter." The norm trendsetter(s) can be an individual, group, or the media (Bicchieri, 2016, pp. 163–207).

beneficial to specifically focus on two studies on global norm diffusion in accounting.

First, Bebbington et al. (2012) analyzed the production of normativity with respect to environmental reporting in Spain and the UK. They explored the reasons behind the differences in the norm acceptance between the two countries from the perspective of the norm diffusion cycle. Bebbington et al. (2012) particularly focused on the tipping point of the norm cascade and put less emphasis on the classification of norm diffusion processes. However, they highlighted three internal conditions during the process: the congruence with the underlying values of previous norms, the perceived integration of the rules in a coherent normative framework, and whether the rule is perceived to provide clarity.

Building upon the research conducted by Bebbington et al. (2012), Larrinaga and Senn (2021) theoretically summarize more recent situations and enhance the framework that explains the role of different actors in the norm diffusion process. Larrinaga and Senn (2021) emphasized the plurality of those actors despite the difficulty in identifying various sources of normativity in the diffusion of environmental reporting (Table 4.1). Whereas the norm diffusion process is neither linear nor smooth (Larrinaga & Senn, 2021, p. 142), it typically progresses from the left (epistemic communities) to the right (regulators and reporters) of Table 4.1. As shown in the far right, when regulators establish a standard that organizations, like corporations, must follow, it usually leads to the internalization of norms. The tipping point marks the moment when norm acceptance or norm cascading occurs. Therefore, the actions of norm entrepreneurs and norm carriers before the tipping point are a matter of concern. In the context of corporate social reporting, Larrinaga and Senn (2021) asserted that the creation of the Global Reporting Initiative (GRI) and the combination of relevant actors (such as epistemic communities, carriers, regulators, and reporters) along with certain conditions (societal context, discourses, analogies, practices, and institutional design) played a significant role in advancing corporate sustainability reporting.

Given the aim of Part II of this book, which examines the generic performativity of globalization and financialization, the focus should be on norm acceptance and internalization. To examine the conditions, Larrinaga and Senn (2021) emphasize the focus on actors, such as consultants, auditors, and professional associations, as the specific

Table 4.1 Actor-centric norm diffusion process[16]

Actors	*Epistemic communities*	*Norm entrepreneurs*	*Carriers*	*Regulators*
Roles	Generate ideas	Innovate, translate, or resist ideas	Diffuse practices	Stabilize and enable the inscription of norms
Examples	Academic researchers, practitioners, experts, and think tanks	International initiatives and academic communities	Consultants, auditors, journalists, and professional associations	Government and its agencies

groups responsible for promoting and enforcing the norms.[17] Following the actor-centered studies on norm diffusion, the subsequent chapters primarily analyze the evolution of accounting standards in Japan, focusing not only on the material texts but also on the actions of powerful regulators such as accounting standard setters (both the former public and the existing private ones). Part II also analyzes both national and domestic organizations and individuals who may influence regulators.

References

Ball, R., Kothari, S. P., & Robin, A. (2000). The effect of international institutional factors on properties of accounting earnings. *Journal of Accounting and Economics, 29*(1), 1–51.

Bebbington, J., Kirk, E. A., & Larrinaga, C. (2012). The production of normativity: A comparison of reporting regimes in Spain and the UK. *Accounting, Organizations and Society, 37*(2), 78–94.

Bello, I. (2016). Cognitive implications of nominalizations in the advancement of scientific discourse. *International Journal of English Studies, 16*(2), 1–23.

Bicchieri, C. (2016). *Norms in the wild: How to diagnose, measure, and change social norms*. Oxford University Press.

[16] This is based on Table 10.3 in Larrinaga and Senn (2021).

[17] Because the GRI itself is not a public authoritative organization but a private one without enforceable power, Larrinaga and Senn (2021) highlighted various actors as norm carriers.

Bieling, H.-J. (2013). European financial capitalism and the politics of (de-) financialization. *Competition and Change, 17*(3), 283–298.

Billig,. (2008). The language of critical discourse analysis: The case of nominalization. *Discourse and Society, 19*(6), 783–800.

Collier, D. (2011). Understanding process tracing. *PS: Political Science & Politics, 44* (4), 823–830.

Collison, D., Cross, S., Ferguson, J., Power, D., & Stevenson, L. (2014). Financialization and company law: A study of the UK company law review. *Critical Perspectives on Accounting, 25*(1), 5–16.

Cooke, T. E., & Kikuya, M. (1992). *Accounting in Japan: An international perspective.* Blackwell Publishers.

Corballis, M. C., & Suddendorf, T. (2010). The evolution of concepts: A timely look. In D. Mareschal, P. C. Quinn, & S. E. G. Lea (Eds.), *The making of human concepts* (pp. 365–384). Oxford University Press.

Cornelissen, J. P., Holt, R., & Zundel, M. (2011). The role of analogy and metaphor in the framing and legitimization of strategic change. *Organization Studies, 32*(12), 1701–1716.

Davis, G. F., & Kim, S. (2015). Financialization of the economy. *Annual Review of Sociology, 41*, 203–221.

Epstein, G. A. (Ed.). (2005). *Financialization and the world economy.* Edward Elgar.

Finnemore, M., & Sikkink, K. (1998). International norm dynamics and political change. *International Organization, 52*(4), 887–917.

French, S., Leyshon, A., & Wainwright, T. (2011). Financializing space, spacing financialization. *Progress in Human Geography, 35*(6), 798–819.

George, A. L., & Bennett, A. (2005). *Case studies and theory development in the social sciences.* MIT Press.

Gunnoe, A., & Gellert, P. (2011). Financialization, shareholder value, and the transformation of timberland ownership in the US. *Critical Sociology, 37*(3), 265–284.

Haiven, M. (2014). *Cultures of financialization: Fictitious capital in popular culture and everyday life.* Palgrave Macmillan.

Harvey, D. (2006). *Spaces of global capitalism.* Verso.

Hopwood, A. G. (2007). Whither accounting research? *The Accounting Review, 82*(5), 1365–1374.

Jackson, G. (2016). Towards a conceptual framework for understanding institutional change in Japanese capitalism: Structural transformation and organizations diversity. *INCAS Discussion Paper, 4*, 1–22.

James, P., & Steger, M. B. (2014). A genealogy of 'globalization': The career of a concept. *Globalizations, 11*(4), 417–434.

Kay, A. (2006). *The dynamics of public policy.* Edward Elgar.

Kikuya, M. (2001). International harmonization of Japanese accounting standards. *Accounting, Business & Finance History, 11*(3), 349–368.
Krippner, G. R. (2005). The financialization of the American economy. *Socio-Economic Review, 3*(2), 173–208.
Larrinaga, C., & Senn, J. (2021). Norm development in environmental reporting. In J. Bebbington, C. Larrinaga, B. O'Dwyer, & I. Thomson (Eds.), *Routledge handbook of environmental accounting* (pp. 137–150). Routledge.
Lavoie, M. (2012). Financialization, neo-liberalism, and securitization. *Journal of Post Keynesian Economics, 35*(2), 215–233.
Lucarelli, B. (2012). Financialization and global imbalances. *Review of Radical Political Economics, 44*, 429–447.
Mader, P., Martens, D., & van der Zwan, N. (2020). *The Routledge international handbook of financialization*. Routledge.
Mahoney, J. (2012). The Logic of Process Tracing Tests in the Social Sciences. *Sociological Methods & Research, 41*(4), 570–597. https://doi.org/10.1177/0049124112437709
Mahoney, J., & Thelen, K. (Eds.). (2010). *Explaining institutional change: Agency, ambiguity and power*. Cambridge University Press.
Martin, J. R. (2008). Incongruent and proud: De-vilifying 'nominalization.' *Discourse & Society, 19*(6), 801–810.
Michaelian, K., & Sutton, J. (2017). Collective memory. In M. Jankovic & K. Ludwig (Eds.), *The Routledge handbook of collective intentionality* (pp. 300–309). Routledge.
Okamoto, N. (2020). Collectively accepted social norms and performativity: The pursuit of normativity of globalization in economic institutions. *Journal of Economic Methodology, 27*(3), 226–239.
Olick, J. K. (1999). Collective memory: The two cultures. *Sociological Theory, 17*(3), 333–348.
Payne, R. A. (2001). Persuasion, frames and norm construction. *European Journal of International Relations, 7*(1), 37–61.
Phillips, N., & Malhotra, N. (2017). Language, cognition and institutions: Studying institutionalization using linguistic methods. In R. Greenwood, C. Oliver, B. Thomas, T. B. Lawrence, & R. E. Meyer (Eds.), *The SAGE Handbook of Organizational Institutionalism* (2nd ed., pp. 392–417). Sage.
Preda, A. (2009). *Framing finance: The boundaries of markets and modern capitalism*. Chicago University Press.
Raymond, G. A. (1997). Problems and prospects in the study of international norms. *Mershon International Studies Review, 41*(2), 205–245.
Rodrik, D. (2018). Populism and the economics of globalization. *Journal of International Business Policy, 1*, 12–33.

Vollmer, H., Mennicken, A., & Preda, A. (2009). Tracking the numbers: Across accounting and finance, organizations and markets. *Accounting Organizations, and Society, 34*(5), 619–637.

Sachs, J. D. (1998). International economics: Unlocking the mysteries of globalization. *Foreign Policy, 110*, 97–111.

Sachs, J. D. (2017). Globalization–In the name of which freedom? *Humanistic Management Journal, 1*(2), 237–252.

Sanders, T. H., Hatfield, H. R., & Moore, W. U. (1938). A statement of accounting principles. New York, NY: American Institute of Accountants.

Sjolander, C. T. (1996) The rhetoric of globalization: What's in a wor(l)d? *International Journal, 51*(4) 603. https://doi.org/10.2307/40203150

Trampusch, C., & Palier, B. (2016). Between X and Y: How process tracing contributes to opening the black box of causality. *New Political Economy, 21*(5), 437–454.

Walsh, V. (2004). *Global institutions and social knowledge: Generating research at the Scripps Institution and the Inter-American Tropical Tuna Commission, 1900s–1990s*. The MIT Press.

Wendt, A. (1999). *Social Theory of International Politics*. Cambridge University Press.

Yamaji, H. (1999). Interaction between Japanese accounting and economic structures. In S. Sunder and Yamaji, H. (Eds.), *The Japanese Style of Business Accounting* (pp. 35–54), Quorum Books.

Young, J. J. (2003). Constructing, persuading and silencing: The rhetoric of accounting standards. *Accounting, Organizations and Society, 28*(6), 621–638.

Zaki, J., Neumann, E., & Baltiansky, D. (2021). Market cognition: How exchange norms alter social experience. *Current Directions in Psychological Science, 30*(3), 236–241.

Zhang, Y., & Andrew, J. (2014). Financialisation and the conceptual framework. *Critical Perspectives on Accounting, 25*(1), 17–26.

Zwan, van der N. (2014). Making sense of financialization. *Socio-Economic Review, 12*(1), 99–129.

In Japanese

Kikuya, M. (Ed.) (2019). *Kaikeigaku to Sozeihō no Genjyō to Kadai*. Zeimu-Keiri Kyokai.

Obinata, T. (2023). *Nihon no Kaikei Kijyun I: Kakuritsu no Jidai*. Chuo Keizai Publishing.

Sakamoto, T. (2011). *Kaikei Seido no Kaimei*. Chuo Keizai Publishing.

PART II

Performative and Counterperformative Institutional Dynamics: Globalization and Financialization of Accounting in Japan

CHAPTER 5

Global Unification of Accounting Standards

Over the past few decades, the global convergence of accounting standards has steadily proceeded. Currently, a set of global accounting standards (IFRS) is used in more than 160 jurisdictions,[1] and the standard-setting body, the IASB, has strong influences on business and accounting practices across those areas. Japan is not an exception. This chapter investigates how the globalization of accounting standards has gained momentum in Japan and considers operative members' actions from the perspective of performative globalization. Put succinctly, Japanese accounting standard setters and relevant regulatory bodies have encountered dilemmas regarding whether they should either embrace global accounting standards or retain the traditional domestic accounting treatments that have long been accepted by Japanese corporations.

This chapter initially focuses on the drastic accounting reforms called "Accounting Big Bang" in Japan in the 1990s, which marked a pivotal turning point in the recent development of Japanese accounting. As mentioned in the previous chapter, the time frame of analysis is limited to the period following these radical accounting reforms. Based on the deductive process tracing method, the present chapter argues that Japanese accounting standard setters and relevant actors have prioritized global standards over domestic standards, which gives credence

[1] https://www.ifrs.org/use-around-the-world/use-of-ifrs-standards-by-jurisdiction.

N. Okamoto, *Institutional Change and Performativity*,
https://doi.org/10.1007/978-3-031-53393-8_5

to the thesis of performative globalization in the context of accounting regulation in Japan.

Hereafter, the first section explains the political background of Japan's Big Bang reforms since the late 1990s and details the process of the rapid changes in accounting standards in Japan. Section 5.2 turns to the recent global convergence of accounting standards and argues that these institutional changes were mobilized by Japanese standard setters' commitment to globalization. Section 5.3 analyzes more recent movements toward globalization while mentioning recent actions that have been counterperformative to the acceleration of the globalization of accounting.

To analyze the sequence of events of these institutional changes, the following chapters rely on the electronic database of Nikkei newspaper articles, Nikkei Telecom 21, which facilitates the searching of and provides the full text of articles on newspapers published by Nikkei since 1975. The database covers all the articles written in national and regional newspapers and papers, such as those in *Nikkei Sangyō Shimbun* (newspaper), *Nikkei Kinyū Shimbun*, *Nikkei Marketing Journal*, *Nikkei Veritas*, and the main paper, *Nihon Keizai Shimbun*.

5.1 Globalization of the Financial Market and the Accounting Big Bang

The Japanese Financial Big Bang After the Bubble Burst

In retrospect, the Accounting Big Bang reforms significantly impacted the development of Japanese accounting standards. However, as Obinata (2023b, p. 254) points out, what the term specifically encompasses is not so obvious. Nevertheless, it at least represents a period during which new accounting standards were rapidly introduced in Japan. This section analyzes the process of radical accounting reform from the perspective of performative globalization.

Before the Accounting Big Bang, Japanese financial regulation significantly changed its direction due to the Financial (*Kinyū*) Big Bang reforms. According to Aoki (2003, p. v), the financial reform was crucial because it radically changed the common Japanese understanding metaphorically represented as the convoy system (*Gosō sendan hōshiki*) in the Japanese financial regulation. Under the traditional convoy system, all financial institutions proceeded at the same speed as the slowest firm, just as in a naval convoy (Toya, 2006, p. 15). More specifically, the regulatory style under the system was characterized by the following policies (Toya, 2006, pp. 15–16): (1) regulations that segmented financial businesses and restricted entry and exit,[2] (2) the reliance on informal policy tools for governmental regulation,[3] and (3) shared expectations that cooperation[4] and stability would prevail. In short, the Financial Big Bang was a policy package introduced by the Japanese government in 1996 to dismantle the traditional convoy system regulations through a series of deregulation and liberalization initiatives in the financial sector (Toya, 2006, p. 2). It had an extensive impact on the banking, securities, and insurance industries, as well as foreign exchange and accounting standards (Toya, 2006, p. 2). In that regard, it is conceivable that the Accounting Big Bang was not an independent phenomenon but rather part of a broader transformation of Japanese financial policies.

As a background, during the recession after the bubble burst, a working group[5] of the Cabinet Office's Economic Council and Action Plan Committee (*Keizai shingikai kōdō keikaku iinkai*) compiled a report titled *For the Revitalization of Japan's Financial System* (*Wagakuni kinyū sisutemu no kasseika no tameni*) in October 1996.[6] It was called the "Ikeo Report," as the chair who led the working group was Kazuhito Ikeo, an economics professor at Keio University at that time. The report had at least some impact on the Financial Big Bang reform because its content, timing, and suggested scope of the proposed reforms closely resembled those of Big Bang initiative put forward by Prime Minister

[2] For instance, from the postwar period to the time of rapid economic growth in the 1980s, the government severely restricted the entry of foreign companies into the Japanese financial industry to protect domestic banks (Kondo, 2011).

[3] For example, there was a shared perception that the soundness of the banks was implicitly guaranteed by the MOF.

[4] This cooperation particularly refers to relations between the MOF, the Liberal Democratic Party (LDP), and domestic financial firms (Toya, 2006, p. 16).

[5] The working group had its origins in a request made by Shusei Tanaka in early 1996 to PM Hashimoto to accelerate deregulation. Mr. Tanaka was the Director-General of the Economic Planning Agency (EPA) and a Sakigake party member at that time. PM Hashimoto requested that Mr. Tanaka make his proposal concrete, and it was decided that the Economic Council, administered by Tanaka's agency, would oversee the task of formulating action plans to speed up deregulation in six major policy arenas (Toya, 2006, p. 167).

[6] https://www5.cao.go.jp/j-j/keikaku/kinyu1-J-j.html.

(PM) Ryutaro Hashimoto the following month (November 1996) (Toya, 2006, p. 167).[7]

In reality, the Financial Big Bang reforms were led by different actors and comprised two phases (Toya, 2006, p. 176). In the first phase, foreign exchange reforms were conducted through cooperation between the Liberal Democratic Party (LDP)'s Administrative Reform Promotion Headquarters (*Gyōsei kaikaku suishin honbu*) and some bureaucrats from the MOF (*Ōkurashō* at that time). By the summer of 1996, as the reform proposal in the first phase had passed the parliament, the threat of a massive capital outflow was very real because the first phase basically proposed deregulating cross-border currency transactions to augment efficient capital flows (Toya, 2006, p. 176).[8] In the second phase, therefore, a series of fundamental reforms of the domestic financial market were mainly led by PM Ryutaro Hashimoto who determined the timing (November 1996), scope (to encompass private finance), and speed (by 2001) of the policies.[9]

Therefore, compared to the Accounting Big Bang, the targeted deadline of the Financial Big Bang was more definite; it was indicated in the plan declared by PM Hashimoto, and the MOF disclosed the detailed plan in July 1997 (Toya, 2006, p. 3). Specifically, it was a three-year plan expected to be completed by the dawn of the twenty-first century. In addition, the Financial Big Bang was far more comprehensive and deeper than the former regulatory reforms because it spanned five financial areas and the measures might have drastically hurt Japanese financial firms' prospects for survival (Toya, 2006, pp. 7–8).

PM Hashimoto's initial message in November 1996 advanced a clear goal of reinvigorating Tokyo as a financial market on par with New York and London by 2001 (Toya, 2006, p. 105). As fair competition

[7] The report also mentioned the significance of introducing market value accounting for financial instruments such as derivatives, which was succeeded to the Big Bang accounting reforms.

[8] The threat was reflected in the interim report titled *Modern Developments and the Improvement of the Trading Environment for International Financial Transactions—New Developments and Deregulation in International Financial Services* (*Kokusai kinyū torihiki ni okeru gendai-teki tenkai to torihiki kankyō no seibi ni tsuite*) issued on June 17, 1996 (https://www.mof.go.jp/about_mof/councils/gaitame/report/1a018f2.htm).

[9] Those messages were clear because PM Hashimoto wanted to personally give the directions to enhance public support of the LDP and his administration at that time (Toya, 2006, p. 176).

in the Japanese financial market was partially restricted by the traditional convoy system of regulation at that time, Japanese financial sectors such as banks were thought to be inefficient and less competitive than their global competitors (Nihon Keizai Shimbun, September 30, 1994, p. 1).[10] For example, the Japanese government restricted entry into the market for derivatives trading and asset-backed securities (ABS). Accordingly, the relative decline of Tokyo's position as an attractive financial market was feared as signifying a "hollowing-out" phenomenon (Toya, 2006, p. 106).

However, the goal of making Tokyo a globally attractive financial center was incompatible with the Japanese industrial policy to enhance the competitiveness of domestic financial sectors. This was simply because an attractive international financial center needed to be indifferent to its actors' nationalities (Toya, 2006, p. 108). Consequently, in areas "where regulations such as foreign exchange controls could mitigate the pressures of globalization, considerations to the 'stability of the financial order,' or the systematic principle of the convoy system of financial regulation, prevailed and reforms were indeed sluggish" (Toya, 2006, p. 110). Hence, radical reforms needed to be implemented in some areas to achieve a "free, fair, and global" market.

Indeed, this slogan of "free, fair, and global" was essential to the Japanese financial reforms.[11] The name "Big Bang" was taken from the reforms led by the Thatcher administration in the UK in 1986.[12] In that

[10] According to the article, Japanese companies' competitiveness was supported by the undervalued yen and wages until the 1970s, which were replaced by the low cost of capital in the 1980s. Moreover, the strong yen kept pressure on interest rates, and the inefficiencies of Japanese corporations did not surface because of the massive sales of their standardized products.

[11] One of the essential policies was to reform the Bank of Japan (BOJ) Act so that it could be more independent and transparent. The governor of the BOJ at that time, Yasuo Matsushita, admitted that "the basic principle of 'free, fair, and global' in the midst of marketization and globalization of finance and economy is a basic credo that is truly appropriate to make our financial markets and system more efficient and flexible to be equivalent to the one in New York and London" (Nikkei Kinyu Shimbun, November 21, 1996, p. 7).

[12] The Japanese Financial Services Agency (FSA) explains the characteristics of the British Big Bang as follows (https://www.fsa.go.jp/p_mof/english/big-bang/ebb24.htm): (1) The relative decline in the status of the British securities market—in 1985, before the implementation of the "Big Bang," the London Stock Exchange's turnover was only 1/13th of the then number 1 ranked worldwide, New York Stock Exchange, and it

sense, the Japanese version of the Big Bang reforms similarly aimed to make the Japanese financial market more global, even if it resulted in a Wimbledon effect.[13] According to the Financial System Planning Bureau (*Kinyū kikaku kyoku*)'s explanations of the financial system reforms,[14] there were three background factors behind Japan's Financial Big Bang: (1) the progress of Japan's financial liberalization and internationalization, (2) the rise and collapse of the bubble economy, and (3) comparisons with the European market. Among these, the third factor reflected Japanese policymakers' strong intention to vie with global financial markets, since their European and U.S. counterparts had steadily continued to progress around that time. In particular, the European financial markets had grown, and the unified currency under the Euro was becoming a reality by the end of the twentieth century. This currency unification drew Japanese regulators' attention more to European financial markets than to their U.S. counterparts. When comparing the market situations of Tokyo's foreign exchange transactions and stock dealings with those of New York and London at that time, the financial market in Tokyo fell behind these two major financial centers.[15] Moreover, the almost 1,200 trillion yen of personal financial assets mostly deposited in bank accounts became an

was found to be only 1/5th that of the number 2 ranked, Tokyo, (2) The development of internationalization and the delayed response of English stock brokers—they were not able to properly deal with the intervention of foreign traders, the majority of whom were from the United States, and regarding their strategy toward internationalization, British traders experienced a decline in position in the financial market, and (3) Technological development and the expansion of transactions outside of the stock exchange—with the advancements in the processing technology of investment and client information and the growth of investment firms made possible with developments in computers and communication technology, there has been a shift toward foreign and over-the-counter block transactions, shaking the foundations of the stock exchange.

[13] Nicole's (2002, p. 7) analogy refers to the fact that although the UK provides the world's foremost arena for tennis at Wimbledon, the winners of the Wimbledon tournament tend to be foreign players. Accordingly, the Wimbledon effect would predict that market deregulation will strengthen the financial center but lead to a situation in which markets are dominated by foreign players.

[14] A 1,200-trillion-yen figure was estimated during the governmental financial system reforms and had been frequently referenced to represent the amount of inefficient personal financial assets in Japan. For instance, see https://www.fsa.go.jp/p_mof/english/big-bang/ebb32.htm. Additional information is available at https://www.fsa.go.jp/p_mof/english/big-bang/ebb2.htm.

[15] According to the data shown on the website of FSA (https://www.fsa.go.jp/p_mof/big-bang/bb4.htm), the average daily volume of foreign currency transactions in 1995 in

essential target to leverage effectively to boost the Japanese economy.[16] Against this background, the priority of the financial system reforms was to revitalize Japan's financial market to be an international one on par with those of London and New York by 2001. On June 1, 1995, the Committee on Financial Systems Research Council (FSRC) (*Kinyū seido chōsa kai*) established the Committee for the Revitalization of Financial Functions (*Kinyū kinou kasseika iinkai*) to study the functions expected of financial services in the twenty-first century (Nihon Keizai Shimbun, June 15, 1996, p. 12).

However, the Japanese economy was experiencing a severe recession at that time. In the face of this economic downturn, radical market-oriented financial reforms might have been catastrophic.[17] Indeed, some politicians supported measures to rescue all troubled banks using public money to maintain financial stability (Nihon Keizai Shimbun, December 14, 1997, p. 2),[18] which might have been consistent with the traditional convoy system financial regulations. However, there was continuous pressure on the MOF from the United States.[19] American manufacturers claimed that the dollar was overvalued relative to the yen and that Japanese financial liberalization could help correct this imbalance (Vogel, 2018, p. 90). In the late 1980s, the MOF took on the segmentation of the financial system, and it eventually decided in 1992 to allow commercial banks and securities companies to enter each other's line of business via separate

Japan was below 200 billion dollars, while that in London was almost 500 billion dollars. The annual volume of stock trading in Tokyo was far less than that in New York.

[16] This amount was less than the total volume of U.S. personal assets over 1,800 trillion yen but much more than that of the UK, Germany, and France. Those three European countries' total personal financial assets amounted to less than 400 trillion yen (https://www.fsa.go.jp/p_mof/big-bang/bb5.htm).

[17] Alternatively, it was also interpreted that neither the MOF nor the banks were in a strong position to resist reforms, as both were thought to be responsible for the burst of the bubble economy and the ensuing financial crisis at that time (Vogel, 2018, p. 90).

[18] For instance, the former PM Kiichi Miyazawa supported the use of public money to maintain local economy as well as the stability of financial system (Nihon Keizai Shimbun, December 14, 1997, p. 2).

[19] The negotiation process between two nations regarding corporate governance and accounting disclosure was investigated in detail in Yonekura et al. (2012). Although Toya (2006, p. 184) mentioned that there is little evidence of any foreign pressure (*gaiatsu*) leading up to the Big Bang despite the increasing presence of foreign financial firms at that time, such pressure from the U.S. government or foreign companies would not always be direct or explicit.

subsidiaries (Vogel, 2018, p. 90). Meanwhile, the MOF phased out fixed stock brokerage commissions, which forced brokerage firms to compete on prices,[20] and it finally eliminated the fixed fee system from securities trading services, which consequently forced competition among securities companies (Vogel, 2018, p. 90). Ironically, the reason why Japan experienced the bubble burst and suffered the financial crisis in the late 1990s was attributed to the increasing competition in the financial sector and financial institutions' greater freedom to make risky investments without increasing prudential supervision (Vogel, 2018, p. 90).

Before the Hashimoto cabinet's public general policy speech that mentioned the Financial Big Bang on November 29, 1996, key persons from the United States (Alan Greenspan and Lawrence Summers) had visited Japan in rapid succession around that time. In November 1996, Alan Greenspan, chairperson of the U.S. Federal Reserve Bank (FRB), spoke at the meeting of the Japanese Bankers Association. In his speech, he emphasized the necessity of financial institutions' measurement of market and credit risk as well as the importance of disclosure. Moreover, Greenspan mentioned a crucial shift in the traditional Japanese convoy system:

> Governments have been given certain responsibilities related to their banking and financial systems that must be balanced. We have the responsibility to prevent major financial market disruptions through development and enforcement of prudent regulatory standards and, if necessary, in rare circumstances, through direct intervention in market events. But we also have the responsibility to assure that private sector institutions have the capacity to take prudent and appropriate risks, even though such risks will sometimes result in unanticipated bank losses or even bank failures. Our goal as supervisors, therefore, should not be to prevent all bank failures, but to maintain sufficient prudential standards so that banking problems which do occur do not become widespread. We try to achieve the proper balance through official regulations, as well as through formal and informal supervisory policies and procedures. (November 18, 1996)[21]

[20] Although stock brokerage commission rates were gradually reduced from 1985 to 1990 and trades over 1 billion yen were liberalized in 1994, it was fully liberalized by the end of 1999.

[21] https://www.federalreserve.gov/boarddocs/speeches/1996/19961118.htm.

He also commented in *Nihon Keizai Shimbun* that "Japanese regulation and practices introduced after World War II have outdated quite some time ago. I support the reform of financial/securities institutions [Japanese version of Big Bang] that Hashimoto administration aspires" (Nikkei Kinyū Shimbun, November 19, 1996, p. 3). Furthermore, on February 28, 1997, Lawrence Summers, the U.S. Deputy Secretary of the Treasury under his political mentor Robert Rubin at that time, visited Japan. He spoke at the event held by the America-Japan Society and criticized the ongoing Japanese financial reforms as slow, fragile, and even contradictory (Nihon Keizai Shimbun, March 1, 1997, p. 1). Summers was arrogant in press conferences and other events during his visit, exuding an attitude that he was going to correct the insufficient Japanese financial system, and some even compared him to General MacArthur after the war (Ohta, 2018, p. 67). In the first week of March 1997, Summers met top-level government officials and explained the significance of competition in the market. For instance, when asked about the possibility of using fiscal spending to address the failures of Japanese financial institutions and non-performing loans, he stated in the interview with Nikkei that "It is important to respond quickly to the issues in the financial sector. In the U.S. experience, the longer the situation is left untouched and the slower the response is, the bigger the wound. Monitoring the soundness of the financial system and economic stability are quite important" (Nihon Keizai Shimbun, March 5, 1997, p. 1). Regarding more specific policies, Summers recommended promoting competition in the Tokyo market while increasing transparency through the improvement of information disclosure and the establishment of a strong financial system (Nihon Keizai Shimbun, March 5, 1997, p. 5).

Accordingly, regarding the accomplishment of the planned Financial Big Bang reform, there was some pressure from key U.S. officials (Ohta, 2018, p. 67). This pressure was crucial because the Japanese government was caught in a dilemma as to whether it should rescue distressed banks by using public money. In November 1997, Hokkaidō Takushoku Bank[22]

[22] Hokkaidō Takushoku Bank went bankrupt in November 1997, and its main operations in Hokkaidō were transferred to Hokuyō Bank. This also revealed the Japanese government's decision not to protect or rescue such a large, troubled bank. As it was a shocking event, some people in Hokkaidō felt that Hokkaidō Takushoku Bank had been made a scapegoat for other troubled banks (Nihon Keizai Shimbun, March 29, 2012, p. 13).

and Yamaichi Securities,[23] both major players in the financial sector at that time, went bankrupt as a result of insufficient risk management. The Minister of Finance at that time, Hiroshi Mizuka, warned that the government would no longer let large banks declare bankruptcy to ward off the public concern about bank failures (Nikkei Kinyu Shimbun, April 3, 1998, p. 1). However, Kiichi Miyazawa, the former Prime Minister, spoke at the Japan Society in the United States in March 1998 and indicated that the government would not protect financial institutions if the market considered that they could not survive (Nikkei Kinyu Shimbun, April 3, 1998, p. 2).

To summarize, the Financial Big Bang in Japan heralded the shift from "coordination and stability" to "competition and transparency," which represented the transformation of the domestic convoy-system financial regulations into a more open market-based financial system (Toya, 2006, p. 283). The reform was particularly led by the slogan of "Free, Fair, and Global" (referring to the market). The Financial Big Bang could be attributed to the initiative of PM Hashimoto (and his staff), the efforts of the MOF, and the support from the LDP's Administrative Reform Promotion Headquarters (*Gyōsei keikaku suishin honbu*) (Toya, 2006, pp. 176–177).[24] These joint efforts also represented a shift in the priority of both the MOF and the LDP from the interests of the private sector to the public interest (Toya, 2006, pp. 176–177).

But what was the public interest at that time? Nobody knew the appropriate policy measures for the Japanese economy under uncertainty, particularly after the burst of the glamorous bubble economy. In this circumstance, the selected solution was abandoning the traditional monitoring system that used to protect the financial industry through the domestic convoy system because it was thought to be the cause of the inefficient Japanese financial system. Put differently, the impetus of the radical financial reform was the belief that emphasized the value of free, fair, and global markets, which was widely accepted in Anglo-Saxon countries such as the United States and the United Kingdom. In addition to

[23] Yamaichi Securities declared that it would cease operations on November 24, 1997.

[24] In the background, before the political initiative of the prime minister, an internal split in the Ministry between those who advocated the reforms and those who opposed them or preferred a more cautious approach was not resolved (Toya, 2006, p. 177).

leading persons' visits from the United States and their insistence, PM Hashimoto and the bureaucrats in the MOF who had devised the original plans of reform were both key norm entrepreneurs, and they finally prioritized the competitive global model operated in Anglo-Saxon countries over the traditional domestic convoy system in the face of the crisis.

Beginning of the Accounting Big Bang in Japan

The Accounting Big Bang was understood as part of the radical and comprehensive financial reforms aimed at achieving free, fair, and global financial markets in Japan. Table 5.1 lists the principal measures conducted during the Financial Big Bang which basically consisted of two pillars. First, liberalization and deregulation were introduced by removing or relaxing the barriers and controls imposed by the government, which intended to expand the competition within the market. Second, in parallel with the expansion of the market and competition, the development of market infrastructure was positioned as a key goal. Among the measures targeted at improving market infrastructure, for example, "global harmonization of accounting standards" and "stricter disclosure rules for banks and securities firms" were directly related to accounting regulation (the underlined parts in Table 5.1).

Furthermore, the introduction of financial holding companies through the removal of the ban on their establishment was closely interconnected with the consolidation accounting standards at that time. The FSRC (*Kinyū seido chōsa kai*) in which the MOF (its Banking Bureau) served as the secretariat (Toya, 2006, p. 193) approved the creation of financial holding companies and relaxed the business restrictions on financial subsidiaries and affiliated companies controlled by those financial holding companies. The deliberation took place primarily within the FSRC's Financial Function Revitalization Subcommittee (*Kinyū kinou kasseika iinkai*). After twenty-four meetings from August 1995, the subcommittee (as well as the FSRC) issued a report in May 1997. With regard to the financial holding company, the report stated that "The lifting of the ban on holding companies will give banks more opportunities. The use of holding companies will enable banks to provide more specialized and sophisticated financial services through spin-offs, and will facilitate banks' entry into new finance-related fields. ... Therefore, the use of such a

Table 5.1 Main policies of Japan's Financial Big Bang (Toya, 2006, p. 120)

(1) Liberalization and deregulation (Enhanced competitions and reduced government control)	• Liberalization of international capital transactions • Product liberalization (securities, investment trusts, derivatives, securitization of loans, and ABS) • Complete deregulation of mutual entry into banking, trust banking, securities, and insurance sectors • Liberalization of bond issuances for commercial banks and non-bank financial institutions • Removal of the ban on financial holding companies • Deregulation of controls on entry into the securities business • Liberalization of fixed brokerage commissions • Abolition of the legalized cartel in the casualty insurance sector • Liberalization of foreign exchange business
(2) Enhancing market infrastructure (Market development, fairness, and transparency)	• Abolition of the monopoly of security exchanges in securities transactions • Strengthening registered markets • Global harmonization of accounting standards • Stricter disclosure rules for banks and securities firms • Creation of a safety net for securities and insurance industries
(3) Other reforms	• Creation of the Financial Services Agency (FSA) (a dismantling of the MOF) • Full revision of the Bank of Japan Law (increased central bank independence) • Change in the style of financial administration toward a rules-based system

holding company is expected to promote competition in the financial sector and increase the efficiency of bank management" (FSRC, 1997).

The establishment of holding companies was possible because the Antimonopoly Law was revised simultaneously in June 1997. In fact, the laws that prohibited financial holding companies were repealed.[25] The admission of financial holding companies whose subsidiaries provided various financial services elevated the significance of rigorous consolidation accounting standards. Almost concurrently, in June 1997, the BAC issued the Opinion on the Revision of the Consolidated Financial Statements System[26] to introduce rigorous consolidation accounting standards with the concept of control. The removal of the ban on financial holding companies thus encouraged a group of companies that had been engaged in various financial businesses to establish a parent holding company, which had to be accompanied by the implementation of rigorous consolidation accounting standards (Obinata, 2023b, pp. 278–289).

As Japanese companies had traditionally prioritized individual financial statements over consolidated ones, the introduction of this set of rigorous consolidation accounting standards was significant (Nihon Keizai Shimbun, August 1, 1996, p. 19). Although there was a system of consolidated financial statements, the choice of which companies should be consolidated was left to a reporting company, and thus, the consolidation accounting at that time was discretionary and superficial (Nihon Keizai Shimbun, August 1, 1996, p. 19). Commercial-Code-based accounting at that time did not have the concept of "corporate group accounting," as it heavily relied on the headquarter's (parent company's) individual "corporate accounting" (Nihon Keizai Shimbun, August 1, 1996, p. 19).

Starting from this introduction of consolidation accounting standards, the global harmonization of Japanese accounting standards gained strong momentum. For instance, on March 17, 1998, the following answer was given by Atsushi Nagano, Director General of the Securities Bureau of the MOF, at a meeting of the Committee on Finance (*Kinyū iinkai*). His speech suggested an inclination to raise Japanese accounting standards to

[25] Before World War II, Japanese industry was controlled by holding companies operated by Zaibatsu (financial conglomerates). However, the establishment of holding companies was prohibited, in principle, with the enactment of the Antimonopoly Law (Article 9) in 1947. The regulation was very strict in that it uniformly prohibited holding companies irrespective of the adverse impact that such prohibition would have on competition (Osaki, 1998, p. 1).

[26] It had previously published the exposure draft of the standards in February 1997.

the level of global standards in line with the International Accounting Standards (IAS) (Obinata, 2023b, p. 290).

> I would like to say that what we are working on now is the global standardization of accounting standards as a separate term from International Accounting Standards (IAS). In fact, there is a movement to make the standards of each country as high as possible while keeping an eye on international trends. International accounting standards are based on the premise that each country uses different standards, but there is a movement to gradually bring these different standards closer to global standards. (March 17, 1998)

After the introduction of the new consolidation accounting standards, other accounting standards were also modified or introduced as part of the Big Bang accounting reforms. As indicated in Table 5.2, major accounting standards in Japan such as the standards for the statement of cash flows, tax-effect accounting, and postretirement benefits were introduced in succession until the mid-2000s.

Table 5.2 Major changes in accounting standards in the Accounting Big Bang

Original date	*Effective date*	*Areas of new/modified accounting standards*
1997.6	1999.4 (Partially, 1998.4)	Consolidated financial statements
1998.3	1999.4	Research and development costs
1998.3	1999.4	Consolidated statement of cash flows
1998.3	2000.4	Interim consolidated financial statement
1998.6	2000.4	Accounting for retirement benefits
1998.10	1999.4	Tax effect accounting
1999.1	2000.4	Financial instruments
1999.10	2000.4	Foreign currency translations
2002.8	2005.4	Impairment for fixed assets
2003.10	2006.4	Business combinations

Source Tsunogaya and Patel (2020, p. 865) and Obinata (2023b, pp. 270–271)

As the background of these consecutive accounting reforms has already been analyzed in detail by Yonekura et al. (2012), Tsunogaya and Patel (2020), and Obinata (2023b), this chapter adds a comprehensive analysis. With regard to the accounting regulations in Japan around this time, the tendency of performative globalization was generally limited to a bilateral relationship, as the U.S. model of global accounting standards was still most influential. Tsunogaya and Patel (2020) described the struggles of relevant actors from the dualistic perspective of external and internal pressures (*gaiatsu* and *naiatsu*, respectively), and accounting regulators in Japan paid close attention to the U.S. standards. Accordingly, as Koga and Igarashi (1999) pointed out, the globalization of accounting standards was still at the harmonization stage before the global convergence and standardization process. A more performative pursuit of globalization that occurred in the twenty-first century in the context of Japanese accounting regulations is analyzed in the next section.

5.2 Global Convergence of Accounting Standards in Japan

Diffusion of Global Harmonization of Accounting Standards

During the Accounting Big Bang, the main counterpart of the Japanese accounting standard setter was the U.S. FASB, and therefore, the influence of the International Accounting Standards Committee (IASC) in Japan was limited during the 1990s.[27] Nevertheless, the significance of the global harmonization of accounting standards was gradually shared by academics and accounting standard setters in Japan (Koga & Igarashi, 1999). In particular, the actions of a global consortium of accounting standard setters in major countries influenced the accounting standard-setting in Japan because accounting researchers and practitioners regarded the consortium's documents as a global model.

In 1993, the Australian Accounting Standards Board (AASB), Canadian Accounting Standards Board (AcSB), Financial Accounting Standards Board (FASB), and UK Accounting Standards Board (ASB) began working on a project with the IASC (Street & Shaughnessy, 1998a,

[27] The IASC was created in 1973 through the efforts of the professional accountancy bodies in the United Kingdom, the United States, Australia, and Canada, among others (Street and Shaughnessy, 1998b, p. 132).

pp. 180–181). The group was called G4+1, and it worked extensively on common accounting issues to achieve the global harmonization of accounting standards (Street & Shaughnessy, 1998a, p. 181). The G4+1 contributed significantly to the development of accounting thought and regulation and cut the time needed to develop global accounting standards. In short, the G4+1 had made substantial progress toward harmonization during the 1990s (Street & Shaughnessy, 1998a, p. 204). Although agenda coordination and cooperation between the IASC and Anglo-Americans did not clearly exist prior to the 1990s, the G4+1 engaged in cooperative endeavors by focusing on common themes in their conceptual frameworks of accounting (Street & Shaughnessy, 1998a, p. 204).

In Japan, the documents issued by the G4+1 were often referenced and discussed by Japanese accounting researchers.[28] Accounting research at that time in Japan was predominated by conceptual and normative studies,[29] which was substantially reflected in accounting education as well as accounting standard-setting activities. Indeed, particularly before the creation of the private accounting standard setter in Japan in 2001, the justification of specific accounting standards had been supported by normative and institutional academic research that played a major role in the deliberations of public organizations such as the BAC in the MOF (Obinata, 2023a, p. 273). In fact, the G4+1 published influential conceptual documents on various accounting topics, such as accounting for leases (McGregor, 1996; Nailor & Lennard, 2000), accounting for stock compensations (share-based payments) (IASC, 2000), accounting for business combinations (IASC, 1998), and reporting financial performance (Johnson & Lennard, 1998).[30] Some of these documents were

[28] It was based on a retrieval of previous studies on Cinii (Scholarly and Academic Information Navigator: https://cir.nii.ac.jp).

[29] Tomo Suzuki highlighted the significance of traditional diversity of accounting research in Japan that includes a type of normative research (Suzuki, 2009).

[30] As the next chapter mentions, with the addition of representatives from France, Germany, Japan, and five Nordic countries to the G4, the Financial Instruments Joint Working Group (JWG) replaced the IASC Financial Instruments Steering Committee. The JWG aimed to produce an international standard by the year 2000 (IASC, 1998). The JWG report was extensively discussed by Japanese accounting researchers and practitioners when accounting standards for financial instruments such as derivatives were introduced in Japan.

translated into Japanese and discussed to deliberate the conceptual consistency of several accounting standards. In sum, the G4+1's conceptual analyses of accounting matters functioned to some extent as the global benchmark before the IASB was established. Therefore, the G4 and the IASC have benefited substantially from their cooperative endeavors.[31] While several other groupings of national standard-setting bodies cooperated to achieve the harmonization of objectives during the 1990s, the efforts of the G4+1 must be deemed the most significant (Street & Shaughnessy, 1998b, p. 255).

In fact, the G4+1 became the foundation of the IASB. This was almost inevitable because "it served as a key catalyst for change by clearly indicating that, if the IASC did not satisfactorily restructure, the G4 could transform itself into a global standard setter. Facing criticism from the International Organization for Securities Commissions (IOSCO), the U.S. Securities and Exchange Commission (SEC), and the G4 national standard setters, the message was clear" (Street, 2006, p. 119).

Foundation of the ASBJ and Steps Toward Convergence

At the end of Accounting Big Bang, there was a movement to establish a private accounting setter in Japan. Before that, the BAC, under the authority of the MOF, had retained the sole authority to set official corporate accounting standards. However, such government-led accounting standard-setting had difficulty in swiftly reflecting the opinions of various stakeholders, such as corporations (Obinata, 2023b, pp. 470–472).

There were several notable backings for the attempt to establish a private accounting standard setter in Japan. Most importantly, the IASC's attempt to reorganize itself to advance a globally prestigious accounting standard setter significantly pushed this initiative. In June 1999, the G7 Finance Ministers gathered at the Economic Summit held in Cologne and prepared a report titled *Strengthening the International Financial Architecture*. In one section of the report, "Enhancing Transparency and Promoting Best Practices," the following declaration was incorporated[32]:

[31] However, their relationship was not always favorable, as there were sometimes turf wars (Street, 2006).

[32] Available at: https://www.mofa.go.jp/policy/economy/summit/1999/g7econo.html.

> We support and commend the efforts being made by private sector bodies to enhance transparency. We welcome the completion by the International Accounting Standards Committee of its core set of international accounting standards, and we look forward to IOSCO, IAIS (International Association of Insurance Supervisors) and the Basel Committee completing their reviews. We urge all those involved in setting accounting standards to work together so that high-quality accounting standards can continue to be developed and agreed upon internationally.

This statement implied several global organizations' support for the creation of a powerful global accounting standard-setting body. In fact, at a regular directors meeting of the IASC held in Warsaw at the end of June 1999, the IASC proposed a reorganization plan that would replace its board members with personnel from national accounting standard-setting bodies (Nihon Keizai Shimbun, July 17, 1999, p. 13). Upon that decision, Shozo Yamazaki, an attendant at the meeting from the Japanese Institute of Certified Public Accountants (JICPA), and Toshiyuki Kenmochi, who attended the same meeting and was an assistant director in the MOF at that time, shared the concern that there were no full-time professional staff members within the BAC who committed themselves solely to establishing Japanese accounting standards. In other words, if the BAC had kept its public organizational status with temporary part-time council members under the MOF, it could have lost the opportunity to attend the newly reorganized global accounting standard setter's meetings (Nihon Keizai Shimbun, July 17, 1999, p. 13).

In response to this concern, in August 1999, the LDP established a subcommittee on corporate accounting (chaired by a former member of the House of Councilors Yasuhisa Shiozaki) within the Financial Problem Research Council (*Kinyū mondai chōsa iinkai*). Meanwhile, the IASC appointed the members of a nominating committee that would select council members with the power to elect the new organization's board members, but none of its seven members included a Japanese representative (Nihon Keizai Shimbun, December 17, 1999, p. 19).[33] Soon after that, on December 21, 1999, the subcommittee led by Mr. Shiozaki published the interim report titled "*Kigyō Kaikei Kijyun Settei Shutai no*

[33] Among those selected seven members was one representative from Hong Kong, which Japanese regulators did not expect (Nihon Keizai Shimbun, February 17, 2000, p. 19).

Kakujyū/Kyōka ni Mukete (Toward the Expansion and Enhancement of Corporate Accounting Standard Setters)," which showed the subcommittee's clear intention to delegate the power of accounting standard-setting from the public to private organization that should be independent from specific interest groups (Nihon Keizai Shimbun, December 25, 1999, p. 2).[34] The JICPA supported the subcommittee's decision and organized a project team to implement the establishment of the private accounting standard-setting body in Japan (Nihon Keizai Shimbun, December 23, 1999, p. 17). The project team issued its opinion on the appropriate accounting standard setter in Japan on March 28, 2000 (Nihon Keizai Shimbun, March 29, 2000, p. 3). Compared to the eagerness of the JICPA and Keidanren to establish a private accounting standard-setting body, which was also globally expected at that time, the MOF was cautious in considering the different factors, such as the delegation of its authority to set accounting standards to other bodies (Nihon Keizai Shimbun, April 13, 2000, p. 3).

Keidanren (Japan Federation of Economic Organizations) supported the establishment of the private accounting standard-setting body. At that time, Keidanren comprised leading Japanese corporations (many of them were multinational corporations) and was quite an influential organization in terms of Japanese economic policymaking. A core member of Keidanren, Yoshiki Yagi, organized the preparatory committee and assumed the position of chairperson in February 2001 to establish a private accounting standard setter. In March 2001, Keidanren urged the reform of Japanese accounting standard-setting body to gain a better international understanding of Japanese conditions.[35] As mentioned above, Keidanren's opinion had a significant influence as well as discursive power on the Japanese economic policymaking. Even after the foundation of the Accounting Standard Board of Japan (ASBJ), Keidanren had repeatedly expressed its opinions that a global convergence of

[34] Yasuhisa Shiozaki commented in the Nihon Keizai Shimbun that "we will have to show other countries our changes before the IASC directors meeting in May 2001" (Nihon Keizai Shimbun, December 25, 2000, p. 30).

[35] According to Benston et al. (2006, p. 173), the establishment of the ASBJ was led by Keidanren, the representative organization of Japanese corporations. It seems that Keidanren was strongly motivated at that time to bolster Japanese corporations' activities by developing global accounting standards. This motivation was reflected in the ASBJ's objective to conform Japanese accounting standards to international ones.

accounting standards was necessary for Japan to ensure the international comparability of corporate financial statements (Keidanren, 2003).

Keidanren was particularly worried about the legend issue (Keidanren, 2001). The "legend" referred to a statement included in the footnotes of financial statements or auditor's reports prepared in accordance with Japanese accounting standards for stakeholders outside of Japan. It informed those readers that "the statements do not present the financial condition, operating results or cash flows that were prepared in accordance with accounting principles and practice that are generally accepted in countries other than Japan." European and American audit firms requested that such an additional note be included in the audit reports for the Japanese GAAP-based financial statements. This requirement, of course, meant that Japanese accounting standards were not trusted internationally (Misawa, 2006). In particular, the insufficient measures by Japanese regulators in response to the non-performing loan problem damaged the reputation of Japan's accounting standards (Obinata, 2023b, p. 163). All in all, the aim of eliminating the legend clause was one of the motivations for the rapid global convergence of accounting standards.

In July 2001, the JICPA and nine other bodies[36] founded the Financial Accounting Standards Foundation (FASF) to contribute to the development of financial accounting practices in Japan. The FASF was created to make recommendations and contributions to the international accounting system through studying, researching, and developing generally accepted accounting standards. The ASBJ was established in 2001 as a core organization within the FASF. Since then, it has been directly responsible for the development of Japanese accounting standards.

With regard to the ASBJ's objective to converge Japanese accounting standards with the global standards, some normative pressures shaped its target. The International Forum for Accountancy Development (IFAD) was created in 1999 as a working group between the Basel Committee, the International Federation of Accountants, IOSCO, large accounting

[36] These included the JICPA, Japanese Stock Exchanges Conference, Japan Securities Dealers Association, Japan Bankers Association, The Life Insurance Association of Japan, The General Insurance Association of Japan, The Japan Chamber of Commerce and Industry, The Securities Analysts Association of Japan, and Corporation Finance Research Institute (COFRI) (https://www.asb.or.jp/jp/fasf-asbj/established_history/2001-0727.html).

firms, the Organisation for Economic Co-operation and Development (OECD), the United Nations Conference on Trade and Development (UNCTAD), and the World Bank, as well as regional development banks. The IFAD's overall mission was to improve market security and transparency and financial stability on a global scale. It was also concerned with the IAS, holding the view that most countries' national accounting standards should be converged to help develop benchmark international accounting standards. As part of its tasks, the IFAD extensively investigated the differences between fifty-three countries' national accounting rules and sixty key accounting measures (including some areas of disclosure) under the IAS. The study highlighted instances where, in December 2000, some countries' rules did not allow, or did not require, IAS accounting treatment. These results were published as "*GAAP 2000: A Survey of National Accounting Rules in 53 Countries*" (Nobes, 2000). This publication was revised after extensive studies, and the revised version was published in 2001. As GAAP 2000 highlighted the differences between Japanese accounting standards and IAS at the time, Japanese accounting professionals and standard setters paid attention to the results (Keegan et al., 2001). As a result, the Chairman of the ASBJ officially approved the proposals of the Theme Advisory Council. Of the recommended proposals, most of the Level 1 issues had already been highlighted by IFAD in GAAP 2000. Thus, the initial agenda-setting of the ASBJ was influenced by these powerful international organizations.

To summarize, in terms of the early stages of Japan's global convergence of accounting standards, the creation of the ASBJ was a crucial step away from the traditional government-led accounting regulations. Several circumstances accelerated this process. First, Japanese regulators and practitioners shared the concern of being isolated from the global political arena of accounting standard-setting during the process of establishing the IASB. In that sense, there was little discussion regarding whether the global accounting standards would be better than the U.S. or Japanese GAAP in terms of their usefulness or the net economic benefits of their use. Second, the strong commitment to harmonizing/converging Japanese accounting standards with international ones was shared, particularly among Keidanren and other influential organizations such as JICPA. Behind these movements, concerns with the legend clause on the audit report and the IOSCO's endorsement of the IAS were also crucial in Japan[37] such that the voice of representative organizations of Japanese corporations, or Keidanren, became much more prominent. Third, the movements and influences of international organizations such as the IFAD greatly affected the ASBJ's stance on convergence of accounting standards. In addition to setting the official Japanese accounting standards, one of the ASBJ's crucial objectives was to have a close relationship with the IASB.[38]

Tokyo Agreement and Acceleration of Global Convergence

Since its establishment in 2001, the ASBJ has regularly modified the Japanese GAAP in line with the development of major internationally recognized accounting standards, especially the IFRS. For instance, the ASBJ announced its mid-term operating policy in July 2004 and stated that it would support the goal of international convergence toward high-quality accounting standards (ASBJ, 2004). The Financial Services Agency (FSA) also supported the ASBJ's efforts and was confident that such efforts would have further positive effects on the assessment of the equivalence of the Japanese GAAP with the IAS/IFRS (FSA, 2004). Against this background, in October 2004, the IASB and the ASBJ started discussing the prospect of working together in the future. Soon afterward, the ASBJ decided to formally launch the joint project for convergence starting at the beginning of 2005. Until June 2006, three conferences were held involving both standard setters. The conference themes comprised the detailed plans for their joint convergence project. At the third conference, in March 2006, the IASB and the ASBJ indicated that a holistic approach[39] would be adopted toward future convergence.

[37] Around 2000, the pressure regarding the international convergence of accounting standards began to heighten in Japan as a result of the effect of the IOSCO's endorsement of the core standards of the IASC in 1995 and the European Union's movement toward the IFRS afterward (Misawa, 2005, pp. 718–720).

[38] At its inception, the IASB established formal liaison relationships with its partner standard setters for the retention of its due process and Japan has been a member of the IASB liaison countries since the foundation of the IASB.

[39] According to the Committee of European Securities Regulators (CESR) (2007, para. 43), the holistic approach emphasizes the decision regarding the equivalence of investors' ability to make similar decisions on investments irrespective of the existence of potential lingering differences in presentation and measurement, as long as such differences are

Through these conferences and close communications, a joint declaration called "Tokyo Agreement" was finally announced by both boards in August 2007 to launch an initiative to accelerate a convergence program between them. The aim of the initiative was to eliminate the major differences between Japan's GAAP and the existing IFRS by 2008, with full convergence between the Japanese GAAP and current IFRS in use by 2011. Following this agreement, members of both boards discussed and confirmed two objectives at a joint meeting in September 2007.[40] The first was to review the convergence program and the shared goal of eliminating major differences between the IFRS and the Japanese GAAP by 2008, with the remaining differences being removed on or before June 30, 2011. The second was to discuss the arrangements for the ASBJ to input its views into the IASB's current work program. This Tokyo Agreement was a historical step toward the foreseeable adoption of the IFRS in Japan.

Considering the above interactions between the two boards, the IASB and the ASBJ were important norm entrepreneurs in accelerating the global convergence of accounting standards at that time. However, the IASB was not the sole actor that could have affected the final Tokyo Agreement. The IASB could have been working with other countries' standard setters at the same time and may not have wanted to spend too much time and resources negotiating only with the ASBJ. Moreover, the IASB did not have any legally enforceable power to require the adoption of the IFRS.

In fact, more important actors were involved in the convergence process in Japan around that time. Normative pressure for the convergence came from the European Commission (EC) and the CESR.

considered in a sensible long-term work program between the standard setters concerned and the IASB.

[40] These discussions included a review of short-term convergence projects, whose goal was to eliminate major differences by 2008 along with considerations of other major projects. In addition, the representatives of the boards exchanged views on the status of their work. The boards also agreed on future arrangements for interaction by the both boards' members and staff to achieve convergence within the agreed timetable. Commenting on the meeting, Sir David Tweedie, Chairperson of the IASB, said "There remains much work ahead of us but I am pleased to report that we are on schedule to achieve convergence between Japanese GAAP and current IFRSs by 2011." Ikuo Nishikawa, the Chairperson of the ASBJ at that time, also stated that "we are pleased with the close co-operation of staff from both boards and the good progress we have made together during the meeting in pursuit of an accelerated convergence program."

Following the receipt of a mandate from the EC (Ref: CESR/04–305), the CESR began considering equivalence between various third countries' GAAPs and the IAS/IFRS (CESR, 2004). Depending on the relevant regulations (the Prospectus Regulation and the Transparency Directive), third-country issuers (non-EU issuers) whose securities had been admitted to trading on an EU-regulated market or who wished to make a public offer of their securities in Europe would be required, as of January 1, 2007, to prepare and present financial statements in accordance with the EU-endorsed IAS/IFRS accounting standards or the third country's national accounting standards if they had been endorsed as equivalent to the IAS/IFRS.[41] For this reason, the EC requested the CESR's advice on this matter.[42]

This decision was quite important because more than 80 large Japanese companies were listing their shares on European securities markets at that time (Nihon Keizai Shimbun, July 13, 2007, p. 19). If both the CESR and the EC decided that the Japanese GAAP was not equivalent to the IAS/IFRS, there was the risk that the corporate financial statements under the Japanese GAAP would need additional adjustments and disclosure.[43] To avoid such undesirable outcome, the Japanese FSA and the ASBJ assumed the role of the main negotiators with the CESR. Whenever the CESR called for comments from interested parties in the deliberation process, the Japanese FSA responded by expressing its opinion in letters. For example, on October 22, 2004, the CESR published a draft concept paper for comments which set out the various principles by which the

[41] These regulations required the EC to establish a mechanism and make the necessary decisions regarding whether a given third country's GAAP was equivalent to the IAS/IFRS.

[42] The EC requested that the CESR's advice be given by June 30, 2005, to allow sufficient time for the parties affected by the application of the Prospectus Directive (which took effect on July 1, 2005) and the Transparency Directive (expected to apply from the Autumn of 2006) to adapt if necessary. According to a provisional timetable, the work would be executed by the operational group, CESR-Fin, chaired by John Tiner.

[43] The assessment process was likely to result in three potential outcomes. At one end of the spectrum, a third-country's GAAP might be found to be equivalent, and no adjustments would be needed. At the other end, there might be a finding of non-equivalence under which restatement was the only solution. Between these two extremes, there were a number of cases where a third country's GAAP could be considered as equivalent subject to remedies.

CESR intended to operate under a mandate received from the European Commission to assess equivalence between certain third-country GAAPs (i.e., the Canadian GAAP, Japanese GAAP, and U.S. GAAP) and the IAS/IFRS and to describe the enforcement mechanisms in place in the considered three countries. The Japanese FSA and the ASBJ sent letters to communicate their arguments that the Japanese GAAP had been rapidly developing, and they believed it had become consistent with and equivalent to international accounting standards (FSA, 2005).[44] Finally, the CESR published its Feedback Statement—Technical Advice on the equivalence of certain third-country GAAPs' and International Financial Reporting Standards in July 2005 (CESR, 2005). According to the statement, the Japanese GAAP needed twenty-six remedies, even though it was accepted as equivalent to the IAS/IFRS.

This result was disappointing for Japanese parties, especially for both the FSA and the ASBJ, the latter of which published its report and expressed deep concern about the remedies indicated, in particular that the differences in Japanese accounting standards should be reduced by continuing the convergence project with the IASB (ASBJ, 2006). Reluctantly accepting the peculiarities of the Japanese GAAP at that time, the ASBJ emphasized the ongoing efforts toward convergence[45] and noted that it would discuss with the IASB how the two boards should proceed with the joint project so that progress could be made by the third joint meeting in March 2006. In June 2006, Keidanren requested the acceleration of the convergence of accounting standards and the mutual acceptance of the standards between the IASB and the ASBJ (Keidanren, 2006). The Japanese government cabinet office also referred to the global convergence of accounting standards in its basic proposal (*Honebuto no Hōshin*) in 2006 (Cabinet Office, 2006) (Nihon Keizai Shimbun, July 27, 2006). Even the BAC's Planning and Coordination Subcommittee (*Kikaku chōsei bukai*) published its official opinion that Japan should proactively advance the convergence of accounting standards and aim for

[44] Before that, some members of the FSA and ASBJ together participated in the open hearing of the CESR-Fin on November 2004.

[45] In light of the importance of the issues that the CESR had delineated, the ASBJ was determined to obtain consensus from constituents in the capital markets to make steady progress by accelerating its efforts toward eliminating differences between its GAAP and the IFRS. The joint project between the ASBJ and the IASB had entered its second year, and sufficient discussions concerning each issue had occurred between both boards (ASBJ, 2006).

higher quality standards by bringing all parties together to establish and strengthen mutual cooperation (BAC, 2006).

In April 2007, the CESR published a consultation paper—CESR's technical advice on a mechanism for determining the equivalence of the generally accepted accounting principles of third countries. The Japanese FSA responded and recommended that CESR consider the Japanese efforts toward the convergence project. At the same time, Keidanren published its opinion again arguing that convergence should be accelerated and achieved quickly as planned in Japan (Keidanren, 2007). Finally, in April 2008, the CESR published a paper saying that the Japanese GAAP was equivalent to the IFRS in consideration of the Tokyo Agreement.

Considering the above efforts by various Japanese organizations such as the FSA, the ASBJ, and Keidanren, it should be noted that the relationship between the IASB and the ASBJ was not only close, but it was also an integral part of the convergence. It is also notable that the equivalence project led by the CESR was quite influential and constructed normative forces of convergence in Japan. From the perspective of performative globalization, even though the norm of global convergence of accounting standards in Japan was not so prominent just after the establishment of the ASBJ, it has gradually changed especially through the interactions with the CESR by way of the equivalence project. In other words, the collective actions of the CESR as the representative of the EU states upheld the global standards (IFRS) in the process of the equivalence project. Through interactions and communications with the CSER, the significance of rapid convergence of Japanese GAAP with the IFRS was gradually shared among organizations such as the ASBJ, FSA, and Nippon Keidanren.

5.3 Partial Adoption of the IFRS and Counterperformative Actions

Political Analysis of the Decision of Voluntary Adoption

Despite their strong commitment to the IFRS, Japanese regulators have not yet fully adopted the IFRS. Rather, only partial voluntary adoption of the IFRS is allowed. Currently, although more than 3,900 firms are listed on the Japanese stock exchange (Japan Exchange Group),[46] only 270

[46] http://www.jpx.co.jp/english/listing/co/index.html.

companies as of March 2024 have voluntarily adopted (or have decided to adopt) the IFRS. Interestingly, in a neighboring country, South Korea, the IFRS has become mandatory for the financial statements of all listed companies since 2011 to settle the Korean discount problem caused by the lack of transparency in financial reporting (Kim & Ryu, 2018, p. 39).[47]

However, Japan has taken a different path to the IFRS. This is understandable because each country has its own accounting norms that are consistent with long-established domestic principles (Waymire & Basu, 2008). Although various reasons underlay the decision to partially adopt the IFRS, a questionnaire survey conducted in Japan in 2005 revealed that nearly 70 percent of senior financial managers in Japanese firms thought that the costs of adopting the IFRS were likely to exceed the benefits (Koga & Rimmel, 2007).

Initially, the BAC was specially appointed by the FSA to work on the introduction of the IFRS in October 2008 (Nihon Keizai Shimbun, October 24, 2008, p. 7). Most BAC members agreed on the initial permission for voluntary adoption (Nihon Keizai Shimbun, October 24, 2008, p. 7). After several months of deliberation, the BAC published the interim report that foresaw the compulsory adoption of the IFRS for the consolidated financial statements of public (listed) companies in 2015 or 2016. To achieve this adoption, the final decision was supposed to be made in 2012 (Nihon Keizai Shimbun, June 12, 2009, p. 4). However, the winds had changed regarding the debate over the extent to which the IFRS should be adopted, since corporations had gradually reckoned the tremendous time and cost of switching their accounting standards from the Japanese GAAP to the IFRS (Nihon Keizai Shimbun, March 4, 2010, p. 18). Indeed, unlisted private companies had little interest in the global wave of the IFRS (Nihon Keizai Shimbun, April 6, 2010, p. 20). Meanwhile, the BAC tentatively decided that the IFRS adoption should be limited to consolidated financial statements (Nihon Keizai Shimbun, August 4, 2010, p. 4). Additionally, in 2009, the BAC of the

[47] For instance, some companies frequently abused the Korean GAAP to manipulate accounting numbers by creating special purpose entities (SPEs). The global credibility of Korean companies diminished because of this fraud (Kim & Ryu, 2018). In examining the data of Korean sample firms, Kim and Ryu (2018) observed a significant negative relationship between mandatory IFRS adoption and the cost of equity capital, which indicates that mandatory IFRS adoption decreased the cost of raising capital in the context of South Korea.

FSA announced its intention to recommend the voluntary adoption of IFRS by publicly traded companies (FSA, 2009) (Nihon Keizai Shimbun, July 12, 2009).

In 2011, the BAC started doubting whether Japan should continue to take steps toward the IFRS, as the U.S. SEC postponed its final decision to adopt the IFRS in April 2011, acknowledging that they had continuously eliminated the differences between the U.S. GAAP and the IFRS over time (Nihon Keizai Shimbun, June 21, 2011, p. 7). Moreover, India's decision to postpone the adoption of the IFRS at that time had no small impact. On June 30, 2011, the BAC held a meeting and agreed upon the direction to apply the IFRS on a limited basis with a careful preparation period (five to seven years). Therefore, the initial prospect of deciding whether to fully adopt the IFRS in 2012 was postponed. Instead, as a compromise, the BAC eased the requirements of voluntary adoption of the IFRS, as there were only nine corporations that had adopted the IFRS at that time (Nihon Keizai Shimbun, April 24, 2013, p. 7).

Counterperformative Reactions: Space for JMIS

As the extent of the adoption of the IFRS was a crucial national matter, the BAC under the FSA deliberated related issues and finally decided to postpone the decision. During that time, although the ASBJ was working on different projects related to various accounting standards, the BAC was not closely involved in the discussion. Meanwhile, on June 12, 2013, the BAC tentatively decided to establish a set of modified IFRS that would be suitable for Japanese companies and ordered the ASBJ to materialize the plan (Nihon Keizai Shimbun, June 13, 2013, p. 5). Both the FSA and the ASBJ were concerned about the low level of IFRS application in Japan at that time and expected that the Japanese version of the IFRS might be a catalyst for Japanese corporations to further increase the number of voluntary adoptions.

On August 27, 2013, the ASBJ established a working group to discuss the Japanese version of the IFRS, assuming that the differences between such Japanese version of the new standards and the official IFRS should be minimized (Nihon Keizai Shimbun, August 28, 2013, p. 15). In November 2013, the major differences between the Japanese GAAP and the IFRS were the accounting for goodwill (amortization versus non-amortization), the accounting for development costs (non-capitalization versus capitalization), and the recycling of gains on the sale of investment securities (Nihon Keizai Shimbun, November 22, 2013, p. 17).

After a year of discussion, in July 2014, the ASBJ published an exposure draft of a new set of accounting standards in Japan known as Japan's Modified International Standards (JMIS). The IASB was reluctant to accept the JMIS as a version of the IFRS because the board believed it was not a Japanese version of the IFRS but rather a different set of Japanese accounting standards (Nihon Keizai Shimbun, July 24, 2014, p. 17). Finally, in June 2015, the ASBJ issued the JMIS, which comprises a set of a few modified IFRS standards and the other endorsed IFRS standards. In particular, the provisions regarding "non-amortization of goodwill" and "items related to recycling of items of other comprehensive income and profit or losses" were subject to deletion or modification under the JMIS.

At this moment (April 2024), no Japanese company uses the JMIS as its accounting standards when preparing official financial statements. In that regard, there seems to be no use in maintaining it. However, one of the former IASB board members, Tatsumi Yamada, said that "If the JMIS is meant to be an efficient way to communicate Japan's claims, such complex situation might be unavoidable during this transitional period [of fully adopting IFRS]" (Nihon Keizai Shimbun, January 14, 2015, p. 27). In that sense, the establishment and the retention of JMIS can be understood as a counterperformative action to the rapid diffusion of the IFRS since the early 2000s, or the globalization of accounting standards.

5.4 Summary and Analysis

The ASBJ and other Japanese operative members have striven to reduce differences in Japan's domestic accounting standards and have achieved global harmonization and convergence of accounting standards. Based on the analysis, the recent development of accounting standards in Japan since the Financial Big Bang reforms can be viewed as a particular case of performative globalization.[48]

This chapter initially investigated the emergence of the Financial Big Bang. During that time, regardless of future costs and benefits, the pursuit of a "free, fair, and global" market was the first priority for recovering

[48] The Financial Big Bang itself may be seen as the overall performance of financialization under the slogan of a "free, fair, and global" market.

from the financial recession after the bubble burst. The Accounting Big Bang reforms occurred in this trend. This chapter then revealed that the Accounting Big Bang reforms can be characterized as reflecting the emergence of global accounting standards led by the G4+1 standard-setting organizations. As their approach to accounting standards was conceptual, it was welcomed by Japanese accounting researchers and relevant operative members took the G4+1's ideas as globally accepted standards. In addition, the reorganization of the IASC into the IASB was a major turning point that forced Japanese regulators to move away from the traditional public accounting standard-setting system led by the BAC under the auspices of the MOF. Since the creation of the private accounting standard setter, the ASBJ, the globalization of accounting standards in Japan has accelerated. The legend issue in global financial markets and the equivalence assessment project led by the EC and the CESR pushed the convergence of accounting standards in Japan.

In summary, around the year 2000, there was a shift in emphasis among Japanese regulators from the U.S. accounting standards to non-American IFRS as a primary set of global standards to which Japanese accounting standards should pay close attention. Starting from the harmonization stage, Japanese accounting underwent the convergence process, and finally, the partial adoption of the IFRS gradually progressed. From an economic point of view, this whole process can be understood as the result of a local accounting standard setter's deliberations that the benefits of embracing global standards would be higher than the costs of adhering to local accounting standards. Otherwise, it would be difficult to rationalize the globalization of accounting standards that has been achieved so far (Wagenhofer, 2013, p. 248).

However, such comparisons of the costs and benefits of replacing local accounting standards with global ones were not able to be seen throughout the standard-setting process analyzed herein. Rather, what this chapter has presented is the collective acceptance among Japanese operative members that it is desirable to somehow catch up with global standards under uncertainty. In particular, this chapter has emphasized the symbolic models of global standards that were supported by powerful individuals and organizations. They constructed performative forces consisting of (1) the value of the "free, fair, global" market, (2) U.S. GAAP and the messages from powerful United States delegates that competition and bank failures are sometimes inevitable, (3) the G4+1's deliberations on appropriate accounting standards, (4) the IASB and its

IFRS, (5) the IFAD's comparative investigation that brought Japan's unique accounting treatments to light, and (6) the decision made by the CESR and EC that the Japanese GAAP were not equivalent to the IAS/IFRS. Obviously, all these factors originated outside of Japan. In short, the forces of performative globalization all came from the outside of Japan.

However, there were counterperformative reactions in Japan. Japanese corporations and regulators wondered and reflected on whether the hasty adoption of the IFRS was truly beneficial to them and Japan as a whole. In addition, the earthquake and tsunami that hit Japan on March 11, 2011, and their extraordinary damage they caused, more or less provoked such reflections. As a result, Japan has not yet made a final decision on the full adoption of the IFRS, and many Japanese companies have decided to continuously use the local Japanese GAAP. More specifically, the establishment of the JMIS, which is not yet globally recognized, can be seen as a counterperformative reaction to globalization. Despite such local actions, to be fair, the pressure to globalize the accounting standards was overwhelming. Given the fact that no Japanese company uses JMIS, there was a general trend toward performative globalization.

In his analysis of the performativity of financial capitalism, Herrmann-Pillath (2013) touched on the globalization trend in relation to accounting standards. Herrmann-Pillath (2013) focused on the development of the IFRS and its penetration into different countries through performative financial capitalism. Here, I argue that the diffusion of the IFRS can be interpreted differently as a performative globalization process. In light of the adoption of the IFRS by listed firms in the EU member states since 2005, the performative globalization logic appears to be more plausible than that of financial capitalism, because different countries whose economic systems demonstrate different levels of financial capitalism have adopted the IFRS. Although performative globalization can assume different levels and degrees, and the process can be interpreted in different ways, considered from an institutional perspective, it primarily refers to the replacement of local accounting standards by global standards without clear evidence or net benefits. Although the use of objective evidence in policymaking drew public attention,[49] and evidence-based policymaking (EBPM) has been in the spotlight recently in Japan, the case of the performative globalization of accounting standards in this particular context casts doubts on the approach.

References

Accounting Standards Board of Japan (ASBJ). (2006, January 31). *Statement on Japan's progress toward convergence between Japanese GAAP and IFRSs: In reference to technical advice on equivalence by CESR.*

Benston, G., Bromwich, M., Litan R. E. & Wagenhofer, A. (2006). *World-wide financial reporting: The development and future of accounting standards.*Oxford University Press.

Committee of European Securities Regulators (CESR). (2004). Call for evidence: *Mandate to CESR for technical advice on implementing measures on the equivalence between certain third country GAAP and IAS/IFRS* (Ref: CESR/04-305).

Committee of European Securities Regulators (CESR). (2005). Call for evidence: *Mandate to CESR for technical advice on implementing measures on the equivalence between certain third country GAAP and IAS/IFRS* (Ref: CESR/04-305).

Committee of European Securities Regulators (CESR). (2007). *CESR's advice on the equivalence of Chinese, Japanese and US GAAPs.* Consultation Paper (Ref.: CESR/07-761).

Financial Services Agency (FSA) (2005, May 27). *FSA's comments on CESR's draft technical advice on equivalence of certain third countries' GAAP.*

Herrmann-Pillath, C. (2013). Performativity of economic systems: Approach and implications for taxonomy. *Journal of Economic Methodology, 20*(2), 139–163.

International Accounting Standards Committee (IASC). (1998). *Recommendations for achieving convergence on the methods of accounting for business combinations.* G4+1 Position Paper.

International Accounting Standards Committee (IASC). (2000). *Accounting for share-based payments.* G4+1 Position Paper.

Johnson, L. T., & Lennard, A. (1998). *Reporting financial performance: Current developments and future directions.* G4+1 Special Report, FASB: Norwalk.

Kim, S., & Ryu, H. (2018). The impact of mandatory IFRS adoption on capital markets: Evidence from Korea. *International Journal of Accounting and Information Management, 26*(1), 38–58.

[49] For example, in 2015, books on the economics of education that quantitatively measured and analyzed the effects of education were in the limelight in Japan.

Koga, C., & Rimmel, G. (2007). Accounting harmonization and diffusion of international accounting standards: The Japanese case. In J. M. Godfrey & K. Chalmers (Eds.), *Globalisation of Accounting Standards* (pp. 218–237). Edward Elgar.

McGregor, W. J. (1996). *Accounting for leases: A new approach, recognition by lessees of assets and liabilities arising under lease contracts*. Special Report. FASB: Norwalk.

Misawa, M. (2005). The Japanese issues and perspective on the convergence of International Accounting Standards. *Northwestern Journal of International Law & Business, 25*, 711–746.

Misawa, M. (2006). A comparative study of US and Japanese Bank directors' duty of disclosure. *Banking Law Journal, 123*(1), 39–79.

Nailor, H., & Lennard, A. (2000). LEASES: Implementation of a new approach. Special Report, FASB: Norwalk.

Nicole, P. (2002). *Foreign penetration of Japan's investment-banking market: Will Japan experience the "wimbledon effect"?* (Working Paper, The Walter H. Shorenstein Asia-Pacific Research Center [Stanford University]).

Nobes, C. (Ed.) (2000). *GAAP 2000–Survey of National Accounting Rules in 53 Countries*. PricewaterhouseCoopers.

Nobes, C. (Ed.) (2001). *GAAP 2001–Survey of National Accounting Rules benchmarked against international accounting standards*. PricewaterhouseC-oopers.

Street, D. L. (2006). The G4's role in the evolution of the international accounting standard setting process and partnership with the IASB. *Journal of International Accounting, Auditing and Taxation, 15*(1), 109–126.

Street, D. L., & Shaughnessy, K. A. (1998a). The quest for international accounting harmonization: A review of the standard setting agendas of the IASC, US, UK, Canada, and Australia. *The International Journal of Accounting, 33*(2), 179–209.

Street, D. L., & Shaughnessy, K. A. (1998b). The evolution of the G4+1 and its impact on international harmonization of accounting standards. *Journal of International Accounting, Auditing & Taxation, 7*(2), 131–161.

Toya, T. (2006). *The political economy of the Japanese financial big bang: Institutional change in finance and public policymaking*. Oxford University Press.

Tsunogaya, N., & Patel, C. (2020). The impact of external pressures (gaiatsu) and internal pressures (naiatsu) on Japan's accounting reforms since the late 1990s. *Accounting, Auditing & Accountability Journal, 33*(4), 857–886.

Vogel, S. K. (2018). *Marketcraft: How governments make markets work*. Oxford University Press.

Wagenhofer, A. (2013). Global convergence of accounting standards. In C. V. Mourik & P. Walton (Eds.), *The Routledge companion to accounting, reporting and regulation* (pp. 246–264). Routledge.
Waymire, G. B., & Basu, S. (2008). Accounting is an evolved economic institution. *Foundations and Trends in Accounting, 2*(1–2), 1–174.
Yonekura, A., Gallhofer, S., & Haslam, J. (2012). Accounting disclosure, corporate governance and the battle for markets: The case of trade negotiations between Japan and the U.S. *Critical Perspectives on Accounting*, *23*(4–5), 312–331.

In Japanese

Accounting Standards Board of Japan (ASBJ). (2004). *ASBJ Chyūki Unei Hōshin.*
Aoki, M. (2003). Prologue to the publication. In T. Toya (Ed.), *Kinyū Big Bang no Seiji Keizai Gaku [The political economy of the Japanese financial big bang: Institutional change in finance and public policy making]* (E. Toya, Trans. & M. Aoki, Trans. Supervised, pp. ii–vi).
Business Accounting Council (BAC). (2006, July 31). *Kaikei Kijyun no Convergence ni Mukete (Opinion).*
Cabinet Office (2006, July 2006). *Honebuto no Hōshin 2006.*
Financial Services Agency (FSA). (2004, June 2004). *Kokusai Kaikei Kijyun ni Kansuru Wagakuni no Seidojyō no Taiou ni Tsuite (Ronten Seiri).*
Financial Services Agency (FSA). (2009, June 2009). *Opinion on the Application of International Financial Reporting Standards (IFRS) in Japan* (Interim Report).
Financial System Research Council (FSRC) (1997, June 13). *Waga Kuni Kinyū Sisutemu no Kaikaku ni Tsuite.*
Keegan, M., Schmidt, H., Yamada, T., Yamazaki, S., & Fujinuma, T. (2001). Zadannkai: IASC Shin-Soshiki Taisei to Kongo no Doukō ni Tsuite. *The JICPA Journal, 13*(6), 44–52.
Keidanren. (2001). *Kigyō kaikei seido ni kansuru teigen. Keiri Jyōhō, 949*, 68–69.
Keidanren. (2003, October 21). *Kaikei Kijyun ni Kansuru Kokusaiteki Chōwa wo Motomeru.*
Keidanren. (2006, June 20). *Kaikei Kijyun no Togo (Convergence) wo Kasokuka shi Ōbei tono Sōgo Shōnin wo Motomeru.*
Keidanren. (2007, August 8). *Kongo no Kaikei Kijyun no Convergence no Susumekata ni Tsuite.*
Koga, C., & Igarashi, N. (1999). *Kaikei Kijyun no Gurōbaru-ka Senryaku.* Moriyama Syoten.
Kondo, M. (2011). Chapter 5: *Kinyū jiyūka.* In K. Iwata & M. Kuroda (Eds.), *Baburu/Defure-ki no Nihon Keizai to Keizai Seisaku. Rekishi-henn (Nihon*

keizai no kiroku: Dai-niji sekiyu-kiki heno taiou kara Baburu houkai made) (Vol. 1, pp. 46–69). Cabinet Office.

Obinata, T. (2023a). *Nihon no Kaikei Kijyun I: Kakuritsu no Jidai*. Chuo Keizai Publishing.

Obinata, T. (2023b). *Nihon no Kaikei Kijyun II: Gekidō no Jidai*. Chuo Keizai Publishing.

Ohta, Y. (2018). *Kinyu Shissaku: Nijyū-nen no Shinjitsu*. Nihon Keizai Shinbunsha.

Osaki, S. (1998). *Mochikabu-gaisya setsuritsu no kaikin to kinyū mochikabu gaisya* (Lifting of ban of establishment of holding companies and financial holding companies). *Nomura Capital Markets Review (Sihon Sijyō Quarterly)*, *1*(3), 2–12 (Nomura Institute of Capital Market Research).

Suzuki, T. (2009). Gurōbarizēisyon to nihon no kaikei kenkyu. *Kaikei, 175*(3), 53–65.

CHAPTER 6

Diffusion and Penetration of Fair Value Accounting

The phenomenon of financialization in Japan has been analyzed from various perspectives (e.g., Dore, 2000; Ogura, 2015; Schaede, 2020; Watanabe, 2018). Although Japanese main bank system was the dominant financial mechanism for corporations during the growth period after World War II, it seemed to be ineffective in the globalized financial markets in which a tremendous volume of financial instruments was traded (Aoki, 2004).[1] This decline of Japan's main bank system and the introduction of free, fair, and global financial market through the Big Bang financial reforms were key factors that accelerated financialization in Japan. This chapter initially outlines the shift from the traditional manufacturing-oriented economy to a finance-oriented one to depict the characteristics of financialization in Japan. In a financialized economy, the significance of financial markets is elevated in society; therefore, the timely market value of tradable financial instruments is of the utmost importance, as it frequently fluctuates depending on various factors under uncertainty. From this standpoint, this chapter discusses performative financialization in terms of the changes in accounting standards for financial instruments in Japan.

[1] This was partly due to the decreasing reliance on bank borrowing and the decline in main banks' screening and monitoring functions (Aoki, 2004, p. 21).

N. Okamoto, *Institutional Change and Performativity*,
https://doi.org/10.1007/978-3-031-53393-8_6

The first section describes a shift in the Japanese economic structure in the long run, which can be characterized as a transition from a manufacturing-oriented economy to a finance-oriented economy, reflecting a financialization process. The second and third sections explain how Japanese accounting regulators (operative members) accepted the penetration of mark-to-market accounting, as Japan had traditionally emphasized historical cost accounting that had long recognized revenues according to the realization principle. However, the financial markets of major developed countries are interconnected and are part of the global financial market.[2] As the pursuit of active, borderless financial markets has been collectively accepted, the performative force of financialization has shaped various accounting standards in Japan to accommodate the introduction of the market-to-market accounting. Nevertheless, some actors tried to secure the significant part of their traditional practices, which represents a counterperformative action to financialization.

6.1 The Shift from a Manufacturing-Oriented to Finance-Oriented Economy

Deregulation of Financial Transactions in Japan

As the previous chapter described, the Financial Big Bang reform in Japan transformed Japanese financial regulation. Before this turning point, Japanese financial regulation had focused on a broad range of stakeholders,[3] including employees, suppliers, trading partners, and banks (Toya, 2006, p. 69).[4] This approach seemed adequate, so far as the Japanese economy rapidly grew in the 1970s and 1980s, as strict financial regulation channeled most corporate finance through the main banks.

[2] Raddant and Kenett (2021) empirically investigated the characteristics of interconnected global financial markets.

[3] Toya (2006, p. 10) called this Japan's unique practice "stakeholder capitalism."

[4] According to Dore (2000), "To be sure, Japanese firms are indeed more prone than those in Anglo-Saxon economies to treat their suppliers as having a stake in trading relationships of long standing which should be respected. When they talk of giving good service to their customers, it is indeed the case that the ratio of earnest honesty to cynical manipulation is quite high. But the stakeholder of which is of overwhelming importance to a Japanese manager is the community of *sha-in*, the 'members of the enterprise community': the firm's regular employees who, like himself, joined the firm, mostly at very early age early age, in the expectation of making a career in it" (pp. 10–11).

Therefore, for those banks, the stock price was much less relevant than steady cash flow that enabled reliable and punctual interest payments on loans (Schaede, 2022, p. 13).

However, after the shocking bubble burst, massive bankruptcies occurred and shook the Japanese government. Suddenly, as mentioned in the preceding chapter, major financial institutions, such as Hokkaidō Takusyoku Bank and Yamaichi Securities, declared bankruptcy.[5] Overall, these bankruptcies were caused by these companies' insufficient risk management and non-performing loans (Onda, 2023). In the end, it was revealed that Yamaichi hid 200 billion yen of off-balance-sheet debt and conducted illegal stock dealings (*Tobashi*)[6] (Onda, 2023, p. 164). From the mid-1990s to the early 2000s, other financial institutions similarly suffered from low profitability due to non-performing loans during the economic downturn, which triggered mergers of banks and securities companies to survive the crisis. For instance, in May 1999, the Industrial Bank of Japan (*Nippon Kogyō Ginkō*), Fuji Bank and Dai-Ichi Kangyō Bank announced a merger of their operations and finally created a financial holding company, Mizuho Financial Group, in 2000. Sakura Bank and Sumitomo Bank also merged in 2001 to establish Mitsui Sumitomo Bank and its parent holding company Sumitomo Mitsui Financial Group was formed in 2002. Likewise, Sanwa Bank and Tōkai Bank merged in 2002 to establish UFJ Bank which was finally acquired by Mitsubishi Bank to establish Mitsubishi UFJ Bank in 2005. These banks currently exist as Japan's top mega banks in terms of size, trade volume, and global networks (Onda, 2023, p. 226), and they now compete with rival global banks in the international financial markets.

This series of bank mergers and acquisitions was the result of market competition in the banking industry in Japan. It is useful to consider how Japanese financial regulation has changed in terms of policy style to enhance market competition. To provide some background, beginning in the 1990s, as Japan's economy fell into two decades of stagnation similar

[5] Moreover, Sanyo Securities and Tokuyo City Bank declared bankruptcy in 1997. In 1998, both the Long-Term Credit Bank of Japan (*Chōgin*) and Nippon Credit Bank were nationalized after the collapse.

[6] This involved temporarily moving worthless assets off the balance sheet at account-closing time by selling them to a firm with a different account-closing date, with the promise to repurchase at some premium. The repurchase undertaking should have been noted but was not (Dore, 2000, p. 83).

to the United States in the 1980s, some identified the lack of market discipline as the culprit (Schaede, 2022, p. 13). The "true believers" of such a market mechanism sought to demonstrate that bureaucratic interference would not help economic growth, which should instead depend on entrepreneurial excellence and open competition (Dore, 2000, p. 42).

During this time, Japanese financial regulations were designed to introduce more risk money/investment. Particularly, the introduction of quantitative monetary easing policy, the U.S.-led globalization of the economy, and the application of information technology to financial transactions facilitated a shift from "savings to investment" (Watanabe, 2018, p. 30). Particularly, the slogan of "choose and focus" (*sentaku to shūchū*) had become a leading catchphrase since the turn of the century (Schaede, 2022, p. 74). Under the helm of Prime Minister Junichirō Koizumi from 2001 to 2006, the Japanese government pushed the market logic and finally achieved the privatization of the Japanese postal service organization, as the postal savings system took in a huge share of savings deposits and financed a substantial amount of government activity via the Fiscal Investment and Loan Program (*zaisei tōyūshi*). It enabled bureaucrats to channel domestic savings toward developmental goals, especially infrastructure investment, and politicians to allocate resources to their constituents. The proponents of the financial reforms contended that Japanese financial markets could not be modernized effectively unless more savings were channeled through private financial institutions and invested in a market-based way (Vogel, 2018, p. 91).

Thus, as a necessary policy, the government at the time proposed a framework in which financial instruments would be traded more actively than before, which culminated in the introduction of the Financial Instruments and Exchange Law (FIEL) (*Kinyū shōhin torihiki-hō*) in September 2007.[7] As this represented a transition in financial regulations from an industry-based approach (different regulations for different sectors of the financial industry) to an instrument-based approach (financial-instrument-based regulation), the FIEL gave experienced investors greater access to sophisticated financial instruments while strengthening protections for retail investors through disclosure requirements, investor protections, and the governance of the stock exchange (Vogel, 2018,

[7] The law was passed and approved in June 2006.

pp. 92–93). In view of the need to respond to the rapidly changing environment of financial and capital markets, these measures were inevitable to protect the users of investment services at that time. One of its objectives was to establish a comprehensive and cross-sectional framework for a wide range of financial instruments and services through a flexible regulatory structure. In other words, the FIEL was intended to bring together diversified financial instruments (shares, mutual funds, government bonds, corporate bonds, financial futures contracts, weather derivatives and investment funds) under the systematic regulation of "financial instruments" (Suzuki, 2006, pp. 2–3). According to Suzuki (2006), there are three layers in the structure of the FIEL. The first layer is a combination of deregulation and the development of a market in which market participants and consumers of financial products are protected by fair rules (Suzuki, 2006, p. 4). The second layer concerns investment services, as the relevant laws at that time only covered financial instruments with the risk of loss of principal (Suzuki, 2006, p. 4). The third layer of the FIEL involved the introduction of internal controls aimed to monitor corporate governance that would prevent financial wrongdoings to protect shareholders and investors. This third regulatory measure was modeled after the Sarbanes–Oxley Act in the United States in 2002.

In short, through extensive financial reforms, Japanese financial regulations have established rules to accept a wide variety of tradable financial instruments in the financial markets. Meanwhile, the protection of consumers of financial instruments and market participants through the exclusion of unfair traders was required. In sum, in the mid-2000s, Japanese financial regulation expanded the sphere of financialization by increasing the types of financial instruments and augmenting the trading volume. Figure 6.1 shows the volume of stock market trading in Japan.

Figure 6.1 indicates the rapid growth of stock trading since 2002, or after the Financial and Accounting Big Bang reforms. Although stock trading shrank after the Lehman Shock and financial crisis for a few years, it recovered in 2013 and has gradually increased since then. Different factors might have contributed to the growth of stock trading, such as the introduction of online trading platforms or the market conditions in each year. However, it is plausible that both the Financial and Accounting Big Bang reforms have heralded the open financial market in Japan and contributed to the increase in trading volume since the early 2000s.

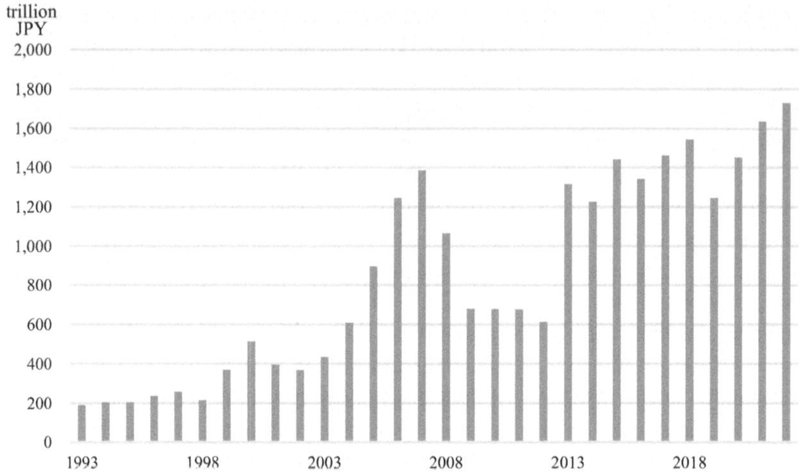

Fig. 6.1 Annual stock trading volume (monetary base) in Japan (*Source* Produced using Nikkei Needs Financial QUEST2.0. Both purchasing and selling amounts were simply combined to calculate total trading volume)

Diffusion of Financialization and Its Implications for Accounting in Japan

As indicated above, from the 2000s onward, various policy measures were introduced to proliferate the financial markets in Japan, resulting in a rapid increase in foreign investors during the early 2000s (Ahmadjian, 2007). Figure 6.2 displays the share ownership ratios among financial institutions, business corporations, foreign investors, and individual investors.

Conspicuously, foreign investors began to expand their ownership in Japanese companies from less than 5% in the late 1980s to above 25% in the mid-2000s, and this proportion has been stable since then. The share ownership by financial institutions was over 40% in the late 1990s but has declined since then and has been stable at around 25%. From 2006 to 2011, individual investors increased their share ownership. After the Lehman Shock and the subsequent financial crisis, the volume of foreign investors' share has gradually increased since 2008. According to Fig. 6.3, which indicates the contrast between the stock trading volumes (monetary base: JPY) of foreign investors and individual investors, the

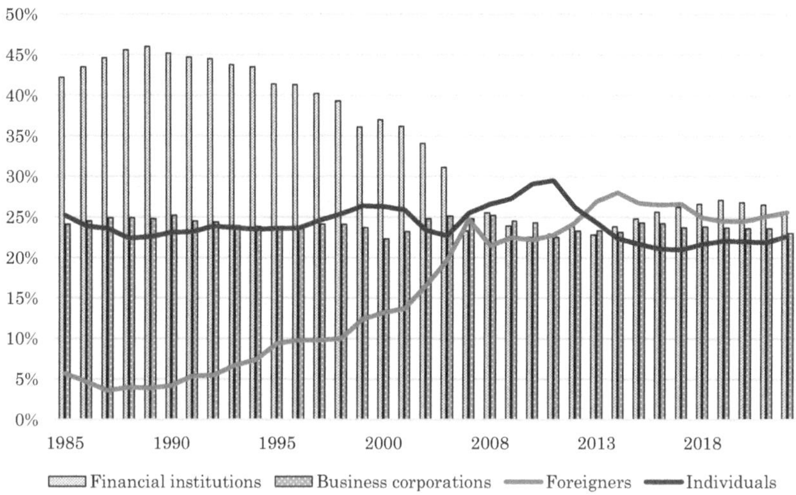

Fig. 6.2 Share ownership ratios among shareholders (1985–2022) (*Source* Japan Exchange Group's Share Ownership Survey. *Kabusiki Bunpu Chōsa*. https://www.jpx.co.jp/markets/statistics-equities/examination/01.html)

trading volume of foreign investors has been larger than that of individual investors since 2004, and the gap has been widening since 2013.

Therefore, it is useful to consider what kind of financial policies were implemented from the 2000s onward. After the introduction of the FIEL, the FSA's Financial Services Council (*Kinyū shingikai*) has assembled a study group (*Kinyū bunkakai*) in January 2007 to strengthen the international competitiveness of the Japanese financial markets. According to Hirofumi Gomi, a former Director General of the FSA, as the FIEL was designed to regulate various investment products with reference to international standards, the FSA also came to realize the necessity of reviewing the Japanese financial system and financial policymaking once and for all from an international perspective (Nihon Keizai Shimbun, December 17, 2007, p. 3). The essence of this plan appeared in his words:

> Strengthening the competitiveness of the Japanese market is not intended to protect or foster domestic financial institutions. The role of the government is to harmonize the regulatory environment as much as possible with international standards and to make the conditions of competition

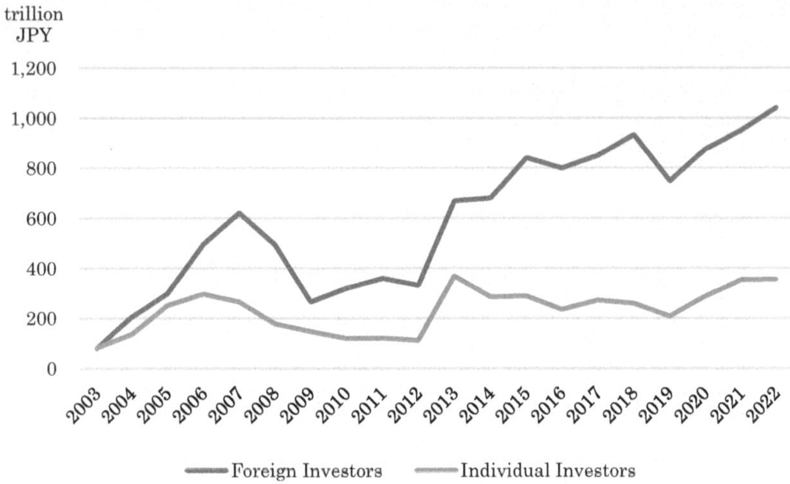

Fig. 6.3 Annual stock trading volume of individual and foreign shareholders (*Source* Produced using Nikkei Needs Financial QUEST2.0. Both purchasing and selling amounts were simply combined to calculate total trading volume)

> as pro-competitive as possible. Thus, it is up to the financial institutions themselves if they can survive the competition. Quality services come from within competition. Our idea was to keep the Japanese market constantly exposed to international competition. (Nihon Keizai Shimbun, December 17, 2007, p. 3)

The first meeting of the study group for the Internationalization of Financial and Capital Markets in Japan (*Waga kuni kinyū sihon sijyō no kokusaika ni kansuru* study group) was convened at the end of January 2007. The chairperson of the study group was Kazuhito Ikeo (a former professor at Keio University) who had previously led the crucial working group that published the Ikeo Report and considered the draft for the Financial Big Bang reforms in the early 1990s. The study group actively held meetings and solicited the views of invited professionals (e.g., directors of banks, thinktanks and various business associations).[8] Indeed, the group held fourteen meetings in five months and published an interim

[8] Among fourteen total meetings, ten were conducted to collect the opinions of professionals (https://www.fsa.go.jp/singi/singi_kinyu/tosin/20070613/05.pdf).

summary of issues that Japanese financial regulation should address (first phase) (Financial System Council, 2007): (1) conditions of attractive markets (e.g., the provision of diverse products and services; self-discipline of market participants), (2) infrastructure including systems (e.g., better regulatory environment; application of rules; market system), (3) physical environment (e.g., urban infrastructure; transportation infrastructure), and (4) market participants (players) (e.g., market operators; fundraisers; individual investors; institutional investors; financial intermediaries; and peripheral services). As this wide range of topics reveals, the target of the FSA's financial regulation at that time was quite diverse. In short, the essence of the attempt was "the enhancement of the international competitiveness of financial and capital markets" (FSA, 2007a, p. 1).

While the study group discussed possible measures to enhance the competitiveness of the Japanese financial markets, the cabinet under the first Abe administration announced the Basic Policies of Economic and Fiscal Reform 2007[9] which consisted of various policy directions including "the plan for enhancing the competitiveness of financial and capital markets [to be decided by the end of 2007]." For example, specific initiatives included the implementation of a comprehensive product line-up at exchanges and the review of firewall regulations on banks and securities firms.[10]

The study group then convened two meetings that were not open to the public (therefore, no minutes were disclosed), and its fifteenth meeting was held on December 19, 2007. In the meeting, the results of the discussions of different government-led groups (including the first and second subcommittees of the Financial System Council, and some study groups in the FSA) were shared. After this all-inclusive meeting, the FSA published a comprehensive report titled *Strengthening the Competitiveness of Japan's Financial and Capital Markets* (*Kinyū-Sihon Sijyō Kyōsōryoku Kyōka* Plan) (the Plan) on December 21, 2007 (FSA, 2007c). To focus on accounting matters, the Plan suggested upgrading the accounting and disclosure systems, stating that "The accounting and disclosure systems are an essential infrastructure for ensuring a high level of confidence in the financial and capital markets" (FSA, 2007c, p. 7).

[9] This document was also called the "Big-Boned Policy" (*Honebuto no hōshin*).

[10] The summary is available at: https://warp.da.ndl.go.jp/info:ndljp/pid/11670228/www5.cao.go.jp/keizai-shimon/english/pamphlet/2007pamphlet-e.pdf (accessed July 16, 2023).

Therefore, the study group thought that improvements to accounting and disclosure would contribute to enhancing the fairness and transparency of Japan's markets through the provision of essential information to investors. To achieve these goals, the international convergence and mutual recognition of accounting standards were highlighted (FSA, 2007c, p. 7). The Plan mentioned the European Union (EU)'s intention to require non-EU corporations to prepare consolidated financial statements in accordance with the IFRS or equivalent standards in its market.[11] Furthermore, it emphasized the necessity of communications with the U.S. Securities and Exchange Commission (SEC) (FSA, 2007c, pp. 7–8).

Although the matter of accounting standards such as the convergence with the IFRS was not discussed so much in the study group, policymakers closely considered one specific accounting matter at that time. In particular, Yoshimi Watanabe, the Minister of Financial Services, established the Financial Markets Strategy Team as a private consultative group (with private-sector practitioners and others) in September 2007 to discuss Japan's financial strategy. Until the end of November 2007, the team held a total of 10 discussions on the subprime-loan problem that had emerged in the international financial markets. The team engaged in discussions, including interviews with experts in credit markets and the U.S. housing market, practitioners in securitization, and rating agencies and finally issued a report proposing several recommendations regarding the problem of expanding subprime loans at that time (FSA, 2007b). Based on interviews with auditors, the team suggested appropriate valuation, and the necessity of proper accounting treatments for securitization products were emphasized (FSA, 2007b, p. 19).

Nevertheless, there was still some pressure to converge Japanese accounting standards to the IFRS at that time. For instance, there was a visit of David Tweedie, the chairmen of the IASB, in August 2007. During the visit, Tweedie had a meeting with the ASBJ, and they agreed to achieve the convergence of the Japanese GAAP with the IFRS by June 2011 (the Tokyo Agreement). Additionally, at that time, South Korea had already announced the adoption of the IFRS for public firms, and as one of the IASB board members from Japan, the successor of Tatsumi

[11] The EU intended to require third-country companies listed in the EU market to prepare consolidated financial statements based on the IFRS, or those standards deemed as equivalent to the IFRS, from 2009.

Yamada was a matter of concern (Yamada's term would end in November 2011) (Nihon Keizai Shimbun, August 15, 2007, p. 2). From the FSA's point of view, since the task of setting accounting standards had already been delegated to the ASBJ at that time, the inclusion of the accounting improvement clause would be one of the feasible measures to enhance the competitiveness of Japanese financial markets at that time. In addition, Ikeo (2008), who headed the study group and was involved in other government-led organizations, proposed the nationwide shift in financial regulation. He emphasized the importance of transforming the traditional "developmental economic model" in Japan into a "market economy model" of finance (Ikeo, 2008).

As the market logic permeated into the Japanese economy, the financialization of corporate assets progressed (Watanabe, 2018, p. 25), which was characterized by the rapid accumulation of financial assets such as deposits, securities, and mutual funds compared to real tangible assets (Watanabe, 2018, p. 26). Shimano (2015) analyzed the shift in the weight of different types of assets held by Japanese large corporations, and Fig. 6.4 displays the weights of assets from 1998 to 2013.

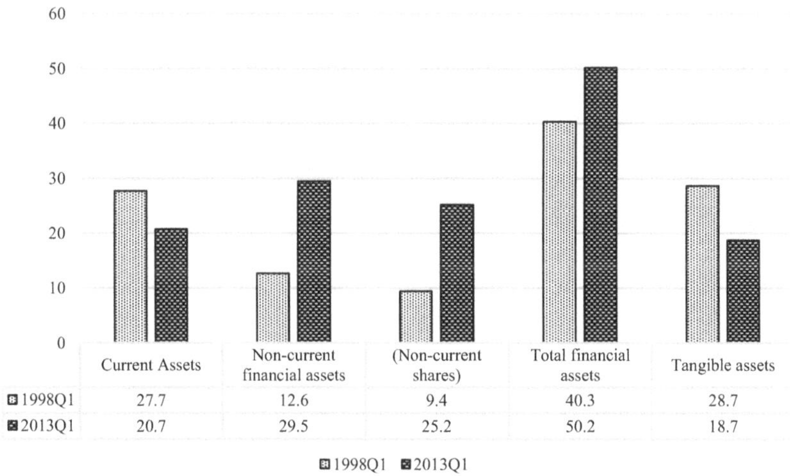

Fig. 6.4 Asset composition of large Japanese corporations (non-financial/insurance) (*Note* This figure is based on Table 1 in Shimano [2016])

For large firms in Japan, the significant increase in the ratio of long-term (non-current) financial assets from 12.6% to 29.5% between 1998 and 2013 could have been mainly due to the sharp increase in the ratio of non-current shares from 9.4% to 25.2% over the same period. The large increase in long-term financial assets resulting from this sharp rise in shares far exceeded the decline in current assets, and total financial assets also increased from 40.3% to 50.2% during the same period. On the other hand, tangible fixed assets declined from 28.7% to 17.8% during the same period. Figure 6.4 indicates that the increase in total financial assets was almost equal to the decline in tangible fixed assets. In other words, the analysis revealed that there was a substitution of assets from physical (tangible) assets to financial assets (non-current shares).

Therefore, it seems that Japanese companies have become to pay more attention to financial markets, especially in terms of shareholder decision-making. Regarding the transition of the Japanese economy, an influential accounting researcher, Ryuji Takeda (1931–2009),[12] theorized the shift from the traditional historical cost accounting to mark-to-market accounting in relation to the change in industrial structure. In his view (Takeda, 2002, 2008), the industrial structure in Japan had changed since the 1980s. In particular, he characterized the feature of the twentieth century as the powerful shift from a "production-oriented market economy (manufacturing companies' products play the central role in the economy and society)" to a "finance-oriented market economy (in which the weight of financial goods such as shares and derivatives has become dominant)."

Under the latter "finance-oriented market economy," the power of markets has grown, which necessarily entails one negative aspect: the explosion of risk (Takeda, 2002, p. 6). The change in the market, or the explosion of risk, likewise changes the measurement of corporate performance. Mark-to-market accounting appears as the measurement basis for the judgments of whether successful risk management is conducted to

[12] Ryuji Takeda was a prominent accounting researcher and former professor Emeritus of Accounting at Kobe University and Osaka Gakuin University. He published more than 200 articles and 50 books in his lifetime. Previously, he had also served as the president of the Japan Accounting Association (2000–2003) and Japan Bookkeeping Association (1990–1993 and 1993–1996) and as the examination board member of the Japanese CPA examination. In addition, he was a member of the BAC of the MOF and played an important role in the development of accounting standards in Japan.

deal with rapidly changing market prices. Therefore, mark-to-market valuation can be a tool to express two characteristics of the market: volatility and feasibility. Reporting capital gains/losses is the expression of the consequences of this volatility and feasibility, and the disclosure of the information can sustain the system of modern society in which corporations act as risk-sharing units (Takeda, 2002, p. 6). Further, Takeda summarized the difference between a P-economy (production-oriented economy) and an F-economy (finance-oriented economy) in one of his latest articles (Takeda, 2008).

As shown in Table 6.1, Takeda characterized the differences between these two types of economy. Although they are not mutually exclusive and, thus, difficult to clearly distinguish, this classification still reflects the gravitational shift from productive to financial forms of capital accumulation (Gunnoe & Gellert, 2011, p. 266) and is particularly useful to analyze the Japanese situation because Japanese "productivism" more or less militates against financialization (Dore, 2000, p. 8). According to Dore (2000):

> One of Japan's Confucian legacies is a well-established "productivism" vocabulary. Everybody understands the distinction between "the culture of making things" and "the culture of making money" (with "things" and "money" being conventionally put in the Japanese equivalent of quotes when the words are written). And those who use the distinction generally imply that the former—a culture geared to serving one's fellow-citizens by providing goods and services—is more worthy than, ethically superior to, a culture geared to "mere" self-enrichment unlinked to any concern with the service or disservice one might be doing to one's fellow-citizens in the process. (Dore, 2000, p. 8)

Takeda (2008) argued that an accounting framework should reflect the differences between these two types because "a material world of the production and a monetary world of finance finally get to different dimensions (different levels of world), and it is a great mistake to treat them equally in accounting" (Takeda, 2008, p. 792). For instance, in the financialized world, the starting point is monetary items such as securities and loans as reality, their replication is repeated, and in the process of replicating replication, we are finally led to the world of replications with

Table 6.1 Takeda's classification of economic sector characteristics

	Production-oriented market economy	*Finance-oriented market economy*
Market characteristics	• Viewpoint of national economy: The relationship between demand and supply determines the price • Viewpoint of individual economy: Price is determined by costs, the prediction of demand, and conditions of competition	• Volatility (price variability) • Feasibility (possibilities of liquidation)
Money characteristics	• The production is provided by the capacity of productive facilities • Consumption never exceeds production	• Free investment in other goods is available as money of free choice • Replicas of replicas can be freely created through the disintegration of risk by financial engineering
Valuation characteristics	• Historical cost = going concern value of the same goods by the capital maintenance	• Current market value = net realizable value = immediate liquidation value
Profit characteristics	• Long-term profit	• Short-term profit
Disclosure	• Theoretical = single-value reporting • Practical = reporting net income	• Theoretical = reporting liquidation values useful for M&As • Practical = the mixture of current market value and historical cost = reporting comprehensive income

no reality (the world of reflecting many mirrors in mirrors). In that situation, the market values on such reflecting mirrors are useful information for replicable financial instruments.[13]

Overall, this subsection has focused on financialization in terms of the shift in Japan's corporate and industrial structure. As Ryuji Takeda proposed, market value accounting for financial instruments was gradually justified during the 2000s in the context of a financialized Japanese economy. However, traditional accounting practices in Japan, which have

[13] Macintosh et al. (2000) similarly pointed out this replicative aspect of accounting for financial instruments, drawing on Baudrillard's perspective on simulacra and hyperreality.

caused some friction in the face of these changes, are examined in more detail in the next subsection.

Issues of Traditional Historical Cost Accounting in Japan

As Japan's economic development progressed after World War II, along with the expansion of Japan's manufacturing sector, a set of Japanese accounting standards relied on historical cost accounting with the realization principle for revenue recognition.[14] In other words, the traditional historical cost accounting fit well with the production-oriented economy for a long time. Or, at least, there was no strong objection to the use of this accounting style. However, as the economy becomes financialized, the significance of mark-to-market accounting has been gradually recognized by regulators.

For instance, the optional selection between the cost method and the lower of cost or market value method for shares held by financial institutions became applicable in 1998 through the Financial System Stabilization Law to address the severe credit crunch among Japanese banks (Nihon Keizai Shimbun, February 14, 1998, p. 5). This optional system was intended to improve financial institutions' capital adequacy ratio because the selection of the cost method could reduce the recognition of the loss from holding the declined shares, and it could enable some financial institutions with solid financial foundations to value their shares at market prices and demonstrate their financial soundness, while others had no choice but to choose to value their shares at cost. As soon as the Accounting Big Bang reforms started, on December 24, 1997, the MOF ironically announced the introduction of the optional measure (which would also cover banks and insurance companies) because of the financial trouble among financial institutions (Nihon Keizai Shimbun, December 24, 1997, p. 1). This decision seemed to have reflected a vestige of the traditional Japanese convoy system regulation because it intended to avoid the bankruptcy of financial institutions in any case. According to Obinata (2023, p. 239), this deferral decision of the MOF severely damaged the

[14] In the case of a production-oriented market economy, accounting theories that take into account the continuous maintenance of the resources necessary for physical production (the diachronic structure) should be developed. According to Takeda (2002, p. 6), historical cost accounting with the realization principle would be appropriate in such a case.

international reputation of Japanese accounting regulations and affected both the legend issue and the EU's equivalence project, as the delay in the introduction of mark-to-market accounting left the room for discretionary profit-taking among financial institutions through the use of the cost method for shares (Obinata, 2023, p. 240).

Despite this time lag, the BAC finally issued its Opinion on the Setting of Accounting Standards for Financial Instruments in January 1999 as part of the Accounting Big Bang.[15] The deliberations of the BAC's Financial Instruments Subcommittee (of which the chairman was Tetsuya Morita, a professor at Nihon University at that time) had begun in July 1996. After more than ten meetings, in a general meeting on June 6, 1997, the Subcommittee compiled the *Interim Report on Issues Related to Accounting Standards for Financial Instruments* that included the introduction of market value accounting for derivatives transactions, securities, and other instruments. However, the Commercial Code, which had traditionally adopted the basis of historical cost accounting, was a barrier to the introduction of mark-to-market accounting for financial instruments (Kato, 2000, p. 200). Therefore, a research group (*Syōhō to kigyō kaikei no chōsei ni kansuru kenkyū-kai*) was organized to study the introduction of market-to-market accounting and its reconciliation with the Commercial Code's traditional historical cost accounting (Kato, 2000, p. 200).

The members of the research group mainly consisted of legal scholars, accounting researchers, and bureaucrats from the MOF and Ministry of Justice (MOJ). As the Commercial Code of Japan had emphasized the significance of creditors, and the distribution of profits was restricted by detailed rules, these two ministries needed to carefully discuss the relationship between the accounting standards and the related rules in the Commercial Code. After these meetings, the research group issued a report (MOF & MOJ, 1998) that underscored the disclosure of useful information to outside parties through financial statements. One of the sections in the report discussed "the introduction of market value to financial instruments" and particularly highlighted "the necessity of market value accounting," "the scope of the entities that needs market value accounting," "the scope of financial instruments under market value accounting," and "the treatment for the changes of market value and

[15] Before that, the BAC had issued accounting standards (the Opinion) for futures and options transactions in 1990, which simply required the disclosure of market value information for futures and options transactions and marketable securities.

the regulation of distribution (of the gains)." The last item was problematic because the unrealized holding gains were not distributable to shareholders, and it contradicted the Commercial Code's function of coordinating the interests of creditors and shareholders (MOF & MOJ, 1998). On this point, the report recommended that the stance on the Commercial Code should be considered after the BAC's decision on accounting standards (MOF & MOJ, 1998, p. 31). Moreover, regarding the regulation of dividend payments, the report indicated that if the assets subject to market valuation were supported by high liquidity, and if market valuation was conducted within the scope of assessing the company's periodic performance, there would be little harm if the Commercial Code did not regulate dividends with regard to unrealized gains or losses (as both unrealized gains and losses were to be reflected in the calculation of distributable income) (MOF & MOJ, 1998, p. 31).

In short, in order to facilitate the introduction of market value accounting, both the MOF and the MOJ have worked together to accommodate it within the existing framework of the Commercial Code to make it acceptable. In particular, the research group's report emphasized the core overlap between the Commercial Code and the Securities and Exchange Law in terms of their objective of taking into account the decision usefulness of the information users (MOF & MOJ, 1998).[16] This joint work was inevitable because the provisions in the Commercial Code had traditionally focused on the calculation of distributable profits, such as restrictions on the scope of dividend payouts (Ebe, 2006, p. 214), which had obviously excluded recognized (unrealized) capital (holding) gains.

All in all, the report jointly prepared and led by the two ministries was not merely a single report of a research group, but rather an influential declaration that attempted to eliminate the long-standing barrier between the Commercial Code and the Securities and Exchange Laws with respect to market value accounting. The Commercial Code was finally modified in line with the discussions of the Council (*Hōsei shingikai*) on March 10,

[16] However, Ebe (2006, p. 211) doubted the core common objective by pointing out the different conceptions of shareholders; the Commercial Code assumed only existing real shareholders while the securities and exchange laws comprehensively assumed existing and future shareholders.

1999, and became enforceable after April 2000.[17] The revised Commercial Code required monetary claims, bonds, and shares to be marked to market, and if the total market value were to exceed the total acquisition cost, the difference should be recorded as unrealized profit, and the distributable profit calculation should deduct the unrealized portion from the net asset value on the balance sheet (Ebe, 2006, p. 221).[18] In terms of the acceptance of market valuation for financial items, the transformation of the Commercial Code can be understood as part of the overall shift toward financialization. The next section focuses on the dynamism of accounting standards for financial instruments.

6.2 Performative Financialization and Fair Value Accounting

Financialization and Market Value Accounting

Freed from the legal hindrance of historical cost accounting stipulated in the Commercial Code, market value accounting was introduced in 1999 with the BAC's accounting standards for financial instruments (BAC, 1999). This introduction was radical because its accounting treatment differed from the traditional practice of historical cost accounting in Japan (Furuichi, 2008, p. 81). Indeed, the tradition made dubious practices possible, including the arbitrary realization of capital (holding) gains on securities, intended to camouflage fluctuating business results (Saito, 1993, pp. 78–80). The new accounting standards for financial instruments were intended to promote more domestic and international investment in Japanese companies by requiring the provision of timely market information about corporate financial instruments (such as securities and derivatives) (Tsuji, 2009, p. 249). For that purpose, the standards were at least in line with the U.S. SFAS 115, 119, and 133 and the IAS 39 (Koga & Igarashi, 1999).

The process of setting the new standard took several steps (Tsuji, 2009, p. 250). As the first step, listed companies were required to disclose

[17] This was initially published as the Draft Law Amending the Commercial Code on January 27, 1999, and submitted to the diet in March 1999 (Ebe, 2006, p. 221).

[18] More detailed treatments regarding market value accounting should refer to the principle of "fair accounting practices" stipulated in Article 32(2) in the Commercial Code (Ebe, 2006, p. 221).

their holding gains and losses of securities, futures, and options in their financial statements in 1991 (BAC, 1990).[19] Secondly, in 1993, the Japanese Bankers Associations (JBA) (*Zenkoku ginkō kyōkai*) considered requiring banks to disclose the "current market value of securities" (Tsuji, 2009, p. 250). In fact, market valuation for specific transactions (trading accounts) held for the purpose of making profits by exploiting short-term fluctuations in financial markets was introduced for financial institutions in 1997 under the Law for Ensuring Sound Management (*Kinyū kikan tō no keiei kenzensei kakuho hō*). This regulation preceded the subsequent wider introduction of market value accounting for financial instruments. As these measures required corporations (particularly, financial institutions) to disclose timely market information of financial instruments while admitting the use of the historical cost for the measurement of corporate assets, these banks could enjoy the benefits associated with the continuous use of the same accounting treatments for these financial assets.

However, since the mid-1990s, public attention has focused on the soundness of financial institutions with respect to non-performing loans, and some have called for accounting treatments that reflect the fair value of financial instruments (Nihon Keizai Shimbun, December 23, 1995, p. 6 and June 14, 1996, p. 6). Moreover, the harmonization of accounting standards for financial instruments was a global trend at that time (Koga & Igarashi, 1999). For instance, on December 16, 1998, there was an IASC meeting in Frankfurt with the main aim of establishing a consensus on accounting standards for financial instruments, IAS 39 (Financial Instruments: Recognition and Measurement),[20] which was the final piece in its core set of international standards. The Japanese representative who attended the meeting was Tatsumi Yamada (an IASC member since 1996), and he voted in favor of the standard. When the IASC embarked on the project of accounting for financial instruments, it agreed to continue to explore the possibility of requiring full fair value measurements for all financial assets and financial liabilities (IASC,

[19] The aim of the BAC (1990) was to require corporations to more accurately disclose the financial condition of companies that were engaged in futures and options transactions. The standards required the disclosure of market value information for those transactions/contracts.

[20] The IASC published an exposure draft ED62 (Financial Instruments: Recognition and Measurement) in June 1998 which was the predecessor of IAS 39 published in December 1998.

1998b). As part of the exploration, for three-and-a-half years, the IASC participated in a Joint Working Group (JWG) of international standard setters on financial instruments, comprised of accounting standard setters representing more than ten countries.[21] The JWG's discussions on setting accounting standards for the recognition and measurement of financial instruments attracted a great deal of attention in Japan.[22] Ultimately, the JWG published a draft report suggesting a model of comprehensive fair value accounting for financial instruments (JWG, 2000).

As mentioned in the previous chapter, a wide variety of reforms of accounting standards in Japan during the Accounting Big Bang period were performatively shaped by globalization. As this new accounting standard for financial instruments established in 1999 was largely affected by the IASC's deliberations on the IAS 39 and the JWG's pursuit of full fair value accounting, it can be regarded as a part of performative globalization. For example, the *Nikkei* newspaper headlined the global move to full market value accounting led by the JWG as unstoppable (Nihon Keizai Shimbun, December 15, 2000, p. 7). Such a global trend mobilized the coordinating support of both the MOF and MOJ to resolve the discrepancies in the prospective accounting standards and the Commercial Code, which enabled the market value accounting for financial instruments in 1999.[23]

However, there was resistance to the idea of the comprehensive application of market value accounting (or fair value accounting) proposed by the JWG. Keidanren, for example, stated that the expansion of fair value accounting would create a number of problems for investors and other users of corporate financial statements, making it more difficult to interpret income statements as indicators of corporate profitability (Keidanren, 2001, p. 69). This opposition sparked a thorough debate that went

[21] Available at https://www.iasplus.com/en/projects/completed/fi/jwg.

[22] The proposal of the JWG attracted global attention too because it was intended to address some of the comparability problems arising from the application of the IAS 39 at that time (Hernández, 2004, p. 177).

[23] The standards allowed mark-to-market valuation with immediate profit/loss recognition for those held for trading securities, mark-to-market valuation without immediate profit recognition for those (tradable but) not held for trading securities, and devaluation for loans receivable. These securities are called available-for-sale securities and the holding gains (and losses) of those securities should be included in the stockholder's equity on corporate balance sheet. The standards also clarified mark-to-market valuation and hedge accounting procedures for derivatives.

beyond the simplistic assumption that fair value accounting is always best. The JICPA (2001) clearly objected to the JWG's proposal draft by mainly stating that (1) the techniques for measuring all financial instruments at fair value had not yet been fully established, and capital markets all over the world had not yet matured enough to respond to them reliably; and (2) not enough public consensus had yet been achieved on the adoption of the comprehensive fair value accounting model (JICPA, 2001, p. 69). In addition, the JBA (2001) opposed the JWG's introduction of full fair value accounting for financial instruments for the following reasons: (1) if non-financial assets would not be within the scope of fair value accounting, it would remain a mixed approach (historical cost basis and market value basis) that the JWG was concerned about; and (2) it considered fair value accounting information to be insufficient in terms of its relevance, reliability (and comparability), understandability, etc. (JBA, 2001, p. 1).

Ultimately, the JWG's (2000) proposal was met with unanimous opposition from business communities and other commentators around the world (Keidanren, 2003). However, there were some accounting researchers in Japan who supported the theoretical consistency of the proposal. For instance, Koga (2003, p. 228) stated that the JWG's idea was groundbreaking in that all financial instruments would be valued at fair value, with unrealized gains and losses recognized in the income statement in principle, and hedge accounting would not even be necessary. Following Takeda's theory, Koga (2003) presented the "finance-oriented accounting theory" under a finance-based economy that focuses on volatility and financial risk, which differs from the traditional cost- and realization-based accounting theories.

Regarding the possible consequences of the introduction of market value accounting, on November 5, 2002, the MOF released an estimate that the switch to the mark-to-market valuation of stocks and other financial instruments held by corporations had reduced corporate pre-tax profits by over 6 trillion yen in FY2001 (Tsuji, 2015, p. 86).[24]

[24] This estimate was based on the figures from Corporate Statistics and a questionnaire survey on the impact of the changes in accounting standards, such as mark-to-market valuation. The survey found that the pre-tax profits of all companies in FY2000 amounted to approximately 7 trillion yen, and that by FY2000, nearly 36,000 companies had introduced mark-to-market valuation, resulting in extraordinary losses of over 6 trillion yen (Tsuji, 2015, p. 86).

Therefore, the introduction of new accounting standards for financial instruments in 1999 undoubtedly had a strong impact in Japan. Although the overall institutional changes described in this section are in the direction of performative financialization, considering the influence of the JWG and the U.S. standards at that time and the negative consequences for Japanese corporations, this standard-setting can also be understood as a part of performative globalization.

Performative Financialization and Globalized Fair Value Accounting

After its foundation in 2001, the IASB worked on accounting for financial instruments as its major project.[25] In particular, the IASB started its joint project with the FASB on fair value accounting in September 2005, which became one of the topics of the memorandum of understanding (MoU) between the IASB and the FASB in February 2006. The goals of the project were (1) to reduce complexity and improve consistency in the application of fair value measurement principles by having a single set of requirements for all fair value measurements; (2) to communicate the measurement objective more clearly by clarifying the definition of fair value; and (3) to improve transparency by implementing disclosures about fair value measurements (IASB, 2011, p. 4).

As a result of the joint project, an independent accounting standard for fair value accounting, the SFAS 157 (Accounting Standards Code Topic 820), was established by the FASB[26] in September 2006 (effective in November 2007), while the IASB issued a similar discussion paper in the same year (IASB, 2006).[27] The basic idea of the standard relies on different levels of inputs to calculate the fair value of different items. The fair value hierarchy consists of three levels of inputs: Level 1 inputs are mainly based on observable market valuations such as quoted prices in active markets; Level 2 inputs include indirectly observable inputs from quoted prices of comparable items in active markets; and Level 3 inputs comprise unobservable subjective information which is often based on

[25] For example, after the publication of the exposure draft in 2002, the revised IAS 39 was issued by the IASB in 2003. The revised standard addressed the measurement of impairment loss on financial instruments.

[26] For a detailed analysis of the development of SFAS 157, see Benston (2008).

[27] This was followed by the issuance of an exposure draft (IASB, 2009a) and the final standard, IFRS 13, in 2011.

theoretical models. In the United States, for instance, Walter P. Schuetze, who was a former chief accountant of the SEC, had written and spoken extensively about fair value accounting to strongly support the extension of its use: "For balance sheets to have relevance to investors and creditors and rating agencies, historical cost of assets and historical proceeds of liabilities need to be replaced with fair value" (Schuetze, 2006, p. 11). This message was a rebuttal to the previous article that had blamed the FASB and its standards on fair value accounting for enabling Enron and other contemporaneous frauds by Qwest, Global Crossing, and Parmalat (Flegm, 2005). Schuetze (2006, p. 11) particularly emphasized that fair value accounting itself was not wrong but that Enron should have relied upon professional independent opinions in its FVA calculation.

Subsequently, however, the subprime mortgage loan crisis occurred in 2007, and the financial crisis thereafter affected the direction of the discussions in the working group of the two boards (FASB and IASB) (Yamada, 2013, p. 334). As a result of severe pressure from outside parties and criticism toward mark-to-market accounting, as a painful decision, the IASB suspended its official due process and urgently revised IAS 39 and IFRS 7 (Financial Instruments: Disclosures) in October 2008. In such a situation where the procyclicality[28] of fair value accounting was being heavily criticized, the pursuit of full fair value accounting might have been difficult. The working group acknowledged that there were many issues to be resolved to achieve the full fair value model, and for the time being, a mixed-measurement attribute model with a mixture of cost and fair value measurement was sought as a tentative solution (Yamada, 2013, p. 342).

Meanwhile, the IASB, in cooperation with the FASB, considered more appropriate accounting treatments for financial instruments and published a discussion paper entitled "Reducing Complexity in Reporting Financial Instruments" (IASB, 2008)[29] as a tentative step toward reforming IAS 39. According to an analysis of the former IASB board member

[28] According to Novoa et al. (2009, p. 24), this procyclicality is based on the tendency that fair value accounting introduces more volatility in earnings and capital during the life of an asset or liability than historical cost accounting and incorporates forward-looking assessments.

[29] This discussion paper also reflected the move away from the heavily criticized rules-based accounting standards and toward principle-based accounting regulation stating that "anecdotal evidence suggests that many users of financial statements and other constituents find the requirements of IAS 39 and the requirements of U.S. GAAP difficult to understand, apply and interpret" (IASB, 2008, para. BD1).

at that time, many other board members on this project expressed the view that "a single measurement attribute model with fair value would improve financial reporting and greatly simplify accounting standards for financial instrument compared to a mixed attribute measurement model" (Yamada, 2013, p. 342). Ultimately, an exposure draft (Financial Instruments: Classification and Measurement) was published on July 14, 2009, to comprehensively replace the previous IAS 39, and the deadline for comment letters was September 14, 2009. The exposure draft basically proposed the use of fair value accounting for financial instruments with some exceptions under which reporting companies could opt for an amortized cost approach in some designated circumstances. Many users of financial statements and other interested parties felt that the requirements of the existing standard (IAS 39) were difficult to understand, apply, and interpret (IASB, 2009b). The new accounting standards for financial instruments, IFRS 9, was finally issued on November 12, 2009. Under IFRS 9, financial assets are classified into one of two measurement categories: fair value or amortized cost. This classification is based on an assessment of how the instrument is managed (the entity's business model) and its contractual cash flow terms. The amortized cost method is only applied to financial instruments with principal amounts that are held for collection or payment of contractual cash flows rather than for sale or settlement through a third party. Therefore, most financial instruments are valued under the fair value method in accordance with IFRS 9, and the resulting changes in their values are generally recognized as profit or loss (fair value through profit or loss: FVTPL). An entity can, on initial recognition of strategic equity investments,[30] elect to record changes in the fair value of the investment as other comprehensive income (fair value through other comprehensive income: FVTOCI).

Obviously, these comprehensive fair value accounting rules had substantial impact in Japan. Initially, the ASBJ published a discussion paper on fair value measurement and its disclosure (ASBJ, 2009), which raised points for discussion regarding the concept of fair value (e.g., if it should be exit (market) value), the treatment of transaction cost, and the appropriateness of fair value hierarchies. Although only 11 interested

[30] "At initial recognition, an entity may make an irrevocable election to present in other comprehensive income subsequent changes in the fair value of an investment in an equity investment within the scope of the standard that is not *held for trading*" (IASB, 2009b, para. 5.4.4).

parties sent comments in response to the ASBJ's discussion paper, they did not clearly reject the introduction of the comprehensive fair value accounting model. Rather, these comments mainly pointed out the ambiguity of the exit price, the necessity of clear guidance, and the unlimited scope of the standard.

Then, the ASBJ issued exposure drafts of No. 43, "Accounting Standard for Fair Value Measurements and Disclosures," and No. 38, "Implementation Guidance on Fair Value Measurements and Disclosures," on July 9, 2010 (ASBJ, 2010a, 2010b). Twenty comment letters were sent to these exposure drafts. Among them, two real estate organizations (The Real Estate Companies Association of Japan and The Association for Real Estate Securitization) strongly opposed the wider application of fair value accounting simply because there was no real estate market in which fair value was observable. They shared concerns about two points: the scope of the standard and the linguistic expressions. First, they argued that the scope of the standard was not clear as the ASBJ excluded accounting standards for inventories and stock options from the scope of the exposure draft. Indeed, Topic 820 by the FASB and the IFRS 13 by the IASB do not only apply to financial instruments, but also cover the fair value measurement of inventories, fixed assets, etc. The exclusion of the application of standards in the ASBJ's exposure draft did not reflect comprehensive convergence. Second, although the ASBJ directly followed the term "fair value" (*kōsei kachi*) in line with the FASB and the IASB in both the discussion paper and the exposure draft, Japanese accounting standards had never used the concept, and it was considered that the Japanese expression of "current (market) value" (*jika*) would be more appropriate and consistent.

Upon the receipt of these comments to the exposure drafts, the ASBJ discussed how it could address them (in its 223rd, 226th, and 227th meetings) from April to June 2011. On this matter, the Technical Committee on Financial Instruments met extensively and discussed supporting the establishment of the standard (e.g., its 81st meeting on May 11, 2011; 82nd meeting on May 20, 2011; 83rd meeting on June 10, 2011; and 84th meeting on July 8, 2011). However, at the June 10 meeting, the committee concluded that it would be better to gather input from practitioners regarding the disclosure of Level 3 inputs for fair value accounting (*Keiri Jyōhō*, 2011, 1285, p. 5). At that time, the ASBJ intended to issue its final standard on fair value accounting in August 2011 (material No. (3)-1 at the 226th meeting on June 16, 2011).

After these several meetings to exchange opinions, on August 9, the 87th meeting of the Technical Committee on Financial Instruments was held. Seven meetings were actually held between July and August in 2011, and major objections were shared (*Keiri Jyōhō*, 2011, 1291, p. 5). In particular, concerns were raised regarding whether strict disclosure requirements for Level 3 input information were really significant and necessary for Japanese companies. During one of the meetings, a committee member asked about the timing of the issuance of the standard, to which the ASBJ responded that its staff of the board would handle the matter but that it would take time to move forward (*Keiri Jyōhō*, 2011, 1291, p. 5).

However, further discussion toward a final decision on the standard was suspended for a long time. Put differently, the ASBJ could not fully address the concerns and comments to the exposure draft. At the 374th ASBJ meeting, more than 6 years after the issuance of exposure draft, the ASBJ retrospectively mentioned that "Although we issued an exposure draft that was consistent with the IFRS 13, as it was a broad suggestion of fair value accounting that attempted to cover assets and liabilities other than financial instruments, our discussion has been suspended since then" (material No. (6)-1 at the 226th meeting on December 5, 2017).[31]

Then, at the time when feedback was being sent regarding the post implementation review (PIR) of IFRS 13, the ASBJ resumed discussions on fair value measurement in December 2017. After one-and-a-half years of deliberation, the ASBJ finally issued its accounting standards for fair value measurements and related practical guidelines on July 4, 2019, which are similar to SFAS 157 (Topic 820) and IFRS 13 (Kunita, 2020, p. 167).

[31] Indeed, the JICPA established the Technical Committee for Fair Value Examination of Nonfinancial Instruments in November 2011 (JICPA, 2013). The committee published a research report in July 2013 that summarized different perspectives of market value (fair value) in various Japanese accounting standards, mentioning that "There are various methods for calculating the fair value of non-financial items, and there are various methods for obtaining the data needed to calculate fair value. Thus, it is difficult to find a single view or conclusion on how to calculate fair value, However, we believe that it is meaningful to publish the progress of the study by the Technical Committee as a research document and provide it here to assist members in their research on the calculation of the fair value of non-financial items" (JICPA, 2013, p. 1).

Nevertheless, Japanese characteristics remained in these standards. First, the new standards did not cover fair value accounting for inventories[32] and tangible assets regardless of the comprehensiveness of the modeled standards (IFRS 13 and Topic 820) established by the IASB and the FASB. Considering that both the FASB and the IASB had been working on the project since 2005, and the former promptly issued SFAS 157 followed by the IASB's issuance of IFRS 13 in 2011, the ASBJ's actions were slow and inconsistent with the decisions of other two major boards. In that sense, the ASBJ's standard-setting on this matter was to some extent counterperformative to financialization (as well as globalization). On this point, during the meeting on April 23, 2019, an ASBJ member argued that the market value of financial instruments and that of non-financial instruments were not similar and that the use of the same terminology would be confusing (*Keiri Jyōhō*, 2018 5.10 and 20, 1512, p. 4). Japanese operative members had been stuck on the difference between using fair value for financial assets and for non-financial assets such as inventories.

Second, the direct Japanese expression of "fair value," or *kōsei-kachi*, was not used but rather "*jika* (current (market) value) was selected, even though the standard states that *jika* can be read as *kōsei-kachi* (fair value). This might be a matter of translation, but the translation in accounting matters, as it is not simply a technical exercise but can entail linguistic and cultural conflicts between dominant and marginalized concepts, traditions, and values (Laaksonen, 2022). It can be considered that the expression of *jika* (current value) would be more appropriate and less misleading in the Japanese context. Thus, the ASBJ's reason for not sticking to the term *kōsei-kachi* (fair value) was, rather, a path-dependent and a counterperformative argument to the concept of fair value. More counterperformative actions are discussed in detail in the next section.

[32] Exceptionally, inventories held for trading are within the scope of the standards.

6.3 Counterperformative Actions from Japan: Securing Local Tradition[33]

Japanese Reactions against the Global Idea

Although the previous sections have discussed how market value accounting has penetrated Japan in terms of financialization, this section highlights counterperformative actions in the context of accounting standard setting, focusing on a specific accounting treatment in the IFRS 9: dividends received from strategic equity investments. The exposure draft (IASB, 2009a, paras. 21–22) stated that "At initial recognition, an entity may make an irrevocable election to present in other comprehensive income subsequent changes in the fair value of investments in equity instruments within the scope of this [draft] IFRS that are not held for trading. If an entity makes that election, it shall recognize in other comprehensive income dividends from those investments when the entity's right to receive payment is established. There would be no transfers from other comprehensive income to profit or loss ("recycling") and hence no impairment requirements" (IASB, 2009a, p. 12). These clauses in the exposure draft were amended prior to the issuance of IFRS 9. The final standard stated that dividends on equity investments could be included in the net income rather than other comprehensive income (OCI), thus indicating that the IASB had changed its position during the four months after the exposure draft was published. This section highlights a set of Japanese counterperformative actions to both the financialized accounting standards and the diffusion of fair value accounting, which was successful from a Japanese perspective.

To examine how such counterperformative actions were made, this section focuses on the lobbying undertaken by interested parties during the four-month period from July 14 to November 12, 2009. This short time frame limited the ways in which interested parties could lobby. In this case, submitting comment letters was one of the few options available to interested parties wishing to present their opinions. Those opinions must

[33] This section is largely based on Okamoto (2017). The author is grateful to Gary Previts who was the editor of *Research in Accounting Regulation* and has permitted the use of the content of the article here.

have been reflected in the comment letters sent to the exposure draft.[34] The following two yes-or-no questions regarding the accounting treatment for equity investment and the dividends from it were included in the exposure draft (IASB, 2009a, pp. 12–13). Accounting treatments for holding gains/losses of equity investment and the dividends from them (into other comprehensive income) were significant in Japan because their insertion into net income has long been embedded in Japanese accounting and business practices.

> (Question 10)
> Do you believe that presenting fair value changes (and dividends) for particular investments in equity instruments in other comprehensive income would improve financial reporting? If not, why?
> (Question 11)
> Do you agree that an entity should be permitted to present in other comprehensive income changes in the fair value (and dividends) of any investment in equity instruments (other than those that are held for trading), only if it elects to do so at initial recognition? If not,
>
> a. how do you propose to identify those investments for which presentation in other comprehensive income is appropriate? Why?
> b. should entities present changes in fair value in other comprehensive income only in the periods in which the investments in equity instruments meet the proposed identification principle in (a)? Why?

After the publication of the exposure draft, 245 comment letters were submitted by various interested parties from 18 countries over the four-month period. All the submissions were classified according to their country of origin. The largest number of submissions (36) came from the United States and the second largest (33) from the United Kingdom, followed by Australia (18) and Japan (16). According to Jorissen et al. (2014), constituents from the G4+1 countries (the United

[34] Several studies have taken a similar method of classifying the arguments presented in comment letters (MacArthur, 1988a, 1988b; Schultz & Hollister, 2003; Tutticci et al., 1994; Yen et al., 2007).

States, Canada, the United Kingdom, Australia, and New Zealand)[35] and countries with a common law background tend to submit the most comment letters to the IASB.

Table 6.2 summarizes the national background of the comment letters and shows the analysis of the responses to the Questions 10 and 11. Notably, almost 90% (14 out of 16) of the comment letters from Japan answered these two questions in the negative, even though more than half the respondents from the United Kingdom and the United States answered in the affirmative. As an example of a typical reason for the uniform objection from Japan, the Security Analysts Association of Japan stated in their comment letter that the proposal was inconsistent in that the opportunity cost of holding stocks (e.g., the interest payments on borrowings used to purchase the stock) would be recognized in net income while the dividend offsetting the cost would be included in other comprehensive income (The Securities Analysts Association of Japan, 2009, p. 4).

Table 6.2 Opinions on the comment letters to the Questions 10 and 11 of IASB (2009a)

Countries[a]	*Total number of submitted letters*	*Number of letters explicitly opposed to the proposal*	*Percentage*[b]
UK	36	13	36
US	33	8	24
Australia	18	11	61
Japan	16	14	88
France	14	11	79
Canada	13	4	31
Germany	12	5	42
Others	103	58	56
Total	245	124	51

[a] If a comment letter was submitted by an international organization whose national attributes were hard to identify, it was classified as "Others"
[b] Numbers are rounded up

[35] As already mentioned in the previous chapter, a group of national standard setters from the Anglo-American countries formed a joint working group (Group of Four) to which the IASC was also invited (+1). From 1994 on, the Group of 4+1 issued a series of discussion papers aiming to influence international standard-setting (Botzem, 2012).

Much of the opposition to the suggested changes proposed in Questions 10 and 11 was also expressed by interested parties in France (79%) and Australia (61%). Thus, an idea of accounting treatment that should include dividends from equity investments in net income (rather than in comprehensive income) might have been shared to some extent by interested parties in those countries as well as in Japan. This coincidental coalition of opinions might have been effective in changing the IASB's decision following the release of the exposure draft.[36] Certainly, at the meeting on October 15, 2009, the IASB board members decided to amend the exposure draft and permit dividends from strategic equity instruments to be presented as profit or loss as long as they represented a return on investment.

However, this analysis reflects the perspective of one country, and it is inconceivable that the IASB modified its decision solely in response to one country's strong objection. As the IASB itself states, it is committed to developing, in the public interest, a single set of high-quality global accounting standards. Thus, the IASB's decisions should be impartial. Nevertheless, which items should be included in net income or comprehensive income is still a contentious topic. There was no consensus among accounting scholars as to which type of income measure (net income or comprehensive income) is superior for the users of accounting information. Bayou et al. (2011) indicated that comprehensive income is inherently ambiguous because it is merely an ideology or myth that coheres with the idea that comprehensive income is useful for predicting corporate cash flows. In this regard, it is reasonable to interpret that the IASB's decision to classify dividends from strategic equity investments in the OCI could be modified through logical and persuasive counterperformative actions.

[36] Although the oppositions from Australian and French to the exposure draft of IFRS 9 were conspicuous among the submitted comment letters, there was no apparent lobbying action regarding the classification of dividend income by actors from Australia and France other than the submission of comment letters to the IASB from July 14 to November 12 in 2009. Only Japanese operative members' reactions were strong during that time.

Counterperformative Actions to Secure Local Practice in Global Context

This IASB's modifications within this short period can be understood as resulting from counterperformative actions to a specific accounting treatment in line with the diffusion of fair value accounting. Japanese actors' actions seemed to effectively persuade the IASB to change its decision to leave room for Japan's traditional accounting treatment. With regard to the opposition to the exposure draft, some Japanese actors were powerful norm entrepreneurs with the idea that dividends from equity investments should be included in net income rather than OCI. Among the 15 board members of the IASB as of December 31, 2010, there was only one Japanese representative, Tatsumi Yamada. Although a majority (nine) of the IASB members represented European and North American countries (the United States and Canada) at that time, Yamada had an opportunity to propagate Japanese accounting norms among those members. During an interview conducted by the author, Yamada commented that Japan's presence on the IASB could be effective in conveying to the IASB the facts, possible consequences, and economic rationale underlying the specific accounting standards.

As stated, many Japanese interested parties objected to the suggetsions in the exposure draft. Their objections were derived from a traditional Japanese accounting practice that dividends from cross-held shares should be recognized in net income. In fact, the practice of cross-shareholding was quite common among Japanese financial institutions (except for trust banks) and other large corporations. The practice declined in the 1990s after the collapse of Japan's "bubble" economy but has remained at a constant level since 2005 in terms of corporations' cross-shareholdings (Ito, 2009, p. 2). The practice of cross-shareholding was also termed "strategic investment" in Japan and was developed as an essential mechanism of Japanese corporate governance (Japan Association of Corporate Directors, 2010). Japanese cross-shareholdings tend to be the result of strategic investment, which expects a return above the market average through, for example, a long-term operational affiliation. Therefore, because the overall outcome of such investment depends on a synergistic effect between the intangible and tangible resources of both investors and investees, it is probably inappropriate to measure the performance of the investment in terms of changes in the market value of the stock (Abe, 2009, p. 95).

Under the Japanese accounting standards at that time, most cross-held shares were usually classified as "other securities" (Kumagai, 2008, p. 53), and changes in their market value were recognized in shareholders' equity. The contentious issue in the IASB's exposure draft was that the dividends from those investments should be included in the comprehensive income (IASB, 2009a). From the Japanese perspective, at that time, the dividends from such strategic investments were thought to reflect the real performance of investment companies in Japan and, thus, included in net income. Based on a projection, if all dividends were recognized in the OCI of listed companies in Japan, at least one trillion yen (about 12 billion USD) of net profit would disappear (Abe, 2009, p. 95), and the impact on these companies would be enormous. This belief was the basis of the opposition to the exposure draft by Japanese interested parties because the norm of net income supremacy in Japan conflicted with the content of the exposure draft.

This Japanese collective opinion was represented by Tatsumi Yamada in an interview with Bloomberg News in August 2009 regarding dividends from equity instruments: "There is no management that does not expect any reward from financing. [Concerning the proposal about dividends in the exposure draft] ... some IASB members take a sympathetic view on this matter" (Okamoto, 2017, p. 134). This comment implied that he had discussed this matter with other IASB board members. Furthermore, the importance of membership in the IASB as a means of voicing national concerns to the board was confirmed in my interview with Mr. Yamada. This point is also consistent with Hansen's (2011) hypothesis that lobbyists with greater access to IASB members are likely to have greater lobbying success.

In addition to Tatsumi Yamada, other Japanese actors assumed the role of norm entrepreneurs and helped persuade IASB members. For instance, the ASBJ not only submitted a comment letter opposing the exposure draft but also made contacts with the IASB through formal meetings such as roundtable conferences with the IASB and the FASB. Actually, the connection between the ASBJ and IASB has become stronger around that time, and they have been working together since 2005 to achieve convergence between the IFRS and Japanese accounting standards.[37] Considering the strong bond between these two standard setters,

[37] This work was formalized in 2007 with the Tokyo Agreement. Additionally, in June 2009, the Business Accounting Council, a key advisory body to the Commissioner

particularly important exchanges between the ASBJ (and other important Japanese political actors) and the IASB regarding IFRS 9 occurred during the IASB's roundtable conferences held in the United Kingdom, the United States, and Japan after the publication of the exposure draft. One meeting, held in Tokyo on September 3, 2009, was aimed at gathering opinions from the Asian region about the exposure draft relating to accounting for the classification and measurement of financial instruments. The ASBJ participated in this meeting as a joint coordinator, and some representatives of the Japanese FSA were also present. One of the main themes of the conference was "Whether exemption should be permitted for equity investments such as cross-shareholdings," and Japanese objections would have been expressed at the meeting. That same day, the ASBJ and FASB held an informal meeting to exchange their views on the exposure draft. In this brief informal meeting, there was a lively discussion of such issues as the accounting treatment for strategic investments. The strong Japanese opposition to the exposure draft was communicated to the FASB members during the meeting.[38]

Furthermore, the ASBJ held its 10th Joint Meeting with the IASB on September 7–8, 2009, in London. The main discussion theme in this meeting was also related to accounting for financial instruments. The ideas underlying the proposed classification models, reclassification,[39] and fair value measurement for unlisted equity securities with reference

of Japanese FSA, approved an interim report—*Application of International Financial Reporting Standards in Japan*. In this report, the BAC proposed allowing certain listed companies to adopt the IFRS early, followed by a final decision about the mandatory adoption of the IFRS around 2012. The interim report also recommended that the ASBJ should accelerate the convergence of accounting standards.

[38] The information source is the ASBJ Newsletter published on October 20, 2009 (https://www.asb.or.jp/asb/asb_j/newsletter/pdf/newsletter11.pdf). The newsletter stated that Marc A. Siege visited Japan on September 3, 2009, and gave a presentation about the ongoing joint project regarding accounting standards for financial instruments. The newsletter also noted that there was a heated discussion about the accounting treatment for strategic equity investments.

[39] With regard to OCI and recycling/non-recycling, the two organizations exchanged views on the concepts of profit and profit presentation in financial reporting, and a concrete proposal for presenting a statement of comprehensive income was put forward by an IASB member.

to the ASBJ's comments on the exposure draft were discussed.[40] One of the ASBJ members presented the Japanese opinion by stating that "Japanese market participants strongly wish to include dividends on cross-held shares in net income, even though recycling of changes in their value is not permitted." One IASB member replied, "Any comments from anyone in relation to specific matters are of considerable concern."

Then, at the IASB meeting held on October 15, 2009, the IASB board members decided to change the requirements outlined in the exposure draft after agreeing to the request that dividends from strategic equity instruments should be shown as profit or loss as long as they represent returns on investments. The IASB's reasons behind this decision are noteworthy. According to the summary of the meeting (IASB Update[41]), "The Board tentatively confirmed the proposal in the ED. However, as a change to the ED proposal, the Board tentatively decided to require recognition of dividends received from these investments in profit or loss, so long as they represent a return on investment (as opposed to a return on investment)."

The essential argument in support of the IASB's decision was that investment in equity instruments could be viewed as being similar to lending. If a bank lends money to a company, the bank expects interest on the loan. Indeed, some Japanese parties argued that dividends from strategic investments are similar to interest payments from borrowers. Generally, investors in equity instruments cannot discretionally manipulate the amount of dividends declared by the companies in which they have invested, and deciding where and how much to invest presents considerable risk for management (Abe, 2009, p. 95). Furthermore, some Japanese interested parties contended that if debt is the source of the investment, it is inconsistent that even though interest payments on the debt are included in the net income calculation, the return on the investment, which is usually in the form of a dividend, is included in the OCI. This simple analogical explanation might have contributed to a change in the IASB's assessment of returns on investments in equity instruments.

[40] This information is based on the newsletter published by the ASBJ. The details of communications between the two organizations, including the minutes of the joint meeting, are available on the ASBJ's website.

[41] Available at https://www.ifrs.org/content/dam/ifrs/news/updates/iasb/2009/iasbupdate16october2009.pdf.

In short, the IASB's decision to modify the exposure draft was largely related to a period in September 2009, only two months after the publication of the exposure draft. The comments presented below are from the IASB meeting held in September 2009. Although the information available from the audio recording of the meeting is limited and detailed information relating to the final vote is not available, this discussion was critical in terms of the sharing of members' opinions on the treatment of dividends. The comments are mostly related to questions 40–44 on IASB meeting Staff Paper 7. In this meeting, the significance of the comments submitted in response to the exposure draft and the IASB's stance on them were discussed.[42]

The coordinator of the meeting directed the IASB members' attention to the questions:

> Well, most respondents agreed that changes in the fair value of some equity investments should be permitted to be presented in OCI. Nearly all respondents criticized at least some aspects of the board's proposals—primarily regarding the dividends—and realized gains and losses would be recognized in OCI...

The Japanese board member, Tatsumi Yamada, was quick to protest the issue:

> So, this is very important in our jurisdiction. In Japan, there has been an emotional reaction. Everybody keeps saying that recycling is necessary, so that is one thing. But this time, I would like to draw attention to the dividends. What I have heard a lot is the need to achieve a strategic relationship with the counterparty. So...what an entity...has in mind is that the dividend, say that is the return on the investment...is a sort of prerequisite to an established relationship. That means that they make an investment to make a huge amount of money. The return is not recognized as part of net income. It's not justifiable. Also, they think that...the benefit from achieving that relationship is the dividend. So...the dividend should be recognized as part of the benefit. That is the strongest argument from the preparers, that is, the holders of the strategic investment.

[42] Background noise in the recording made some words quite difficult to comprehend. However, this is not critical because the meaning of the comments was clear.

His intent in this comment was to highlight the inconsistent treatment of risks and returns (i.e., the costs of cross-holdings and the dividends from the cross-held shares, respectively). Several other board members signaled their support for Yamada's view on the basis of information obtained during their "outreach." The audio recording of the meeting confirmed that the IASB members often referred to their "outreach" information to bolster their opinions. This information included specific interested parties' comments or opinions from various jurisdictions.

From this analysis, it can be inferred that the appeal of Japanese norm entrepreneurs was aggressive and that political contact with other organizations, such as the exchanges during the roundtable meetings with the FASB and the ASBJ was important. With regard to the inclusion of dividend income from strategic investments in net income, the former chairman of the IASB, Sir David Tweedie, admitted that the number of comment letters from Japan opposing the change was unexpectedly large (Nihon Keizai Shimbun, October 15, 2009, p. 14). Furthermore, it was reported that John Smith, one of the IASB board members at the time, had commented that the Japanese interested parties were most concerned regarding the accounting treatment of strategic investments and that he would like the Japanese opinion to be taken into account (Nihon Keizai Shimbun, September 4, 2009, p. 14).

To summarize, while the Japanese interested parties accepted the mark-to-market accounting for cross-held shares (strategic investments), they successfully avoided the introduction of the provision that would include dividends from those shares in the OCI. This case in the context of accounting standard setting can be seen as a counterperformative action within a broader trend of performative globalization and financialization.

6.4 Summary and Analysis

This chapter has considered the political process of setting accounting standards for financial instruments in Japan. Particularly since the Financial Big Bang reforms, financialization has accelerated as a result of the deregulation of financial transactions and the modifications to the Japanese Commercial Code that had traditionally protected creditors, such as banks, and strictly restricted the distribution of corporate capital. For that reason, historical cost accounting based on the realization principle was suitable for Japanese companies (especially, manufacturing companies) to reflect their growth after World War II.

However, as the volume of global business transactions augmented and the global financial market became increasingly important, the traditional emphasis on historical cost accounting did not fit well with the financialized economy that strongly emphasized shareholders and financial markets. As the global financial markets have become so influential, mark-to-market accounting, or fair value accounting, has begun to play a central role in the global accounting regulations. In particular, during this period, formal institutions such as laws and accounting standards were transformed to present timely valuations of financial instruments. The slogan of the Financial Big Bang in the late 1990s in Japan was to achieve a "free, fair, and global" market, and until the early 2000s, as the preceding chapter highlighted, the globalization of accounting standards was performative. Along with the trend, the globalization of market value accounting progressed in Japan. Besides, from the early 2000s to the mid-2010s, the Japanese accounting standard setter continued to make efforts to embrace fair value accounting in its standards. In the context of accounting standard setting in Japan, the IFRS and U.S. accounting standards had been influential, and the opinions of global organizations, such as the JWG and the IASB, were powerful. The previous chapter focused on Accounting Big Bang reform in the period from the collapse of the bubble economy to the 2000s, which was mainly driven by global harmonization and convergence of accounting standards in Japan. Since the mid-2000s, especially after Japanese accounting standards became less internationally differentiated, the reform of accounting standards in Japan has been noticeably aimed at promoting financial transactions and financial markets. These major institutional changes can be interpreted as a case of performative financialization led by operative members, such as the FSA and the ASBJ.

Nevertheless, there were some counterperformative actions taken by Japanese actors. First, some norm entrepreneurs, such as the former Japanese IASB board member, Tatsumi Yamada, and Keidanren, actively participated in the IASB's standard-setting activities to secure Japanese traditional practices and interested parties' interests by modifying the exposure draft issued by the IASB. More specifically, in order to avoid the negative impact on Japanese corporations' financial statements, these Japanese actors requested that the IASB include the dividends from equity investments in net income, as had been common and traditional in Japan with the practice of cross-shareholding. If the dividends from cross-held shares had not been classified as a part of net income, the practice of cross-shareholding would evaporate, being meaningless.

References

Ahmadjian, C. (2007). Foreign investors and corporate governance in Japan. In M. Aoki, G. Jackson, & H. Miyajima (Eds.), *Corporate governance in Japan* (pp. 125–150). Oxford University Press.

Aoki, M. (2004). The Japanese firm as a system of attributes: A survey and research agenda. In M. Aoki & R. Dore (Eds.), *The Japanese firm: Sources of competitive strength* (pp. 10–40). Oxford University Press.

Bayou, M. E., Reinstein, A., & Williams, P. F. (2011). To tell the truth: A discussion of issues concerning truth and ethics in accounting. *Accounting, Organizations and Society, 36*(2), 109–124.

Benston, G. J. (2008). The shortcomings of fair-value accounting described in SFAS 157. *Journal of Accounting and Public Policy, 27*, 101–114.

Botzem, S. (2012). *The politics of accounting regulation–Organizing transnational standard setting in financial reporting*. Edward Elgar.

Dore, R. P. (2000). *Stock market capitalism: Welfare capitalism: Japan and German versus the Anglo Saxons*. Oxford University Press.

Financial System Council. (2007, June 13). *Interim summary of issues (Phase 1): Study Group on the internationalization of Japanese financial and capital markets*.

Flegm, E. H. (2005). Accounting at a crossroad. *CPA Journal, 75*(12), 16–22.

Gunnoe, A., & Gellert, P. (2011). Financialization, shareholder value, and the transformation of timberland ownership in the US. *Critical Sociology, 37*(3), 265–284.

Hernández, F. G. H. (2004). Another step towards full fair value accounting for financial instruments. *Accounting Forum, 28*, 167–179.

International Accounting Standards Board (IASB). (2006). *Fair Value Measurements part 1: Invitation to comment and relevant IFRS guidance* (Discussion Paper).

International Accounting Standards Board (IASB). (2008, March). *Reducing complexity in reporting financial instruments* (Discussion Paper).

International Accounting Standard Board (IASB). (2009a). *A proposed IFRS for financial instruments: Classification and measurement* (Exposure Draft).

International Accounting Standard Board (IASB). (2009b). *International Financial Reporting Standard 9: Financial instruments*.

International Accounting Standard Board (IASB). (2011, May). *IFRS 13 Fair Value Measurement* (Project Summary and Feedback Statement).

International Accounting Standards Committee (IASC). (1998). *IAS 39: Financial Instruments: Recognition and measurement*.

Japanese Institute of Certified Public Accountants (JICPA). (2001). JWG dorafuto kijyun "Kinyu Syōhin oyobi ruiji kōmoku" ni taisuru nihon kōnin-kaikeishi kyokai no komento ni tsuite. *JICPA Journal, 13*(11), 69–77.
Joint Working Group of Standard-Setters (JWG). (2000). *Financial instruments and similar items*. International Accounting Standards Committee.
Jorissen, A., Lybaert, N., Orens, R., Tas, L. (2014). Constituents' participation in the IASC/IASB's due process of international accounting standard setting: A longitudinal analysis. In R. Pietra, S. McLeay, & J. Ronen, *Accounting and regulation* (pp. 79–110). Springer.
Kunita, K. (2020). "Jika no santei ni kansuru kaikei kijyun" no tekiyō hanni no kakudai-kanōsei: "Kinyū syōhin ni kansuru kaikei kijyun" to "tanaoroshi shisan no hyōka ni kansuru kaikei kijyun" tono kentō kara. *Sensyū Syōgaku Ronsyū, 110*, 167–176.
Laaksonen, J. (2022). Translation, hegemony and accounting: A critical research framework with an illustration from the IFRS context. *Critical Perspectives on Accounting, 89*, Article 102352.
MacArthur, J. B. (1988a). An analysis of the content of corporate submissions on proposed accounting standards in the UK. *Accounting and Business Research, 18*(71), 213–226.
MacArthur, J. B. (1988b). Some implications of auditor and client lobbying activities: A comparative analysis. *Accounting and Business Research, 19*(73), 56–64.
Macintosh, N. B., Shearer, T., Thornton, D. B., & Welker, M. (2000). Accounting as simulacrum and hyperreality: Perspectives on income and capital. *Accounting, Organizations and Society, 25*(1), 13–50.
Novoa, A., Scarlata, J., & Solé, J. (2009). *Procyclicality and fair value accounting* (IMF Working Paper, WP/09/39).
Okamoto, N. (2017). Norm entrepreneur lobbying and persuasion: A case study involving the IASB's modification of an exposure draft. *Research in Accounting Regulation, 29*(2), 129–138.
Raddant, M., & Kenett, D. Y. (2021). Interconnectedness in the global financial market. *Journal of International Money and Finance, 110*, 102280.
Schaede, U. (2020). *The business reinvention of Japan: How to make sense of the new Japan and why it matters*. Stanford University Press.
Schaede, U. (2022). *The digital transformation (DX) and the financialization of Japan: A case study of private equity* (IMES [Institute for Monetary and Economic Studies] Discussion Paper, No. 2022-E-18). Bank of Japan.
Schuetze, W. P. (2006). In defense of fair value. *CPA Journal, 76*(2), 11–12.
Schultz, S. M., & Hollister, J. (2003). Lobbying FASB on accounting for investments. *Journal of Applied Business Research, 19*(2), 85–97.

The Securities Analysts Association of Japan. (2009). *Comment letter to the exposure draft of a proposed IFRS for financial instruments: Classification and measurement (CL 8).*

Toya, T. (2006). *The political economy of the Japanese financial big bang: Institutional change in finance and public policymaking*. Oxford University Press.

Tutticci, I., Dunstan, K., & Holmes, S. (1994). Respondent lobbying in the Australian accounting standard-setting process: ED49. *Accounting Auditing and Accountability Journal, 7*(2), 86–104.

Vogel, S. K. (2018). *Marketcraft: How governments make markets work.* Oxford University Press.

Yen, A. C., Hirst, E., & Hopkins, P. E. (2007). A content analysis of the comprehensive income exposure draft comment letters. *Research in Accounting Regulation, 19*, 53–79.

In Japanese

Abe, Y. (2009). IFRS ga nihon no kigyō Keiei ni ataeru eikyō. *Keiri Kenkyū, 53*, 84–99.

Accounting Standards Board of Japan (ASBJ). (2009). *Kousei Kachi Sokutei oyobi sono Kaiji ni Kansuru Ronten no Seiri.*

Accounting Standards Board of Japan (ASBJ). (2010a). *Kōkai Sōan (exposure draft) No. 43: Kousei Kachi Sokutei oyobi Kaiji ni kansuru Kaikei Kijyun.*

Accounting Standards Board of Japan (ASBJ). (2010b). *Kōkai Sōan (exposure draft) No. 38: Kousei Kachi Sokutei oyobi Kaiji ni kansuru Tekiyō Shishin.*

Business Accounting Council (BAC). (1990, May 29). *Sakimono Opusyon tō Torihiki no Kaikei Kijyun ni Kansuru Ikensyo ni Tsuite.*

Business Accounting Council (BAC). (1999, January 11). *Kinyu Shouhin ni Kakaru Kaikei Kijyun no Settei ni Kansuru Ikensyo.*

Ebe, H. (2006). Syōhō to kigyō kaikei no chousei ni kansuru kenkyū kai houkokusyo (1998) no igi. *Gendai Shakai Bunka Kenkyu, 37*, 209–224.

Financial Services Agency (FSA). (2007a, June). *Wagakuni Kinyū-Sihon Sijyō no Kokusaika ni kansuru Study Group Chūkan Ronten Seiri (Dai-ichiji)* (Interim Discussion Paper: Phase I).

Financial Services Agency (FSA). (2007b, November). *Kinyū Sijyō Senryaku Team no Dai-ichiji Hōkokusyo.*

Financial Services Agency (FSA). (2007c. December). *Kinyū-Sihon Sijyō Kyousōryoku Kyouka Plan.*

Furuichi, M. (2008). Kaikei seido kaikaku no seika to kadai: kono jyū-nen wo furikaette. *Kinyū Kenkyū, 27*(9), 53–90.

Hansen, T. B. (2011). Lobbying of the IASB: An empirical investigation. *Journal of International Accounting Research, 10*(2), 57–75.

Ikeo, K. (2008). How to improve the quality of Japanese financial markets? [Kōshitsu na kinyu shihon sijyō no kakuritsu ni mukete]. *Keio Journal of Economics, 101*(1), 13–27.

Ito, M. (2009). Kaisyō ni mukaunoka, nihon kigyō no kabushiki Mochiai-Mochiai kōzō no suikei: Year 2009. *Report of Capital Market Analysis of Daiwa Institute of Research, 23*, 174–201.

Japan Association of Corporate Directors. (2010, June 30). *Ginko no Seisaku Hoyū Kabusiki ni Tsuite* (Report).

Japanese Bankers Association (JBA). (2001). *Comments on the JWG Draft Standard "Financial instruments and similar items."*

Japanese Institute of Certified Public Accountants (JICPA). (2013). Jika no santei ni kansuru kenkyū siryō. *Kaikei Seido Iinkai Kenkyu Siryō, 4*, 1–62.

Kato, A. (2000). *Shin Kaikei Kijyun no Kanzen Kaisetsu–IOSCO no Eikyō to Saranaru Seido Kaikaku no Houkō*. Chuo Keizai Publishing.

Keidanren. (2001). Kigyō kaikei seido ni kansuru teigen. *Keiri Jyōhō, 949*, 68–69.

Keidanren. (2003, October 21). *Kaikei Kijyun ni Kansuru Kokusaiteki Chōwa wo Motomeru*.

Koga, C. (Ed.). (2003). *Finance-gata Kaikei no Tankyū*. Chuo Keizai Publishing.

Koga, C., & Igarashi, N. (1999). *Kaikei Kijyun no Gurōbaru-ka Senryaku*. Moriyama Syoten.

Kumagai, S. (2008). Mochiai kabushiki no jika hyōka to haitō kisei: "Kinyū syōhin kaikei kijyun" no hi-ronrisei to sore wo oshisusumeru mono. *Rikkyo Economic Review, 61*(4), 51–63.

Ministry of Finance & Ministry of Justice (MOF & MOJ). (1998). *Syohō to Kigyō Kaikei no Chōsei ni Kansuru Kenkyu-kai Hōkokusho*.

Obinata, T. (2023). *Nihon no Kaikei Kijyun II: Gekidō no Jidai*. Chuo Keizai Publishing.

Ogura, S. (2015). *Financialization—Kinyūka to Kinyūkikan-kōdō*. Sakurai Shoten.

Onda, Y. (2023). *Jitsuroku Baburu Kinyū Hishi*. Kawade shobō shinsha.

Saito, S. (1993). Nihon no kaikei kijyun to disclosure seido. *Kinyū Kenkyū, 12*(3), 75–96.

Shimano, T. (2015). Kinyū ka ga nihon-keizai no shihon-chikuseki ni ataeru eikyou ni kansuru Jisshō-bunseki: Nihon-kigyō ni okeru "kabunushi-kachi-shiko" shinto no kanten kara. *Kikan-Keizai-Riron, 51*(4), 70–82.

Shimano, T. (2016). Nihon keizai ni okeru shihon chikuseki no yousiki no henka no youin: nihon no hi-kinyū hoken-gyo no kinyu-ka ni chyakumoku sita jissyō bunseki. *Kikan Keizai Riron, 53*(3), 81–93.

Suzuki, Y. (2006). Kinyū shouhin torihiki-hō no rekishiteki igi. *Shōkei Ronsō* (Kanagawa University), *41*(3–4), 1–15.

Takeda, R. (2002). Seido riron ni okeru Frame of Reference. *Kigyo Kaikei, 54*(41), 4–11.

Takeda, R. (2008). Fukusei jidai no kaikei syuhō. *Kigyo Kaikei, 60*(6), 78–797.
Tsuji, M. (2009). Kinyu shouhin kaikei kijyun no tekiyō to kigyō gyōseki eno eikyō (1). *Waseda Shōgaku, 418/419*, 1–31.
Tsuji, M. (2015). *Kaikei Kijyun to Keieisha Kōdō*. Chuo Keizai Publishing.
Watanabe, M. (2018). Nihon keizai no kinyū-ka to kaikyū-teki haken no koutai. *Kikan Keizai-Riron, 55*(1), 25–35.
Yamada, T. (2013). *IFRS Settei no Haikei–Kinyū Shōhin–*. Zeimu-Keiri Kyōkai.

CHAPTER 7

The Pursuit of Better Corporate Governance

So far, Chapter 5 has explained how accounting standards in Japan have been performatively shaped by the collectively accepted norms of globalization in recent decades, especially after the Big Bang financial reforms. Although the benefits of adopting a unified set of global accounting standards and reducing differences in local standards were not clear, the development of accounting standards in Japan during the recent period has consistently followed the U.S. GAAP and the IFRS. In the particular context of accounting for financial instruments, Chapter 6 described that financialization has perfromatively shaped the relevant accounting standards for financial instruments in Japan. Assuming that the wider application of fair value accounting is part of financialization, it has gained momentum over the past two decades.

Accordingly, it seems that both globalization and financialization have overlapped and shaped relevant accounting institutions. While the former mobilizes operative members to prioritize global standards over local domestic practices/standards under uncertainty, the latter tends to incentivize operative members to support the expansion of financial markets and the proliferation of financial transactions. But the story is not that simple. Think of Islamic countries, which still maintain their way of

N. Okamoto, *Institutional Change and Performativity*,
https://doi.org/10.1007/978-3-031-53393-8_7

financing that does not accept the accrual of interest.[1] Some of those countries are more or less globalized but are less financialized in the sense that they lack the assumption of the time value of money, one of the foundations of modern finance theories.

Beyond formal accounting standards, the collective norms of globalization and financialization have reached the sphere of corporate governance in Japan. With this in mind, this chapter focuses on the recent corporate governance reforms in Japan. Because the corporate governance is thought to be crucial to the success of a company's business activities, social scientists from various disciplines (e.g., economics, legal studies, accounting, and finance) have investigated its mechanism and functions. However, as the style of corporate governance reflects the local traditions and cultural practices of different countries, the regulation or standardization of corporate governance tends to be complicated. This chapter examines the recent regulatory measures toward reforming corporate governance in Japan by applying the theoretical framework of performative globalization and financialization.

The first section considers the trend of corporate governance in Japan, particularly after the Financial Big Bang reforms. Specifically, it highlights that the traditional Japanese model of corporate governance differs significantly from the Western model, which has emphasized the interests of shareholders. Section 7.2 focuses on a unique Japanese form of corporate governance: the practice of cross-shareholdings. Although this practice was developed in a unique Japanese context, it has been perceived as an unusually inefficient practice in the more globalized and financialized world. Accordingly, Japanese regulators have been trying to reduce the volume of cross-shareholdings. Lastly, Sect. 7.3 highlights

[1] As the time value of money and discounting are generally calculated with reference to interest rates under modern accounting standards such as the IFRS, they appear to conflict with the outlawing of interest charges (*riba*) under Shariah law (PricewaterhouseCoopers, 2010, p. 8). Therefore, while conventional banking generally relies on a contractual liability to recover monies exchanged as loans and deposits, together with an interest margin for the lender, Shariah-compliant banking requires an underlying physical asset or trading transaction and may at times be more akin to either profit sharing or an agency/investment management contract (PricewaterhouseCoopers, 2010, p. 3). The IASB has tried to translate such differences within the IFRS framework using the notion of "substance over form" (IASB, 2016).

and analyzes the wave of shareholder-oriented corporate governance that has extended to accounting regulation and disclosure requirements to eradicate the remaining cross-shareholdings, which is considered to be achieving "better" corporate governance.

7.1 The Development of Corporate Governance in Japan

The Traditional Japanese Corporate Governance Model

In the context of Japan, the term "corporate governance" first appeared in *Nihon Keizai Shimbun* in May 1991, in which a professor at Hitotsubashi University (a former assistant professor at Harvard Business School who received his Ph.D. from the University of California at Berkeley), Hirotaka Takeuchi, argued regarding the concept of corporate governance that the various stakeholders involved in the operation of a corporation have rights and responsibilities (Nihon Keizai Shimbun, May 13, 1991, p. 23). This article suggested Japanese corporations to incorporate external perspectives, such as those of outside directors, in addition to their internal viewpoints. Since this first public appearance of the term, articles on corporate governance have gradually increased in Japan. For instance, according to the CiNii (Citation Information by NII: National Institute of Informatics) article database in Japan, the number of articles with "corporate governance" in the title skyrocketed from 13 in 1994 to 945 in 2000; subsequently, this number reached 2,694 in total during the period of 2010 to 2020.

Although the theme of corporate governance gained popularity in the 1990s, the differences in the corporate structures of Japan and other countries had been recognized long before. For instance, from the perspective of the variety of macroeconomic capitalism, the types of economy are generally categorized into two models: the liberal market economy (LME) model with a free-market system and the coordinated market economy model (CME) (Katada, 2020, p. 38). The former assumes that the outcomes of firm behavior are usually produced through the demand and supply conditions of the competitive market, while the latter assumes that firms and other actors strategically interact to produce outcomes (Katada, 2020, p. 38). Institutional settings such as financial systems (stock-market-based versus bank-based), legal systems (formal contracts versus informal relations), employment protections (low versus high), and innovation styles (rocket versus incremental development) are starkly different between these two models (Katada, 2020, p. 38). While countries such as the United States, the United Kingdom, and other commonwealth countries subscribe to the LME model, Japan has traditionally been categorized as utilizing the CME model, similar to Germany (Katada, 2020, p. 38).

Historically, discussions of corporate governance in postwar Japan were dominated by reactive (*mamorino*) governance (preventing fraud and ensuring legality) rather than proactive governance, and the authority of the internal supervisor (or the audit and supervisory board) (*Kansayaku*) was strengthened in response to corporate scandals (Hayashi, 2022, p. 81).[2] As briefly discussed in the previous chapter, corporate governance in postwar Japan is characterized by (1) monitoring by the main bank, (2) weak shareholder influence, (3) the alignment of executive and supervisory roles on boards of directors, and (4) a high employee presence (Kawamoto, 2022, p. 31).[3]

Among these, the first two factors were particularly unique to Japanese corporate governance. First, in the postwar period, the financing for large Japanese corporations was mainly based on banks' lending (Kawamoto, 2022, p. 36). This main bank system in Japan represents a long-term relationship between a specific company and a specific bank. In this bilateral relationship, the main bank was typically the largest creditor and a stable shareholder of the company, sending directors to the board and

[2] According to an analysis of the organizing body of *Kansayaku* (the Japan Audit and Supervisory Board Members Association) on its website, "The system of '*Kansayaku*' was developed uniquely in Japan and no similar system is found in other countries (other than in a few Asian countries). This uniqueness means that it can be difficult for people outside Japan to correctly understand the structure of the corporate governance system in Japan and the function and role of '*Kansayaku*' and '*Kansayaku-kai*'. As a result, '*Kansayaku*' often find it difficult to carry out their activities outside Japan, such as auditing overseas subsidiaries of Japanese companies. In addition, overseas investors are not able to understand how '*Kansayaku*' contributes to corporate governance in Japan and, as a result, often have a negative impression of corporate governance in Japan." To summarize, they finally recommended "Audit & Supervisory Board Member" for the translation of *Kansayaku* and simply defined its role as the supervisory function targeted at monitoring executive directors' management (Japan Audit and Supervisory Board Members Association, 2012, p. 3).

[3] Interestingly, the characteristics of prewar Japanese corporate governance can be summarized as (1) strong shareholder authority, (2) weak bank monitoring, (3) a highly liquid labor market, and (4) active M&A activity (Kawamoto, 2022, p. 31).

monitoring corporate activities (Kawamoto, 2022, p. 37). In addition, the main bank earned fee income by conducting multifaceted financial transactions with the partner company. As a result, the main bank carefully monitored the partner company's business transactions, thereby reducing the monitoring costs of other non-main banks with which it may have transactions (Kawamoto, 2022, p. 37). Aoki et al. (2004) viewed this main banking system as a "bundle of relationships" which consisted of three types: "various financial, informational, and managerial relationships between specific firms and their correspondent banks," "the relationships among major banks," and "the relationships between the regulator (MOF) and the BOJ and the financial industry." In other words, from a functional perspective, the main bank system alleviated the information asymmetry between firms and banks (investors) and facilitated flexible governance according to firms' business conditions (Kawamoto, 2022, p. 38).

Second, stable cross-shareholdings were in place in the 1990s (particularly, the main banks and their counterparties), allowing for stability in the following three aspects: stability of management, stability of transactions, and stability of revenue (risk sharing) (Kawamoto, 2022, p. 39). Thus, these cross-shareholding practices ensured the long-term prevention of hostile takeovers and stock price fluctuations, and the reduction of various pressures from active shareholders (Kawamoto, 2022, p. 38). According to Itami (2000), Japanese companies, especially since the postwar period, have traditionally been employee-oriented rather than shareholder-oriented, and their cross-shareholdings have been held as a symbol of strong business relationships, with cross-shareholding partners speaking only to improve trading conditions, rarely exercising their right to speak otherwise, and basically being silent stable shareholders.

Therefore, the imperfection of the equity market has significantly diminished shareholders' bargaining power to demand dividends (Yamaji, 1999, p. 47) in relation to the dominance of the main bank system in Japan. However, it was not until the 1990s that regulators and relevant actors (operative members) in Japan acknowledged the need to reform the traditional Japanese corporate governance.

The Penetration of Corporate Governance in Japan

In parallel with the implementation of the Big Bang reforms in finance and accounting, there was a widespread belief, especially in the twenty-first century and beyond, that differences in corporate governance might explain the revival of the U.S. economy and the improved U.S. corporate performance in the 1990s as well as the declining Japanese economy and corporate performance (Hayashi, 2022, p. 81).

Four factors are thought to have contributed to the demand for corporate governance reform in Japan (Kawamoto, 2022, pp. 43–47). First, the actual corporate performance of Japanese firms was sluggish. Second, the financial liberalization and deregulation brought about by the Big Bang financial reforms and the increase in banks' non-performing loans resulting from the bursting of the bubble economy weakened the banks' operational strength, and the effectiveness of the main bank's governance declined rapidly. The close relationships with the main bank provided mutual stability, which could explain the slow diversification of management away from traditional operations (Shimpo, 2006, p. 139). Third, and related to the second factor, the introduction of mark-to-market valuation for cross-shareholdings, which accompanied the retreat from the main bank system, prompted the sale of bank shares by business companies. As for the main banks, to generate profits, partner companies' shares were sold in the market, which led to a decline in cross-shareholdings. Consequently, the traditional corporate governance conducted through monitoring by main banks was outdated. Fourth, the proportion of foreign investors has increased rapidly since the 1990s. With the collapse of the main bank system, banks and corporations sold their cross-held shares, and foreign investors became the buyers of many of them. The active nature of these foreign investors was quite different from that of the traditional main banks and passive shareholders in Japan.[4]

All these four factors have led to a heightened awareness among operative members of the need for corporate governance reform in Japan. Figure 7.1 shows the long-term trend of Japanese firms' average return on equity (ROE) from 1997 to 2021 based on the MOF Policy Research

[4] Japanese shareholders' passive investment style was also highlighted in the Ito Report as follows: "many (70 to 80%) institutional investors holding Japanese shares (e.g., pension funds) mainly depend on passive investment styles" (METI, 2014, p. 11). The report also urged investors to make mid-/long-term investments in companies through dialogue/engagement with companies rather than being excessively passive.

Institute's Financial Statements Statistics of Corporations. Beginning in the late 1990s, the average ROE of Japanese firms was rarely above five percent until 2012; in particular, it hit bottom and was below zero in 2001. However, after both the Financial and Accounting Big Bang reforms, the average ROE has improved quickly until 2006.

However, as is clear in Fig. 7.1, the average ROE declined suddenly and was below two percent in 2008 and 2009. Even considering the influence of the global financial crisis in 2008 and 2009, the profitability of Japanese corporations was lower than their Western counterparts at that time, and corporate governance became the target of reform for policymakers. The collective awareness became evident when the Financial System Council (*Kinyū shingikai kinyū bunkakai*)'s study group on the internationalization of Japanese financial and capital markets began in October 2008 (chaired by Professor Kazuhito Ikeo from Keio University).

The study group held sessions on the state of corporate governance in public companies. As a result of its deliberations, on June 17, 2009, the study group published a report entitled *Toward Stronger Corporate*

Fig. 7.1 The long-term trend of the average ROE of Japanese firms (*Source* The data were collected from the MOF Policy Research Institute's Financial Statements Statistics of Corporations [*Hōjin kigyō tōkei chōsa*]. The total amount of equity was used to calculate the ROE)

Governance of Publicly Listed Companies.[5] Under the slogan of "stronger (or better) corporate governance," the report highlighted the transition of Japanese corporate governance. In particular, two general issues were raised to be addressed in the improvement of Japanese corporate governance[6]: the dominance of internal logic in the management of Japanese corporations and Japanese corporations' inability to change in the face of challenges.

Notably, the report proposed many policy measures to address these concerns from different angles, which proved the study group's commitment to reforming Japanese corporate governance. The report started with the issues on corporate capital policies (raising capital by issuing new shares, squeezing-outs, the governance of group companies, and subsidiary listings and cross-shareholdings), followed by recommendations regarding the corporate governance structure (e.g., the independence of outside directors as auditors, effective structure of the board of directors), management monitoring mechanisms, and a framework for governance disciplines (FSA, 2009). More importantly, what I would like to highlight here is the following concluding message:

> In Japan, there has been a move towards a market-based financial system under the slogan "from savings to investment"... In the future, if the capital market succeeds in assuming the role primarily as a place for raising capital, companies will naturally be inclined to pay more attention to investors and shareholders, resulting in the strengthening of corporate governance practices. Conversely, if good corporate governance is not ensured, investor confidence in capital markets will not improve, in which case progress on "from savings to investments" will be unachievable. In this way, the fate of the transition "from saving[s] to investments" and "strengthening of corporate governance of listed companies" is entwined, and the effort to attain these objectives must therefore be strenuously and simultaneously pursued. (FSA, 2009, p. 20)

This message clearly emphasizes two keywords: "savings to investment" and the "strengthening of corporate governance practices." The government, or the FSA, clearly acknowledged the need for Japanese citizens

[5] A tentative English translation is available on the Keidanren's website (https://www.keidanren.or.jp/english/policy/2009/038.pdf).

[6] Although this report also addressed detailed issues related to capital policies, this subsection focuses on structural issues related to corporate governance in Japan.

to use the personal money (savings) in their bank accounts. These operative members expected a tremendous amount of money to be invested in Japanese corporations through stock investment. To achieve this, they believed that a strong corporate governance mechanism should be established.

The Establishment of Corporate Governance Code

Under the second Abe administration, the Japan Revitalization Strategy[7] (revised) was approved by PM Abe and the Cabinet Secretariat in June 2014. One of the strategies clearly mentioned the improvement of corporate governance through the issuance of the Corporate Governance Code (CGC). The CGC was intended to increase corporate profits by improving productivity and to ensure that these increased profits led to increased wages and reinvestment as well as the return of profits to shareholders (Cabinet Secretariat of Japan, 2014, p. 34). More clearly, the beginning of the strategy stated:

> What should be done to increase the earning power of Japanese firms, that is, their profitability and productivity in the medium to long term, and to distribute the fruits of such an increase evenly to the people (households)? First, it is important to strengthen the mechanism to enhance corporate governance and reform corporate managers' mindset so that they will make proactive business decisions to win in global competition in order to achieve targets, including globally acceptable levels of return on equity. Particularly, companies that have achieved the highest earnings in several years should be encouraged to use their earnings proactively for new capital investment, bold business realignment, mergers and acquisitions, and other deals, instead of accumulating internal reserves...The time has come to further advance the environment for companies' demonstration of corporate governance and implement specific measures to improve the companies' "earning power"... At the same time, banks, institutional investors and other financial players must maintain healthy tension with companies and play positive roles in creating values in the long term and

[7] This document is known as the third of the three arrows launched by the Abe administration under the label of Abenomics. The primary goals were to restore the self-confidence of corporate managers and individual citizens, encourage them to believe in their future, and induce them to take specific actions to tackle the challenge of innovation. The full document is available online at https://www.kantei.go.jp/jp/singi/keizaisaisei/pdf/honbunEN.pdf.

improving their "earning power". (Cabinet Secretariat of Japan, 2014, pp. 5–6)

Accordingly, the objective of proactively increasing the earning power of Japanese companies became a major goal of corporate governance reform. This reform was based on the belief that better corporate governance would lead to higher profitability for Japanese companies. How such a goal could be achieved with detailed measures depended more on the specific results of policymaking.

In particular, the Council of Experts on the Corporate Governance Code (*Yūsikishya kaigi*), organized with the support of the Tokyo Stock Exchange and the FSA as joint secretariats, formulated the basic ideas for the CGC. With the Abe administration's approval of the strategy, the council was established in August 2014. The experts met nine times since August 2014 to develop preliminary ideas into a set of standards known as the "Corporate Governance Code (Final Proposal)." As the strategy stipulated that the formulation of a code should be based on the OECD's Principles of Corporate Governance (OECD, 2015),[8] the Council carefully considered those principles so that the Japanese CGC would be consistent with them. Furthermore, before finalizing the Code, the Council circulated a draft prepared in both Japanese and English for comment and received suggestions from 80 individuals/organizations in Japanese and 41 individuals/organizations in English. Taking these suggestions into account, the Council revised and completed the Code.[9]

The establishment of this new CGC in Japan represented the introduction of a new style of proactive governance, which is distinct from traditional and other countries' codes of reactive corporate governance. While reactive governance generally aims to prevent corporate misconduct and fraudulent behaviors and reduce risk, proactive governance seeks positive returns from corporate earning power (Horie, 2015, p. 40). What is the goal of proactive governance? How could it be achieved?

[8] The first version was adopted by the OECD Council on July 8, 2015, and revised on June 8, 2023.

[9] Japan's CGC was detailed and comprehensive and has been revised several times. A comprehensive explanation of the code is not the purpose of this book and is therefore omitted. Put simply, the Code was a breakthrough in the history of the Japanese market, accomplished by former Prime Minister Abe, and was highly regarded by domestic and foreign market participants as a great structural reform (Nihon Keizai Shimbun, July 20, 2022, p. 6).

One member of the Council of Expert stated that the draft code did not overemphasize avoiding and controlling risks or preventing misconduct in the company, but rather focused on encouraging sound entrepreneurship, promoting the company's sustainable growth, and enhancing corporate value in the medium to long term (Horie, 2015, p. 41). In short, the central concern in the Council at that time was Japanese corporations' low profitability (see Fig. 7.1) and its targets were further continuous improvement of ROE and the engagement with shareholders/investors in the financial market (Nihon Keizai Shimbun, March 20, 2015, p. 5). In other words, the target was to support shareholder activism,[10] which had not been embraced previously in Japanese corporate governance.

Another member of the Council noted that there was strong support for the implementation of the CGC and the Stewardship Code in Japan (Oguchi, 2015, p. 18) to be found in the Ito Review, compiled through the efforts of over 40 business executives, investors, market professionals, and academics. The review report was completed by Kunio Ito, then an accounting professor at Hitotsubashi University, and consisted of basic proposals and detailed targets. The basic proposals of the Ito Review were as follows: (1) departing from practices and legacies that impede sustainable growth, (2) becoming a "model nation-state" in the simultaneous realization of innovation and high profitability, (3) creating sustainable value through "collaborative creation" by companies and investors, (4) working toward a capital efficiency revolution in which ROE exceeds the cost of capital, (5) becoming a "dialogue-rich country" that pursues high-quality dialogue between companies and investors, and (6) reforming and optimizing the "investment chain." More practical and detailed suggestions were also included in the review report that clearly mentioned the target of making Japanese corporations more profitable through good corporate governance:

> Despite a slight recovery last year, the average ROE of Japanese companies has been below 5% for a long time, even though their cost of capital is well above that level. This demonstrates the very low capital efficiency of Japanese companies, and can be taken as a structural problem. As the pillar

[10] This refers to shareholder (investor) behavior that forces management reforms that result in increased corporate value (Shimpo, 2006, p. 195).

> of any capitalist economy, a public company can only create corporate value and sustainable growth if it can generate a return on equity that exceeds its cost of capital over the medium to long-term. The capital markets will naturally eliminate companies that fail to do so. A key tenet of capitalism is to maximize the capital efficiency while carefully considering labor's share of income. Although the actual cost of capital varies from company to company, the first step to being recognized by global investors is for a company to commit to achieving a minimum ROE of 8%. Needless to say, this 8% ROE is a minimum level and companies should strive to achieve higher ROE. (METI, 2014, pp. 7–8)

The Ito Report's target of 8% of ROE was recognized and shared by many Japanese companies. For instance, the surge in share buybacks from 2015 to 2016 was expected to have been influenced by this 8% target, which the Ministry of Economy, Trade and Industry proclaimed through the Ito Review as indicating a company's competitiveness (Nihon Keizai Shimbun, November 25, 2016, p. 5). But why did 8% become the target? Put simply, 8% was considered the magic number because the data about Japanese companies demonstrated that when ROE exceeds 8%, PBRs tend to rise sharply (Nihon Keizai Shimbun, November 25, 2016, p. 5).[11] Moreover, the JPX Nikkei 400, a new stock price index introduced by the Tokyo Stock Exchange in 2014, might have been set a high average ROE over the past three years as a criterion for inclusion (Nihon Keizai Shimbun, August 26, 2014, p. 16).

Overall, Japan's corporate governance reforms, undertaken to pull the country out of the economic doldrums since the 2000s, have shifted from a style that emphasized so-called inter-corporate relationships based on the traditional Japanese main bank system to one that emphasizes financial markets. Although it is not yet possible to accurately measure the positive impact of this transition on Japan's economy and prosperity, it did introduce corporate governance practices adopted primarily in the United Kingdom[12] and the United States that were underpinned by high

[11] In a later interview with Tomo Suzuki (Waseda University), Kunio Ito noted that he was not necessarily stuck on the 8% figure. In other words, he wanted to send a clear message by announcing "8% ROE" and expected the number to speak for itself (Ito & Suzuki, 2018, p. 35).

[12] The series of governance reforms that became a top priority of the Abe administration's economic policy (so-called Abenomics) adopted the British corporate governance model and significantly impacted the subsequent institutional design (Hayashi, 2022, p. 1).

profitability (e.g., high ROE). In that sense, the recent introduction of the CGC represents a hybrid of performative globalization and financialization. Regarding the global norm diffusion in the context of corporate governance, members of the Council of Experts who established the code were the norm entrepreneurs or carriers who promoted Western corporate governance model in Japan. As the CGC has been revised several times since its original version, the next section examines a more specific set of practices and standards and their changes during the recent corporate governance reform.

7.2 The Rise and Fall of the Corporate Cross-Shareholding Practice

The Traditional Cross-Shareholding Practice in Japan

As indicated in the previous section, the transformation of Japanese corporate governance has become the target of regulatory reform to improve Japanese corporations' profitability and to encourage the utilization of personal financial assets that have been saved and accumulated in bank accounts. Although various factors compose the corporate governance mechanism, this chapter focuses on the practice of cross-shareholding in Japan, because it has attracted widespread attention in Japan in the context of corporate governance reform.

Traditionally in Japan, it was common for multiple firms to hold each counterpart's shares to maintain close relationships with partner firms and banks. These firms occasionally shared the same industrial group, suppliers, customers, creditors, and borrowers (Scher, 2001). This type of arrangement has been described as "quiescent stable shareholding, which may be held in trilateral, multilateral, or otherwise stable arrangements among companies, usually based on group and/or transactional relationships" (Scher, 2001, p. 1). This corporate cross-shareholding is generally defined as a situation in which two publicly traded companies hold shares in each other,[13] and it has both advantages and disadvantages. In

More specifically, the Ito Review modeled the 2012 Key Review in the United Kingdom (METI, 2014).

[13] *Nihon Keizai Shimbun* defined cross-shareholding as the practice of publicly traded financial institutions and non-financial companies strategically seeking ownership of each

the first place, corporate cross-shareholding can strengthen the relationships between firms. Compared to typical companies in other countries (e.g., Western counterparts), Japanese corporations tend to place greater emphasis on corporate relationships. The practice of cross-shareholdings reached its apex in the form of the *Keiretsu*[14] conglomerates that formed a dominant partnership network after World War II (Milhaupt & West, 2004, p. 14). According to Genay (1991, p. 27), such industrial groups were important to the development of Japan's blossoming industries during the period when the Japanese economy was highly regulated and isolated from international markets. In short, the Japanese *Keiretsu* and the main bank system were considered not only key to Japan's postwar recovery but also superior forms of industrial and financial organization (Scher, 2001). According to Kagono and Yamada (2016), long-term corporate relationships, such as those underpinning the *Keiretsu* system, produced relational trust and contributed to reducing transaction costs (e.g., the cost of monitoring partner firms).

The large volume of cross-shareholdings by banks was justified for several reasons. From a historical perspective, cross-shareholding arrangements in the postwar period functioned as tacit mutual agreements designed to insulate management from any market-based threat of a hostile takeover (Scher, 2001, p. 62). Consequently, interrelated firms and banks often did not exercise their shareholder (or voting) rights to improve the management of partner firms. Therefore, stable shareholding relationships functioned as a corporate management strategy to limit the shareholder governance of the firm (Scher, 2001, p. 2), and it worked well while the Japanese economy continued to grow steadily.

Although such relational industrial groups were not unique to Japan (France, Germany, Korea, and Spain had similar industrial groups), the Japanese main banking system was distinctive (Genay, 1991, p. 20). In Japan, the complex relationships among firms within relational industrial groups were characterized by cross-shareholdings. Historically, these

other's shares (Ogishima & Kobayashi, 2000, p. 3). However, this definition is too circumscribed, as a publicly traded corporation unilaterally owning stock in another publicly traded company for strategic purposes could be similarly regarded as cross-shareholding.

[14] *Keiretsu* is a traditional Japanese conglomeration of businesses linked by cross-shareholding to form a stable corporate structure. It was traditionally based on long-term transactional relationships among constituents, such as those between assemblers and suppliers.

groups typically had close ties with a particular main bank that provided most of a firm's debt financing (Genay, 1991, p. 20). In other words, the main banks were key players in Japanese corporate cross-shareholdings at the time, and the practice was intended to strengthen relationships between firms.

This type of cross-shareholding practice is uncommon in Anglo-American companies, as it would mean that management cannot effectively utilize shareholders' invested capital. To understand the different attitudes toward cross-shareholdings in different countries, it is useful to compare the rate of floating stock in the financial market by dividing tradable public stocks by market capitalization. According to Kanda (2001, p. 134), more than 20 years ago, this ratio was 94% in the United States and 92% in the United Kingdom, while it was 65% in Japan, whose financial market was the largest among non-Western countries at the time.[15]

Growing Pressure to Reduce Cross-Shareholding

During the economic downturn following the collapse of the bubble economy and the decline of the main bank system, the unique practice of cross-shareholdings was viewed with suspicion. Because the key players in cross-shareholdings were financial institutions by virtue of the embeddedness of the main bank system around that time, the economic downturn after the banking crisis roused suspicion that the monitoring mechanism by the main banks was not functioning effectively in the globalized shareholder-oriented Anglo-American financial market.[16] This concern was evident in the following conversation that Dore (2000, p. 112) had with the retiring president of a large trading company in Japan:

> —Our cross-holdings are running down and I've been encouraging tendency.
> Dore: Why?
> —Well, when I go to your country or to America and meet our foreign investors they all ask me: why do you keep such unprofitable

[15] In France and Germany, where code-law financial regulations had long dominated the market, these rates were 65% and 64%, respectively (Kanda, 2001, p. 134).

[16] Regarding the development of the main bank system in Japan, Hoshi (1994) is insightful.

> assets on your balance sheet? Look at the miserable returns. Why don't you get rid of them. And I don't know how to answer.
> Dore: But why do you need foreign investors anyway, when Japan is awash with savings?
> —I think a global company should have global investors.

As shown in Fig. 7.2, the volume of cross-shareholdings in Japan has declined since the mid-1990s, and this figure divides the long-term decline in cross-shareholding in Japan into two phases. The reduction during the first phase was mainly caused by the sale of cross-held shares by Japanese banks after the bubble burst from the late 1990s to the early 2000s. Around that time, cross-shareholding was mainly carried out by the main banks and corporations (the banks' main partners) that had close ties with them. The second phase, which will be discussed in the Sect. 7.3, began after the 2008 financial crisis and is ongoing.[17]

The first phase covers the period from the late 1990s to the early 2000s, and the key actors in the widespread cross-shareholding phenomenon in Japan during that time were banks. To add more data (Scher, 1997), in 1987, or when the bubble economy emerged, cross-shareholdings represented 15.2% of the outstanding corporate shares issued in Japan by non-financial companies and 22.7% when financial institutions were included, and cross- and stable shareholdings comprised between 65 and 70% of all the stock issued by publicly traded corporations in Japan; only the remaining minority of shares were freely traded on stock exchanges (Scher, 1997, p. 62).

In fact, criticism of cross-shareholdings existed early on. When the bubble economy burst, the Economic Planning Agency (EPA) in Japan was skeptical of Japanese cross-shareholding practices. In its 1992 annual economic report, the EPA acknowledged the positive effects of the practice, stating that "transferring the residual claim right to the management side (cross-shareholding) can contribute to the long-term stability of the management by eliminating the threat of hostile takeovers and releasing the management from excessive pressure from the capital market" (EPA, 1992, 3.1.3). The EPA further stated that "the stocks held by each other also have the characteristics of 'hostage' and 'collateral' and exchanging the 'hostage' is a potential deterrent to betraying the relationship of

[17] The phased analysis here also appears in Okamoto (2024).

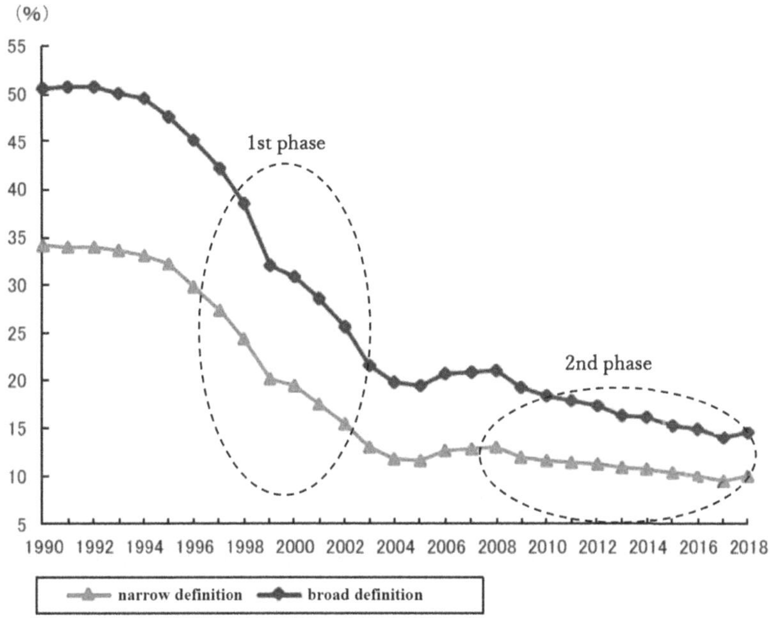

The graph is based on the data in Nishiyama (2019). It is calculated by dividing the market value of public companies' cross-held shares of other public companies by the total market value of stock market. The broad definition includes the sample of insurance firms.

Fig. 7.2 The percentage of cross-shareholding in Japan

trust. By promoting long-term inter-relational transactions, mutual information sharing among those firms will encourage progress and produce synergistic effects" (EPA, 1992, 3.1.3). At the same time, the EPA acknowledged the side effects of cross-shareholdings:

> Even if cross-shareholdings have the above-mentioned functions, inefficient transactions may occur if they create a 'collusive' relationship. Moreover, when a company selects a business partner, the presence or absence of cross-shareholdings is taken into consideration regardless of individual goods or services. Futhermore, when a cartel-like relationship arises between competitors because of that, there is a significant risk of restricting competition. (EPA, 1992, 3.1.3)

Since then, Japanese regulatory agencies have recognized that corporate cross-shareholding can cause inefficient corporate management. According to Okabe (2002), in the late 1990s, the practice of cross-shareholding gradually lost its advantages, and some disadvantages appeared to be recognized. The main reason for this shift was the diminishing benefits of the practice. For both banks and corporations, the direct rate of return generated by cross-held shares declined or became negative during an unprecedented recession in the 1990s (Okabe, 2002, p. 31), during which the stocks held in the portfolios of financial institutions (such as banks) and corporations became so-called non-performing assets. Consequently, these assets were sold on a performance basis to reallocate funds more efficiently (Okabe, 2002, p. 32). Moreover, from the banks' perspective, the increase in the risk sensitivity of shareholdings was conspicuous. The decline in the value of portfolio stocks due to falling stock prices meant the erosion of the banks' capital base, which increased anxiety about being unable to meet the international capital adequacy standard (Basel Capital Accord[18]) (Okabe, 2002, p. 32).

Thus, reducing the volume of corporate cross-shareholding was the political target of Japanese economic policy at the time and one of the political reforms implemented after the bubble burst in Japan. In particular, the removal of three factors potentially hindering the efficiency of the financial market proved to be of special significance—cross-shareholding, the main bank system, and the Ministry of Finance-led Convoy System of Financial Administration—all of which were characteristics or peculiarities of the Japanese economy (Okazaki, 2014, p. 104). In addition, the Capital Markets Research Institute (*Sihon sijyō kenkyū kai*) established a research committee that held eight meetings in 1999 and completed a research report (Kanda, 2001).

According to a research report prepared by the committee, in the context of cross-shareholding, the introduction of market-value-based accounting standards for cross-held shares in Japan had an enormous impact on the sale of cross-held shares by banks and businesses (Kanda,

[18] The Basel (Capital) Accord imposed uniform regulations on internationally active banks. Historically, financial crises, such as bank failures, have led to the recognition of the need to impose uniform international regulation. It was first introduced in 1988, stipulating that by the end of 1992, banks with international operations must have a capital adequacy ratio of at least 8% and banks with domestic operations must have a capital adequacy ratio of at least 4%. For the more detailed information, see Quillin (2008).

2001, p. 192). Regarding formal accounting standards, one of the Big Bang accounting reforms in 1999 was a turning point. As discussed in the previous chapter, the new accounting standard for financial instruments was established to introduce market value accounting. The new valuation method required corporations to classify securities according to the purpose of their holdings. Cross-held shares are not classified as tradable or held-to-maturity; rather, they are regarded as "other" available-for-sale securities. Those securities are required to be marked at market value, and capital gains or losses must be reported in the section of shareholders' equity on a corporate balance sheet. This new accounting standard appears to have accelerated the sale of shares in corporate portfolios (Okabe, 2002, p. 33).[19]

Regarding the introduction of the new accounting standard, the Japan Association of Corporate Executives (*Keizai Dōyūkai*) estimated in April 1999 that the ROE of the 1,200 corporations listed in the first section of the Tokyo Stock Exchange (excluding financial institutions) would decrease by about 0.32%, or from 2.96 to 2.64, if all the cross-held shares held by them were deemed "other securities" and marked at market value (Okabe, 2002, p. 34). Considering this estimation, it was reasonable for Japanese firms at that time to sell cross-held shares and allocate the proceeds to other investments or to pay off debt rather than holding them (Okabe, 2002, p. 34).

Therefore, it can be understood that the rapid decline in the volume of cross-held shares in the first phase (late 1990s—early 2000s) was triggered by the introduction of market value accounting (financialization). Regarding the accounting standards for available-for-sale securities, the aim of the standards was to reflect market values on corporate balance sheets to provide more timely financial information about financial assets. In addition, another type of actor exerted excessive pressure on Japanese corporations to sell their cross-held shares: foreign investors. In fact, according to Fig. 7.3, from 1995 to 2015, the weight of foreign shareholding (on monetary value basis) increased steadily and has stabilized at around 30% since then. In other words, foreign investors bought the dissolved cross-held shares in the market. Further, it appeared that those major foreign investors were large financial institutions such as State Street and Chase Manhattan whose asset classes were U.S. pension assets (Nihon

[19] The Japan Association of Corporate Directors (2010) made the same argument.

Keizai Shimbun, January 28, 1997, p. 19). As Dore (2000) indicated, an increasing number of foreign investors at that time doubted the ability of investees who held cross-held shares to maintain stable relationships with other corporations (Nihon Keizai Shimbun, April 8, 1997, p. 9).

Therefore, it seems that the Japanese traditional practice of cross-shareholding dissolved as a result of the intermingled influence of globalization and financialization.[20] Assuming that the introduction of market value accounting was a part of performative financialization, the reduction in cross-held shares among Japanese firms in the first phase can be seen as the result of financialization. It was also due to the globalization of accounting, as the accounting standard for financial instruments established in 1999 followed the global trends at that time.

However, as Fig. 7.2 indicates, the cross-shareholdings did not completely disappear and remained at a certain level. According to an

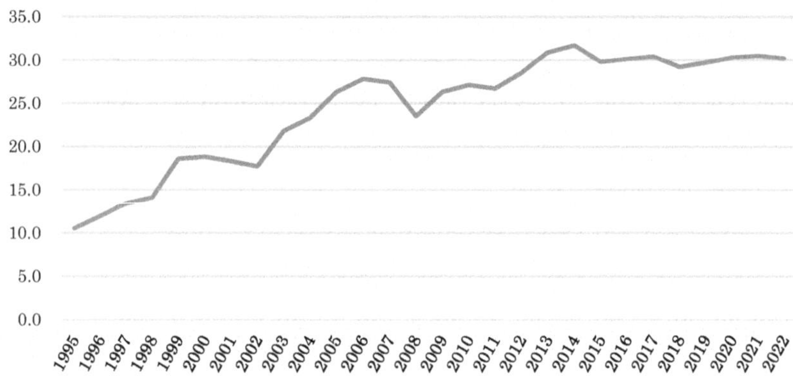

Fig. 7.3 The percentage of foreign shareholdings in the Japanese Market from 1995 to 2022 (*Source* Data were collected from JPX and are based on the shares listed on JPX)

[20] In the more recent past, Japanese financialization has been analyzed in terms of the growing financial power of financial institutions (Ogura, 2015), hedge fund activism (Buchanan et al., 2012), and an increasing number of foreign investors (Ahmadjian, 2007). These studies have illuminated the changes in Japanese corporate practices during the wave of global financialization and the pressure of the global convergence of such practices.

empirical study that analyzed Japanese cross-shareholding practices, Miyajima and Kuroki (2007) concluded that, after the 1997 banking crisis in Japan, banks sold the shares of firms with large growth opportunities (large Tobin's q) and held shares of firms with which they had a main bank relationship. They also predicted that cross-shareholding among firms would not be dissolved on a large scale, as corporate ownership of shares has its own economic rationale, and they stated that there was no indication that it had negatively affected corporate governance (although corporate block holding has, in fact, played a positive role) (Miyajima & Kuroki, 2007, p. 118). As indicated above, the practice of cross-shareholdings in Japan is relational in nature, and its effects are difficult to accurately measure because of the long-term nature of cross-shareholdings. This relational ambiguity has become a target of criticism again in the waves of globalization and financialization, which will be discussed in the next section.

7.3 The Globalization and Financialization of Corporate Governance

The Problematization of Cross-Shareholding

As shown in Fig. 7.2, the second phase in the long-term trend of reducing Japanese cross-shareholdings covers the period from 2008 to 2020, after the Lehman Shock and the subsequent financial crisis. As mentioned earlier, a concerted attempt by the government to reform the Japanese corporate governance system in the form of the Financial System Council's study group for the Internationalization of Financial and Capital Markets in Japan (*Waga kuni kinyū sihon sijyō no kokusaika ni kansuru study group*) played a significant role. Led by Kazuhito Ikeo, the study group started discussing the issue of the corporate governance of Japanese corporations on October 21, 2008 (from the study group's 16th meeting). At the beginning of the meeting, the Vice Minister of State for Financial Affairs of the Cabinet Office, Tatsuya Tanimoto, shared the aims of this new theme: "It has been pointed out that corporate governance problems are a factor that discourages investment in the Japanese market and undermines the market value of Japanese companies."

From then on, the study group held seven more meetings until June 2009. Among various topics regarding the mechanism of corporate governance, corporate cross-shareholding was discussed several times.

For instance, in the 22nd meeting held on May 27, 2009, an invited professional practitioner stated,

> Regarding cross-shareholdings, it is no exaggeration to say that Japan is probably the only developed country in the world that has a cross-shareholding system, compared to Europe and the United States. On the one hand, some investors deny the existence of cross-shareholdings and demand the dissolution of cross-shareholdings. On the other hand, understanding that it is a Japanese business practice, some people do not demand the dissolution of cross-shareholdings, but often expect the disclosure of the stocks, number of shares, holding period, reasons and merits of cross-shareholdings.

The uniqueness of Japanese cross-shareholding was also mentioned in the 23rd meeting, which was also the last:

> As you are probably aware, Germany, for example, had many cross-shareholdings between banks and business companies, but these were dissolved around 2001 and 2002 due to the decline in stock prices, and Japan is probably the only developed country with the cross-shareholdings. This is a factor that is always difficult to explain to investors. One of the potential consequences of the elimination of cross-shareholdings would be an improvement in the governance and the disclosure of management, which would in turn encourage individuals and other investors to invest in the company.

The discussion in the meeting was reported the next day: *Nikkei* hit the headline "A series of arguments for limiting cross-shareholdings" and explained the study group's negative stance toward cross-shareholdings (Nihon Keizai Shimbun, June 11, 2009, p. 4).

Based on its deliberations, on June 17, 2009, the study group published a report titled *Toward Stronger Corporate Governance of Publicly Listed Companies.*[21] Under the banner of "stronger (or better) corporate governance," the report proposed the reform of Japanese corporate governance to address several issues. Among them, corporate cross-shareholding was specifically mentioned:

[21] The report is downloadable at https://www.fsa.go.jp/en/news/2009/20090618-1/01.pdf.

> Cross-shareholdings had been on a decline since the 1990s, but the trend reversed in recent years. A number of issues have been raised regarding this practice, including the resultant hollowing out of capital and voting rights, and reducing the governance function performed by shareholders to a mere formality. Furthermore, cross-shareholdings between listed companies may possibly affect their management, and therefore information concerning such cross-shareholdings [is] important for investors when they make investment decisions. (FSA, 2009, p. 8)

Clearly, the study group viewed opaque cross-shareholding practices as problematic. To tackle this issue, it turned its attention to corporate disclosure. The report states that "some companies have already begun voluntarily disclosing the status of their cross-shareholdings, and it is appropriate to promote this kind of disclosure. Further consideration should be made to institutionalize the disclosure requirement so that it would be possible to obtain information on cross-shareholdings that occur under explicit or implicit agreements to hold shares reciprocally or multilaterally" (FSA, 2009, p. 8).

Following this suggestion, the FSA decided to require listed corporations to disclose the volume of their cross-shareholdings and their reasons for continuing to hold those shares (Nihon Keizai Shimbun, July 5, 2009, p. 1). In February 2010, the FSA published the draft to amend the Cabinet Office Ordinance on the Disclosure of Corporate Affairs (*Kigyō naiyō tou no kaiji ni kansuru naikaku-furei*) which required listed companies to disclose information related to corporate governance. Specifically, the amendments required the disclosure of the following information for those shares held primarily for strategic purposes (not for trading) in the securities reports: (i) the number of such issues and their total amount on the latest balance sheet and (ii) detailed information about publicly traded cross-held shares.[22] This was a radical shift, as the new rules required companies to disclose not only detailed information about cross-held (or strategically held) shares but also their specific reasons for holding them. Since then,

[22] Detailed information is required for strategically held (not for the purpose of pure investment) publicly traded shares if the total amount of each issue exceeds 1% of the capital reported on the balance sheet. When it was introduced, the disclosure requirement was necessary for the top 30 largest amounts of those shares. Particularly, the number of shares held, a detailed description of the purpose for holding them, and the amount of the shares on the balance sheet with respect to each issue were required.

listed Japanese companies have had to carefully consider their reasons for holding cross-held shares.

The FSA solicited comments on the draft from the public for one month and then issued the summary of the received comments and their responses (FSA, 2010a, 2010b). In total, 520 comments were sent to the FSA during that short period, which demonstrated stakeholders' high level of interest in the issue. In their responses to many comments, particularly to the skeptical questions regarding the disclosure requirements for cross-held shares, the FSA strategically maintained its neutral position on corporate cross-shareholding, stating the following:

> There has been a tradition of reciprocal and multilateral cross-shareholding among listed companies in Japan. Some investors take the negative view that such cross-shareholding by companies is not an efficient investment, while others make the point that the cross-shareholding has positive aspects, such as allowing companies to maintain and explore good business relationships, and further contributing to their profitability, which are not necessarily reflected in financial statements. (FSA, 2010b, pp. 2–3)

The official disclosure rule became effective on March 31, 2010, with the publication of the FSA's analyses and responses to the comments. In particular, regarding the shares held primarily for any strategic purpose, the order required corporations to disclose a list of issues (a) within the top thirty largest amounts on the balance sheet of the company in either the latest or the preceding fiscal years or (b) whose amount reported on the balance sheet exceeded one percent of the capital in either the latest or the preceding fiscal years. It also required the disclosure of the number of shares held by the company, a detailed description of the purpose of holding them, and the amount of the shares on the balance sheet with respect to each issue.

To review the effects of this disclosure requirement for cross-shareholding practices, Fig. 7.4 depicts the trend of the shareholding proportions of three groups of main shareholders from 2010 to 2018: stable, institutional, and individual (and others). Stable shareholders include corporations that own cross-held shares. Between 2010 and 2013, when the disclosure requirement took effect, the percentage of stable shareholders decreased slightly by 2.3%. As the weight of individual shareholders was stable from 2010 to 2013, it was inferred that the cross-held

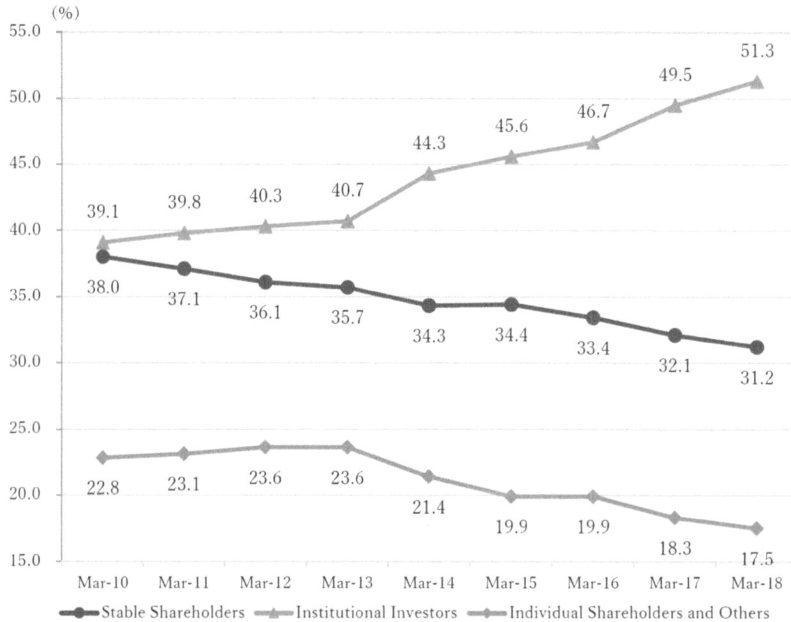

The original data were obtained from Ueda (2019) and Japan Investor Relations and Investor Support, Inc. The sample firms are Nikkei 225 firms and the data were adjusted with the amount of treasury stocks.

Fig. 7.4 Shareholding percentages by various investors in Japan

shares sold in the same period were largely purchased by institutional investors.

The Recent Reduction in Cross-Shareholding: The Introduction of Disclosure Requirements

However, the volume of cross-held shares did not decrease drastically in the years immediately following the introduction of the disclosure requirements in 2010, which indicated that the institutional device requiring the corporate disclosure of strategically held shares did not reduce the volume of cross-held shares quickly as the FSA intended. Rather, the declining trend gained momentum after 2014, which coincides with the introduction of the CGC in Japan in 2015. According to the members of the expert panel who led the development of the

CGC, the basis for the Code was the Revitalization Strategy of Japan approved by the Cabinet in 2014 (Takei, 2021, p. 23). In particular, the aim of the CGC was to change the mindset of the managers of Japanese corporations by strengthening corporate governance, and to encourage management decisions that would enable companies to compete globally by, for example, achieving a global level of ROE. In addition, the issuance of the CGC was to some extent dependent on the Japanese version of the Stewardship Code, which was formulated as part of the 2013 Growth Strategy, and has promoted the significance of the dialogue between investors and companies to improve profitability and capital efficiency (Takei, 2021, p. 23).

Among the various principles and rules in the CGC, the most relevant clause for this chapter is included in the principle "1–4 Cross-Shareholdings." It requires companies holding shares of other listed companies as cross-shareholdings to disclose their policies on doing so. In addition, their boards should examine the mid- to long-term economic rationale and prospects of major cross-shareholdings on an annual basis while taking into consideration both the associated risks and returns. This annual examination should provide a detailed explanation of the purpose and rationale behind cross-shareholdings. Therefore, companies were required to establish and disclose a clear stance on voting rights in relation to their cross-shareholdings.

However, these principles in the CGC are not a set of strict mandatory rules: rather, it is designated as a soft law that adopts a principles-based approach. Therefore, if a company does not want to disclose specific information concerning its cross-shareholding practices, it can provide a reasonable explanation for its decision. Yet, regarding the normativity of this code in Japan, Miyamoto (2018, p. 15) mentions that "Although it was a voluntary code, it was, in effect, compulsory due to the inclusion of the 'comply or explain' rule." With regard to the cross-held shares, as the required disclosures in the CGC became stricter (even the prospects and rationale for cross-shareholdings were to be disclosed), many officials in the listed companies seemed to have feared the new code (Nihon Keizai Shimbun, December 23, 2014, p. 15).

Furthermore, in June 2018, the CGC was revised, and new supplemental principles were added to Sect. 1.4.1: when cross-shareholders outside of a company indicated their intention to sell their shares, the company was expected not to hinder the sale of the cross-held shares by, for instance, implying a possible reduction in business transactions.

Companies were also expected to avoid engaging in transactions with cross-shareholders that could harm the interests of other companies or the common interests of their shareholders by, for instance, conducting transactions without carefully examining the underlying economic rationale. As follow-up guidance, the FSA published "Strategically held Shares: Points for Ideal Disclosure for Shareholders" in 2019. This document presents models of real companies' disclosures that detailed the goals, rationales, and effects of holding cross-held shares. As a supplement to the revised CGC, this guide implicitly encouraged the further dissolution of cross-held shares that provided no clear benefits or return to the holding company.

Overall, the informal soft law contained in the CGC, combined with the required disclosure of the reasons for cross-shareholding practices, was meant to function as a mixed institutional device to reduce the volume of cross-held shares. In that sense, the terms "corporate governance reform" or "better corporate governance" have been catchphrases in the second phase (since 2008) of corporate governance reform. As the OECD's corporate governance principles were used as the model for the Japanese CGC, prioritizing better corporate governance in Japan can be interpreted as a part of globalization.

The introduction of the CGC pressured corporations to reduce cross-held shares to achieve better corporate governance and has performatively shaped relevant institutions and changed corporate behaviors in Japan.[23] To illustrate this phenomenon, corporate qualitative disclosures were examined and a search was conducted using the full-text search system on PRONEXUS's eol database[24] for the terms "strategically-held" and "cross-held," which are relevant for explaining the purposes for corporate cross-shareholding in the annual securities reports prepared by Japanese listed firms. The data on the firms that used these terms were collected and classified into three periods (2010, 2015, and 2020). Overall, the data reveal the number of firms that have directly mentioned or

[23] The introduction of the CGC was expected to change the actual behaviors of Japanese corporations regarding the practice of cross-shareholding. This expectation was based on some analyses that argue that cross-shareholding practices are not beneficial. For instance, Tsumuraya (2020) empirically demonstrated that firms with more cross-holding shares tend to have lower profitability, which does not lead to the maintenance or strengthening of subsequent business relationships.

[24] The database is available at: https://www.pronexus.co.jp/english.

explained the purpose for holding cross-held shares and have substantially complied with the revised CGC. The results are 74 (2010/01–2010/12), 73 (2015/01–2015/12), and 1,896 (2020/01–2020/12) respectively. Although there were more than 3,000 listed firms in the Japanese market from 2010 to 2015, only a few of them directly mentioned either strategically held (holding) or cross-held (holding) shares in their securities reports. In the recent securities report in 2020, however, the situation changed suddenly, and many more firms reported their purposes for holding these shares.[25] These data imply that large-scale corporate governance reform was successful in altering corporate disclosure practices in Japan. It can be said that more shareholder-oriented global corporate governance is becoming more prevalent in Japan.

The rapid global convergence of corporate governance has been analyzed from the perspective of performativity by Veldman and Willmott (2020). Their concept of the modern corporation as a social construct is based on the understanding that theory may be used to bring about change in the world rather than merely explaining or enabling an understanding of it (Veldman & Willmott, 2020, p. 410). According to this analysis, agency theory in textbooks and academic journals has fostered and disseminated theoretical ideas related to agency (Veldman & Willmott, 2020, p. 416). Such a shift toward agency theory is evident in the formulation and spread of CGCs and the idea of shareholder value maximization (Veldman & Willmott, 2020, p. 417). In their concluding remarks, Veldman and Wilmott (2020) argue that the theoretical stabilization of notions such as agency-theory-based corporate governance through the enactment of national and transnational rules, regulations, policies, and institutions must be analyzed in terms of the political economy. This chapter's findings and argument regarding regulatory

[25] However, it is important to be cautious when acknowledging this result, as it is completely inconsistent with the analysis of Tsumuraya (2020), who investigated the securities reports of the listed firms issued in 2011 and found that more than 90% of the companies admitted that they were holding shares primarily for strategic purposes. This 90% figure comes from his own reading of the reports and calculations. According to the regulation enacted in 2010 (mentioned above), although listed companies were required to disclose information about shares held primarily for strategic purposes, many companies typically reported them as "shares held for purposes other than pure investment," which obscures the purpose of holding the shares and is regarded as passive compliance with the requirement. As Tsumuraya (2020, p. 110) also points out, the corporate disclosures regarding strategically owned shares appeared to be boilerplate responses and did not provide useful information.

changes in cross-held shares during Japan's corporate governance reforms are in line with their analysis.

7.4 Summary and Analysis

This chapter has considered the introduction and diffusion of corporate governance in Japan, which has been largely supported by shareholder-oriented Western ideas. It focuses in particular on the unique traditional practice of cross-shareholdings and the pursuit of better corporate governance from the perspective of performative globalization and financialization. Simply put, the Japanese CGC, introduced in 2015 and revised several times, has shaped the ideal model of corporate governance, which tends to exclude Japanese relational cross-shareholding practices.

Through the reduction in cross-held shares and related institutional changes in Japan, Japan has gradually shifted toward pursuing a more globally homogenous financial market. In the first phase, or from the late 1990s to the early 2000s, radical reforms in accounting standards and the pursuit of the global comparability of corporate profitability were significant themes. Further, it can be concluded that regarding the classification and valuation of assets, the institutional device of accounting standards assisted the sale of cross-held shares between banks and corporations. During the second phase, particularly after the financial crisis, the movement toward an Anglo-American type of corporate governance was intense. Better corporate governance was prioritized, which contributed to the dissolution of traditional Japanese cross-shareholding practices.

More specifically, in the first phase, crucial differences in domestic accounting standards were collectively recognized by interested Japanese parties, and the relevant actors expected the clear benefits of reducing such local differences and following global standards for global investors. As Chiapello (2016) highlighted the performative aspects of global accounting standards from the viewpoint of financialization, "catching up" with American (or global) accounting standards (harmonization) was envisioned in Japan around that time. Instead of the global convergence or adoption of accounting standards (which could be more comprehensive than harmonization), an incremental approach was taken in the first phase.

In contrast, during the second phase (from late 2000s to early 2020), several regulatory actions advanced corporate governance reform, and this movement has recently become influential in Japan. During this period, specific important actions were taken to further reduce the volume of cross-held shares. For example, the requirement for extensive disclosures about cross-shareholdings requests corporations to disclose the details of the shares and reasons and rationales for continuing the practice. Through these actions, the concept of better corporate governance has been effectively performative. During this process, formal disclosure rules and informal guidance-based institutions were used to achieve better corporate governance. This understanding is in line with the thesis of the convergence of corporate governance (Veldman & Willmott, 2020), and it implies that the global penetration of financialization has also occurred in Japan through the proliferation of shareholder-centric corporate governance. Although Veldman and Willmott (2020) emphasize that a cautious approach to "convergence" must be maintained, as this chapter indicates, Japan's recent pursuit of better corporate governance and reduction in cross-held shares fit well with the thesis of convergence. However, notably, recent corporate governance reform in Japan has been accomplished without a thorough examination of the costs and benefits of cross-shareholdings.

How can we look at this set of institutional changes in terms of performativity? In the context of corporate cross-shareholding practices, the generic performativity of financialization has been conspicuous, as relevant institutions have shifted in the direction that cross-shareholding is inefficient and should be reduced from the perspective of shareholders who play a central role in the financial market. It is also due to performative globalization since the ideal "better corporate governance" (effective self-fulfilling performativity) comes from Western countries. It is therefore reasonable to assume that both globalization and financialization have been generically performative.

It is uncertain whether Japanese firms should further reduce the number of remaining cross-held shares.[26] An interesting case recently arose in Japan involving representative railway companies (East Japan Railway, Central Japan Railway, West Japan Railway, and Kyushu Railway)

[26] In 2015, Kazuhiko Toyama, one of the members of the Council of Experts on the Corporate Governance Code, participated in a panel discussion on "Changing Corporate Governance in Japan," which was organized by the Asia-Pacific Research Center (APARC) at Stanford University. During the discussion, he remarked that "the quality of most of the activists coming to Japan is very low." If financialization, or corporate governance reform, has been driven by these (low-quality) activists, emphasizing shareholder primacy is not an ideal scenario for the Japanese people.

that had increased the volume of their cross-held shares as of 2020. These holdings covered about 1% of each company's outstanding shares, up from about 0.2%, and JR East, JR Central and JR West each held more than 1% of JR Kyushu. According to Nikkei Asia,[27] the rail operators explained that these moves were meant to promote the sharing of information regarding disaster responses and the development of new technologies in addition to facilitating the implementation of new mobility services combining railway and other transit methods for more efficient transportation. "Cross-shareholdings are an effective method of fostering trust," JR Kyushu President Toshihiko Aoyagi told Nikkei. This action can be seen as a rare counterperformative response to performative financialization and globalization in this context.

References

Aoki, M., Patrick, H., & Seard, P. (2004). The Japanese main bank system: An introductory overview. In M. Aoki & H. Patrick (Eds.), *The Japanese main bank system: Its relevance for developing and transforming economies* (pp. 3–50). Oxford University Press.

Ahmadjian, C. (2007). Foreign investors and corporate governance in Japan. In M. Aoki, G. Jackson, & H. Miyajima (Eds.), *Corporate governance in Japan* (pp. 125–150). Oxford University Press.

Buchanan, J., Chai, D. H., & Deakin, S. (2012). *Hedge fund activism in Japan: The limits of shareholder primacy*. Cambridge University Press.

Cabinet Secretariat of Japan. (2014, June 24). *Japan revitalization strategy revised in 2014–Japan's challenge for the future* (Provisional translation).

Chiapello, E. (2016). How IFRS contribute to the financialization of capitalism. In D. Bensadon & N. Praquin (Eds.), *IFRS in a global world* (pp. 71–84). Springer International.

Dore, R. P. (2000). *Stock market capitalism: Welfare capitalism—Japan and German versus the Anglo Saxons*. Oxford University Press.

Financial Services Agency (FSA). (2009). Toward stronger corporate governance of publicly listed companies. *Report by the Financial System Council's Study Group on the Internationalization of Japanese Financial and Capital Markets*.

Financial Services Agency (FSA). (2010a, February 19). *Outline of disclosure items concerning corporate governance*. https://www.fsa.go.jp/en/news/2010/20100219-2/01.pdf

[27] The article is available at https://asia.nikkei.com/Business/Transportation/JR-companies-defy-US-investor-by-boosting-cross-shareholdings (accessed February 9, 2021).

Financial Services Agency (FSA). (2010b, March 26). *Outline of disclosure items concerning corporate governance*. https://www.fsa.go.jp/en/news/2010/20100326-1/01.pdf

Genay, H. (1991). Japan's corporate groups. *Economic Perspectives, 15*(1), 20–30.

Hoshi, T. (1994). Evolution of the main bank system in Japan. In M. Okabe (Ed.), *The structure of the Japanese economy* (pp. 287–322). Macmillan.

International Accounting Standards Board (IASB). (2016). Staff Paper (Outreach on Shariah-Compliant Instruments and Transactions). *Issues in the Application of IFRS 9 to Islamic Finance*.

Japan Audit and Supervisory Board Members Association. (2012, September). *Background and goals: New recommended English translation of "Kansayaku" and "Kansayaku-kai"*.

Katada, N. S. (2020). *Japan's new regional reality: Geoeconomic strategy in the Asia-Pacific*. Columbia University Press.

Ministry of Economy, Industry and Trade and Industry (METI). (2014, August). Final report. *Ito Review of Competitiveness and Incentives for Sustainable Growth–Building Favorable Relationships between Companies and Investors.*

Ogura, S. (2015). *Financialization—Kinyūka to Kinyūkikan-kōdō*. Sakurai Shoten.

Okabe, M. (2002). *Cross shareholdings in Japan: A new unified perspective of the economic system*. Edward Elgar.

Okamoto, N. (2024). Financialisation in the context of cross-shareholding in Japan: The performative pursuit of better corporate governance. *Journal of Management and Governance, 28*(1), 337–357.

Okazaki, T. (2014). Financial market globalization and its influence on Japanese firms. In N. Kambayashi (Ed.), *Japanese management in change: The impact of globalization and market principles* (pp. 99–112). Springer.

PricewaterhouseCoopers. (2010). *Open to comparison: Islamic finance and IFRS*.

Shimpo, Y. (2006). *Kōporeito Gabanansu no Rekishi-teki Tenkai*. Chuo Keizai Publishing.

Yamaji, H. (1999). Interaction between Japanese accounting and economic structures. In S. Sunder & H. Yamaji (Eds.), *The Japanese style of business accounting* (pp. 35–54). Quorum Books.

In Japanese

Economic Planning Agency (EPA). (1992, July 28). *Nenji Keizai Hōkoku: Chōsei wo Koete Aratana Tenkai wo Mezasu Nihon Keizai*.

Hayashi, J. (2022). *Kōporeito Gabanansu no Rekishi to Sasutenabiritī*. Bunshindo Publishing.

Horie, S. (2015). *Corporate governance code*. Nihon Keizai Shinbun-sha.

Itami, T. (2000). *Nihon gata Kōporeito Gabanansu*. Nihon Keizai Shimbun-sha.

Ito, K., & Suzuki, T. (2018). The end of accounting: *Hatashite "kigyō kaikei no saisei" ha kanō ka. Kigyō Kaikei, 70*(12), 17–39.

Kagono, T., & Yamada, K. (Eds.). (2016). *Nihon no Business System: Sono Genri to Kakushin*. Yūhikaku.

Kanda, H. (Capital Markets Research Institute) (Ed.). (2001). *Tettei Tōron: Kabushiki Mochiai no Kaisyō no Riron to Jitsumu*. Zaikei Shoho Sha.

Kawamoto, S. (2022). *Dēta Bunseki de Yomitoku Nihon no Kōporeito Gabanansu Shi*. Chuo Keizai Publishing.

Milhaupt, C. J., & West, M. D. (2004). *Economic organizations and corporate governance in Japan: The impact of formal and informal rule*. Oxford University Press.

Miyajima, H., & Kuroki, F. (2007). The unwinding of cross-shareholding in Japan: Causes, effects, and implications. In M. Aoki, G. Jackson, & H. Miyajima (Eds.), *Corporate governance in Japan: Institutional change and organizational diversity* (pp. 79–124). Oxford University Press.

Miyamoto, M. (2018). *The new Japanese firms as a hybrid organization*. Springer.

Nishiyama, K. (2019, Autumn). *Wagakuni jyōjyō kigyō no kabushiki mochiai jyōkyō* (2019 *nendo*). *Nomura Sihon Sijyō Quarterly*, 123–129.

OECD (2015). *G20/OECD Principles of Corporate Governance*. OECD Publishing.

Ogishima, S., & Kobayashi, T. (2000). *Nihon no kabushiki mochiai to kabuka* (Cross-shareholdings and equity valuation in Japan). Working Paper (Center for International Research on the Japanese Economy, University of Tokyo), CIRJE-J-36.

Oguchi, T. (2015). Kōporeito gabanansu code he no kitai to kadai-Chūchyōkiteki na Kigyō Kachi no kōjyō ha kaisya to kikan tōshika no kyōdō sekinin. *Securities Analysts Journal, 53*(8), 13–23.

Quillin, B. (2008). *International financial co-operation: Political economics of compliance with the 1988 basel accord*. Routledge.

Scher, J. M. (1997). *Japanese interfirm networks and their main banks*. Palgrave Macmillan.

Scher, J. M. (2001). *Bank-firm cross-shareholding in Japan: What is it, why does it matter, is it winding down?* (DESA Discussion Paper, pp. 1–21). United Nations.

Takei, K. (2021). *Corporate governance code no jissen 3rd edition*. Nikkei BP.

The Japan Association of Corporate Directors (2010, June 30). *Report: Ginkō no seisaku tōshi kabushiki ni tsuite*.

Tsumuraya, S. (2020). *Seisaku Hoyū Kabushiki no Jissyō Bunseki: Ushinawareru Kabushiki Mochiai no Keizaiteki Koka*. Nihon Keizai Shimbun Press.

Ueda, R. (2019). Seisaku hoyū Kabushiki no genjyō to kōporeito gabanansu jyō no kadai No. 1. *Corporate Governance, 1*, 38–43.

Veldman, J., & Willmott, H. (2020). Performativity and convergence in comparative corporate governance. *Competition and Change, 24*, 408–428.

CHAPTER 8

Conclusion

As mentioned in the introduction, this book is interdisciplinary in nature and aims to derive some theoretical and conceptual implications through the analysis of cases of accounting reform in Japan. First, in Part I, this book distinguishes between institutions and norms. In particular, based on the perspective of the social ontology of institutions, it presents the viewpoint that formal institutions are composed of different types of collectively accepted norms. Among these different types, this book focuses particularly on the belief-based collective norms (informal norms) that shape agreement-based institutions (formal norms). Relevant actors, or operative members, tacitly accept such informal social norms and occasionally rely on them in the face of uncertainty. Therefore, such comprehensive type of collective norms can be identified by observers, such as social scientists, potentially offering new insights into the ontology of institutions and norms.

Second, in order to explain the mechanism of normativity of collective social norms, this book has introduced a perspective of performativity. Social norms are obviously social constructs, existing through linguistic expressions. From this perspective, performativity describes the power of a certain linguistic representation that encourages individuals to act in the same way. The aim of this book is, therefore, to analyze the nature of comprehensive generic performativity in society (MacKenzie, 2006). However, in trying to capture the broad performative forces, the

N. Okamoto, *Institutional Change and Performativity*,
https://doi.org/10.1007/978-3-031-53393-8_8

identification of an observable norm tends to be subjective and arbitrary. To mitigate this risk, the book has taken a linguistic approach and, based on some data, has identified generically performative norms in contemporary society. Although two types of linguistic representations, globalization and financialization, were specifically selected for the analysis of accounting regulation in Japan in Part II, a more appropriate method for selecting the specific type of norm could be explored in future studies.

Part II grapples with the task of narratively explaining the cases of performative (and counterperformative) institutionalization in the context of accounting regulation in Japan. The design of appropriate institutions in a particular regulatory context can never be perfect. Different individuals and organizations (regulatees) have their own interests and goals, which change dynamically, making the process of institutionalization of regulators difficult and complicated. In a medical context, for example, there would be common, widely shared goals: eradicating disease and improving the health of patients. In contrast, in the context of corporate financial accounting, the common goal is less clear because corporations involve various stakeholders, such as shareholders, creditors, and employees. In addition, the interests of users of financial accounting information are often conflicting, making it difficult to set optimal accounting standards.[1] Then, one of the most difficult tasks for the accounting standard setter is to consider which stakeholder's interests should be prioritized for a particular accounting matter. In other words, accounting standard setters' decisions are inevitably political. Predicting and comparing the net benefits to stakeholders of a particular accounting standard would be critical to the accounting standard setter's decisions. However, how different stakeholders will react to a particular accounting standard is uncertain. Under such uncertainty, accounting standard setters, or operative members, implicitly follow collectively accepted norms in society. Although the objectives of accounting standard setters include, for example, improving the usefulness of accounting information for investors' decision-making and reducing the costs of producing accounting information for companies, these objectives are limited to the sphere of accounting. Generic performativity goes beyond accounting and is more pervasive in society. Through the repeated appearance of similar discourses in different forms of texts, the forces of generic

[1] Almost five decades ago, Demski (1973) pointed out the impossibility of setting the best accounting standards among alternatives through the normative deliberations.

performativity become stronger and social institutions converge in a particular direction through their changes.

Accounting standard-setting in Japan has become increasingly global in the sense that it consistently followed global accounting standards set by the IASB and the FASB. Local differences in traditional Japanese accounting standards have been reduced and replaced by those global standards. In parallel with the globalization of accounting standards, the expansion of the domestic financial market and its connection with global financial centers such as New York and London became the target of Japanese financial and accounting regulation. The present book considered the pursuit of an active financial market as the core of financialization. From that standpoint, the institutional reforms in Japan have consistently prioritized shareholders as the significant actors standing at the center in the financial markets. It was exemplified in the introduction and the expansion of market value (or fair value) accounting that requires the revaluation of most financial instruments. For instance, many financial instruments such as derivatives have become marked to market, and the gains and losses are recognized every business period, as those items are often traded in the active financial market. More recently, globalization and financialization have culminated in the reform of corporate governance in Japan. Japanese corporate governance style was traditionally unique with its emphasis on the relational main bank system. However, through the introduction of the Corporate Governance Code, a set of new institutional mechanisms has been put in place for the benefits of shareholders. For example, the Code now requires Japanese listed corporations to explain economic rationales for cross-shareholdings. As the clear financial benefits of traditional Japanese cross-shareholdings were not obvious, the Code aims at reducing the volume of Japanese companies' inefficient cross-held shares to achieve better corporate governance. Simply put, under the slogan of proactive better corporate governance, the relational Japanese business practices were replaced by the Anglo-Saxon model of corporate governance.

In short, this book focuses on the changes in accounting institutions in Japan since the late 1980s and views them through the lens of the performativity of globalization and financialization, while shedding new light on the dynamics of accounting institutions. Although the discussion is based on interpretation, the narrative analyses in Part II have described certain movements of performative changes in accounting, including counterperformative resistances. In this regard, it would be useful to reconsider the globally converging Anglo-Saxon model of accounting regulation, which has emphasized the prosperity of the financial market.

Although the performances of collective social norms of globalization and financialization have been conspicuous in the recent development of accounting in Japan, Japanese regulators and stakeholders have not accepted it with open arms every time. There were several counterperformative actions. Chapter 5 particularly highlighted that the establishment of the JMIS was not to replace the IFRS but to inscribe the unacceptable differences between Japanese GAAP and the IFRS. Chapter 6 revealed that although the relevant actors, such as Tastumi Yamada and the members of the ASBJ, generally accepted market value accounting for cross-held shares, they did not concede to the classification of dividend income from cross-held shares in the comprehensive income and resisted the IASB's proposal in the exposure draft. They finally obtained the IASB's concession on this matter, as the IASB finally changed the proposal to accept the classification of it in the net income in the final standard. In addition, the consistent disuse of the term "fair value accounting" in the accounting standards for market value accounting also reflects a vestige of traditional Japanese accounting regulation that used to emphasize the historical cost accounting and the aversion to the use of "fair value." With regard to the corporate governance reform in Japan, as the trend of global convergence of corporate governance style that aims a shareholder-oriented market has been so strong, Chapter 7 briefly mentioned a recent case of strengthened cross-shareholding relationship that can be recognized as a counterperformative action.

Overall, the chapters in Part II have shown that globalization and financialization have shaped accounting regulation in Japan, regardless of its clear benefits to the Japanese economy or society. Of course, the existence of powerful accounting standard setters, such as the IASB and the FASB, are important actors leading the trend of global accounting standard-setting. This book emphasizes that although globalization and financialization are two different phenomena, based on the above analysis of institutional changes in Japanese accounting regulation, the performativity of these collective social norms is closely related. At first glance, they appear to be overlapping phenomena, and they are not mutually exclusive. Thus, it might be possible to conclude that a hybrid performativity of globalization and financialization has shaped the development of accounting standards in Japan over the previous decades.[2] According to Miller et al., (2008, pp. 944–945), accounting is constantly engaged in a dual hybridization process: seeking to make visible and calculable the hybrids that it encounters, while at the same time hybridizing itself through encounters with a range of other disciplines." Following this analysis, it is possible to say that this book has revealed that the development of accounting in Japan might have made visible the performative forces of globalization and financialization. This also enables us to pay more attention to counterperformative actions that tried to resist the influences of globalization and financialization. The matter we need to consider further then is whether those counterperformative actions can change operative members' cognitive frames that filter collective social norms.

There are several limitations in this book. First, this book could not address why globalization and financialization are so performative and normative. Therefore, how a particular discourse becomes collectively accepted is still an important issue to be addressed from a different angle. Although it could be analyzed to some extent within the framework of the norm diffusion process, this book did not address why certain norm entrepreneurs or carriers are more committed to some norms than others, even though they are likely to be in the same epistemic community with similar cognitive frameworks. Second, the application of the concept of performativity needs to be better-structured. In this book, I have emphasized the linguistic aspect of norms that shape individual and organizational behavior through the concept of generic performativity. Some previous studies of performativity have emphasized material aspects of cases in limited contexts (e.g., MacKenzie, 2009; Pinch & Swedberg, 2008). As this book has shown, the generic performativity is broad and all-encompassing, and the selection of texts representing performative globalization and financialization was subjective. Nevertheless, they were complemented by detailed analyses of the political process of standard-setting in the course of narrative analysis.

Of course, these are not the only shortcomings of this book. However, as mentioned at the beginning, this book was an ambitious challenge to

[2] Expanding their viewpoint of economic analysis to the social one, Cochoy et al. (2010) state that the performativity of society involves studying the hybridization between the political language of society on the one hand and the working of social devices, processes, and hard facts on the other.

examine the relationship between social dynamics and accounting changes from an interdisciplinary perspective. Although I am not sure to what extent this book has fulfilled its original goal, it will be a great pleasure for me as the author if the contents of this book can help you in your future research.

References

Cochoy, F., Giraudeau, M., & McFall, L. (2010). Performativity, economics and politics. *Journal of Cultural Economy, 3*(2), 139–146.

Demski, J. S. (1973). The general impossibility of normative accounting standards. *The Accounting Review, 48*(4), 718–723.

MacKenzie, D. (2006). *An Engine, not a Camera: How Financial Models Shape Markets*. MIT Press.

MacKenzie, D. (2009). *Material Markets: How Economic Agents are Constructed*. Oxford University Press.

Miller, P., Kurunmäki, L., & O'Leary, T. (2008). Accounting, hybrids and the management of risk. *Accounting, Organizations and Society, 33*(7–8), 942–967.

Pinch, T., & Swedberg, R. (Eds.). (2008). *Living in a Material World: Economic Sociology Meets Science and Technology Studies*. MIT Press.

Index

A

Abe administration, 141, 185, 186, 188

abstraction, 71

Accounting Big Bang, 85, 97–100, 107, 110, 111, 113, 126, 137, 147, 148, 152, 170, 183

accounting regulation, 2, 79, 80, 87, 155, 170, 179, 214

in Japan, 3, 4, 68, 69, 80, 82, 83, 87, 98, 111, 148, 212–214

accounting standard(s), 1, 2, 4–6, 10, 33, 80, 82, 85–87, 91, 97–99, 107, 109–118, 120, 121, 123–128, 133, 134, 142–144, 147–153, 155–158, 160, 163–166, 169, 170, 177, 178, 194, 195, 205, 212–214

unification of, 1, 5

Accounting Standards Board of Japan (ASBJ), 113, 115–122, 124–126, 142, 143, 156–159, 165–167, 169, 170

Actor-Network Theory (ANT), 10, 20, 22–24, 59

agency(ies), 23, 24, 55, 99, 178, 204

agency theory, 204

agreement-based norm(s), 37, 38

amortized cost method, 156

anomaly, 52

asset-backed securities (ABS), 101

assignment of function, 25

Austin, John L., 46, 48, 50, 56, 58, 59, 70

available-for-sale security(ies), 152, 195

B

bank finance, 1, 2

Bank of Japan (BOJ), 101, 135, 181

Barnes, Barry, 52

Barnesian performativity, 52

Basel Accord, 194

Basel Committee, 114, 116

belief

-based norm(s), 35–38, 58, 73, 74, 80

N. Okamoto, *Institutional Change and Performativity*,
https://doi.org/10.1007/978-3-031-53393-8

collective, 38, 50, 58, 59, 68, 72
individual, 14
Berger, P.L., 13, 14
Bicchieri, Christina, 30–32, 36, 89
boundary of institutions, 11
brute fact(s), 25
bubble burst, 98, 99, 104, 126, 135, 192, 194
bubble economy, 2, 4, 102, 103, 106, 170, 182, 191, 192
Business Accounting (Deliberation) Council (BAC), 86, 87, 109, 112–114, 122–124, 126, 144, 148–151, 165, 166
business sector(s), 76

C

capital base, 194
capitalism, 37, 38, 77, 127, 179, 188
capitalization, 73, 125, 191
causal inference, 81–83
causal relationship, 55, 83, 84
cognitive institutionalism, 18
cognitive institution(s), 18, 24
cognitive schema(s), 80
cognitive system, 16, 18
collective acceptance, 2, 3, 5, 9, 10, 26–28, 32, 33, 38, 50, 54, 56, 67, 68, 72–77, 126
collective belief, 50, 58, 59, 68, 72
collective intentionality, 25–27, 33
collectively accepted norm(s), 45, 84, 177, 211, 212
collective memory, 72, 73
collective norm(s), 3, 10, 31, 32, 45, 46, 55, 56, 60, 62, 63, 67–70, 73–75, 82, 87, 211
comment letter(s), 156, 157, 160–163, 165, 169
Commercial Code, 3, 86, 148–150, 152, 169
Committee for the Revitalization of Committee on Finance, 103
Committee of European Securities Regulators (CESR), 118–122, 126, 127
Committee on Financial Systems Research, 103
communication, 17, 18, 20, 61, 70, 102, 119, 122, 142, 167
Company Law(s), 79
comparability, 116, 152, 153, 205
complexity(ies), 61, 154
comply or explain, 202
conceptual framework, 76, 79, 80, 112
conditions of causality, 84
conditions of understandability, 84
consolidation accounting standards, 107, 109, 110
constative utterance, 46
constitutive rules, 25–27
constitutive view, 13–15
constraint(s), 12–14, 16, 28
contingent effect(s), 48, 49
convention(s), 16, 19, 27, 59, 60, 70
convergence, 5, 23, 74, 111, 113, 118, 119, 121, 122, 126, 142, 157, 165, 196, 205, 206
of accounting standards, 5, 97, 98, 111, 116–119, 121, 122, 125, 126, 166, 170
of corporate governance, 204, 206, 214
convoy system (*gosō sendan hōshiki*), 98, 99, 101, 104, 106, 107, 147
coordinated market economy (CME), 179, 180
Corporate Accounting Principles (CAP), 85, 86
corporate governance, 5, 103, 137, 164, 178–189, 197, 198, 202–206, 213

code, 6, 185, 186, 206, 213
convergence of, 204, 206, 214
corporate law(s), 13, 80
corporate profitability, 52, 152, 205
counterperformativity, 52–56, 59, 60
creditor(s), 148, 149, 155, 169, 180, 189, 212
cross-held share(s), 5, 164, 165, 167, 169, 171, 192, 194–196, 199–207, 213, 214
cross-shareholding(s), 5, 6, 164, 166, 170, 171, 178, 179, 181, 182, 184, 189–194, 196–203, 205–207, 213, 214
culture, 1, 11, 12, 18, 63, 85, 145

D
declaration(s), 29, 56, 113, 119, 149
deductive approach, 57, 81
deductive process tracing, 83, 97
Denzau, A.T., 16–19, 21
deontic power, 10, 28, 29
deregulation, 99, 102, 107, 134, 137, 169, 182
derivative(s), 37, 55, 79, 100, 101, 112, 137, 144, 148, 150, 152, 213
descriptive norm(s), 31
desire, 13, 20, 26, 29, 30, 58, 61
desire-independent reason(s), 29, 30
De Soto, Fernando, 37, 38
diagnostic evidence, 81
discourse(s), 3, 12, 17, 30, 46, 49–51, 53, 55, 56, 58–60, 63, 67–71, 73, 90, 212, 215
discursive practice, 21
domestic standards, 82, 97

E
earning power, 185, 186
Economic Council, 99
Economic Council and Action Plan Committee, 99
economic model, 16, 48, 143
economic rationale, 164, 197, 202, 203, 213
economist(s), 3, 52, 75
effective performativity, 51–53
eight percent (8%), 188, 194
epistemic community(ies), 90, 91, 215
equilibrium, 14, 17
equity investment(s), 156, 160, 161, 163, 164, 166, 168, 170
equivalence project, 122, 148
European Commission (EC), 119–121, 126, 127
evidence-based policy making, 128
experiment(s), 21, 50
explicable social norm(s), 35, 36

F
failure of performativity, 55, 60
fair value accounting, 150, 152–160, 164, 170, 177, 214
fair value hierarchy, 154
fair value of the investment as other comprehensive income (FVTOCI), 156
fair values are generally recognized as profit or loss (FVTPL), 156
fallibility, 55
feedback loop(s), 52
felicitous condition(s), 5, 56–59
finance-oriented (market) economy (F-economy), 134, 144–146
Financial Accounting Standards Board (FASB), 3, 80, 85, 111, 154, 155, 157, 159, 165, 166, 169, 213, 214
Financial Accounting Standards Foundation (FASF), 116

Financial Big Bang, 98–100, 102, 104–108, 125, 134, 140, 169, 170, 178
financial center, 101, 102, 213
financial cognition, 80
financial crisis, 78, 103, 104, 137, 138, 155, 183, 192, 197, 205
financial holding company, 107, 135
Financial Instruments and Exchange Law (FIEL), 136, 137, 139
financialization, 2, 4–6, 51, 75, 77–80, 82, 83, 87, 89, 90, 125, 133, 134, 137, 138, 143, 145, 146, 150, 154, 159, 160, 169, 170, 177, 178, 189, 195–197, 205–207, 212–215
financial market(s), 2, 4, 47, 69, 70, 77, 79, 83, 98, 100–104, 107, 126, 133–139, 141–144, 151, 170, 177, 187, 188, 191, 194, 205, 206, 213, 214
financial model(s), 47, 80
Financial Problem Research Council, 114
financial regulation, 79, 80, 98, 101, 103, 106, 134–137, 141, 143, 191
financial stability, 103, 117
Financial System Council, 141, 197
Financial System Research Council, 103
Fiscal Investment and Loan Program, 136
fixation of belief, 68, 72
flat ontology, 23, 24
flexible governance, 181
foreign investor(s), 138, 139, 182, 191, 195, 196
formal institution(s), 12, 19, 31, 34, 60, 62, 80, 170, 211
formal rule(s), 34–36
free, fair, and global, 69, 70, 101, 106, 107, 125, 133, 170

G
G4+1, 112, 113, 126, 161
GAAP 2000, 117
gaiatsu (external pressure), 3, 103, 111
game theory, 14
genealogy, 74, 76
generic performativity, 4, 46, 50–59, 68, 70, 77, 80, 82, 84, 87, 90, 206, 211–213, 215
German accounting, 85
globalization, 2, 4–6, 51, 72–78, 80, 82, 83, 87, 89, 90, 97, 98, 101, 111, 122, 125–128, 136, 152, 154, 159, 169, 170, 177, 178, 189, 196, 197, 203, 205–207, 212–215
global standard(s), 82, 97, 110, 113, 116, 122, 126, 177, 213
government, 3, 25, 86, 91, 99, 101, 104–107, 113, 117, 121, 135–137, 139, 141, 143, 184, 197
Greenspan, Alan, 104
gross domestic products (GDP), 54
Guala, Francisco, 19–21, 48

H
Hashimoto, Ryutaro, 100
harmonization of accounting standards, 107, 111, 112, 151
Herrmann-Pillath, Carsten, 127
historical cost accounting, 86, 134, 144, 147, 148, 150, 155, 169, 170, 214
holding company, 108, 109, 135, 203
hollowing-out phenomenon, 101
homo economicus, 16

homo sociologicus, 16
hostile takeover, 181, 190, 192
human actor(s), 16, 22
human uncertainty principle, 55
hybridization, 215
hypothesis building, 81

I
identification of norm(s), 5, 46, 212
ideology, 163
Ikeo, Kazuhito, 99, 140, 143, 183, 197
Ikeo Report, 99, 140
illegal stock dealing, 135
illocution, 48, 49
illocutionary act(s), 46, 48, 49
illusions of knowledge, 47
imagination, 58
imitation, 19, 60, 62
individual intention, 26, 27, 33
individualism, 12
inductive approach, 56
industry group(s), 86, 106, 136
infelicitous condition(s), 58, 63
informal norm(s), 12, 31, 37, 211
informal rule(s), 10, 33, 35–37, 45
injunctive norm(s), 31, 32
institutional change(s), 4, 18, 45, 46, 49, 54, 56, 57, 60, 62, 63, 68, 70, 81–85, 98, 170, 205, 206, 214
institutionalization, 13, 22, 32, 61, 68, 69, 212
institutional reality, 10, 25–29, 45, 56, 69, 74
institutional regress, 59
institutional theory, 9–11, 13, 20–25, 57
institution(s), 1–5, 9–21, 24, 25, 27, 28, 30, 32–34, 37, 45, 47, 50, 54, 57, 59, 60, 62, 63, 67, 68, 75, 76, 79, 82, 84, 98, 104–106, 135, 136, 138, 139, 147, 151, 177, 191, 192, 194–196, 203, 204, 206, 211, 213
  r-institution(s), 33
  s-institution(s), 33
internal control, 137
International Accounting Standards Board (IASB), 4, 5, 80, 97, 113, 117–119, 121, 122, 125, 126, 142, 154–157, 159–170, 178, 213, 214
International Accounting Standards Committee (IASC), 111–115, 118, 126, 151, 152, 162
International Accounting Standards (IAS), 110, 117, 118, 120, 121, 127
  IAS 39, 150–152, 154–156
International Federation of Accountants, 116
International Financial Reporting Standards (IFRS), 1, 87, 97, 118–127, 142, 160, 166, 170, 177, 178, 214
  IFRS 7, 155
  IFRS 9, 156, 160, 163, 166
  IFRS 13, 154, 157–159
International Forum on Accountancy Development (IFAD), 117, 118, 127
Internationalization of Financial and Capital Markets in Japan, 140, 197
International Organization for Securities Commissions (IOSCO), 113, 114, 116–118
international relation(s), 75

J

Japan's Modified International Standards (JMIS), 124, 125, 127, 214
Japanese accounting regulation, 3, 4, 68, 69, 82, 83, 87, 111, 148, 214
Joint Working Group (JWG), 112, 152–154, 170

K

Kansayaku, 180
Keidanren, 115–118, 121, 122, 152, 153, 170, 184
Keiretsu, 190

L

language, 17, 19, 21, 28, 33, 46, 49, 71, 89, 215
Latour, Bruno, 22, 24
learning, 17, 18
legend issue, 116, 126, 148
legitimacy, 69, 89
Liberal Democratic Party (LDP), 99, 100, 106, 114
liberalization, 99, 102, 103, 107, 108, 182
liberal market economy (LME), 179, 180
linguistic expression(s), 21, 59, 73, 89, 157, 211
  performance of, 3
linguistic representation(s), 21, 45, 53, 54, 56, 69–72, 81, 211, 212
local tradition, 160, 178
long-term relationship, 180
long-term stability, 192
Luckmann, Thomas, 13, 14

M

MacKenzie, Donald,A., 46, 47, 50, 52–55, 58, 211, 215
main bank system, 133, 180–182, 188, 190, 191, 194, 213
manufacturing-oriented economy, 133, 134
marketable security(ies), 79, 148
market cognition, 80
market competition, 135
marketization, 75, 101
market value accounting, 5, 100, 146, 148–153, 160, 170, 195, 196, 214
mark-to-market accounting, 134, 144, 147, 148, 155, 170
material actor(s), 59
mental model(s), 16–19, 21, 24, 61, 62
Mertonian performativity, 52
Ministry of Finance (MOF), 86, 99, 100, 103, 104, 106, 107, 109, 112–115, 126, 144, 147–149, 152, 153, 181
Ministry of Justice (MOJ), 148, 149, 152
moral norm(s), 10, 32

N

national economy, 146
natural scientist(s), 21
negotiation(s), 13, 103
neoliberalism, 77, 80
Nishikawa, Ikuo, 119
nominalization, 68, 70–74
non-amortization of goodwill, 125
non-human actor(s), 22
non-human entity, 22, 23
non-knowledge, 47
non-operative member(s), 33, 34, 38, 60, 61, 63, 68, 70, 72, 76, 80

non-performing loan, 105, 116, 135, 151, 182
norm acceptance, 88–90
normality, 30
normativity, 2, 3, 5, 9, 10, 20, 21, 24, 27, 29, 30, 32, 34, 36, 45, 46, 49, 52, 74, 87, 90, 202, 211
norm carrier(s), 90, 91
norm diffusion, 83, 87, 89–91, 189, 215
norm entrepreneur(s), 89–91, 107, 119, 165, 169, 170, 189, 215
norm internalization, 88, 89
North, D.C., 12, 16–19, 21

O
observable social norm(s), 35–37, 45, 46, 49, 52, 54, 56–58, 60, 62, 63, 71, 73, 84, 87
observer-relative, 35, 36, 50, 57
observer(s), 25, 26, 45, 49–51, 57, 62, 70, 78, 84, 211
off-balance-sheet debt, 135
operative member(s), 33, 36, 38, 45, 56, 57, 60–63, 68, 70, 76, 80, 82, 84, 88, 89, 97, 125, 126, 134, 159, 163, 170, 177, 181, 182, 185, 211, 212, 215
option-trader(s), 47
Organisation for Economic Co-operation and Development (OECD), 117, 186, 203
other comprehensive income, 125, 156, 160–162
outside director(s), 179, 184

P
performance of norm(s), 214
performative force(s), 5, 6, 46, 50, 53, 56, 60, 70, 81, 84, 87, 126, 134, 211
performative globalization, 5, 97, 98, 111, 122, 125, 127, 128, 152, 154, 169, 178, 189, 205, 206, 215
performative utterance, 46, 50, 58, 59
performativity, 3–5, 36, 37, 46–50, 52, 53, 59, 67, 68, 214
  and institutional change(s), 4, 81, 84
  of financialization, 5, 133, 150, 154, 170, 196, 207
  of globalization, 5, 97, 98, 111, 122, 125, 127, 128, 152, 154, 169, 178, 189, 205, 206, 215
perlocution, 48, 49
perlocutionary act(s), 46, 48, 50
personal financial asset(s), 102, 103, 189
poverty, 75
private accounting standard setter, 112, 115, 126
private property right(s), 38
proactive governance, 180, 186
process tracing, 81–83, 97
production-oriented (market) economy (p-economy), 144–147
pseudo-knowledge, 47

R
reactive governance, 186
realized gains, 168
reciprocity, 14, 35, 36, 88
recycling, 37, 125, 160, 166–168
reflexivity, 20, 55
regulative institution(s), 13, 21
regulative view, 14, 15, 18
regulator(s), 2, 4, 6, 57, 69, 82, 84, 90, 91, 102, 111, 114, 116, 117, 122, 126, 127, 134, 147, 178, 181, 212, 214
relevance, 153, 155
reliability, 80, 153

representational redescription, 17, 19
return on assets (ROA)/return on invested capital(ROIC), 52
return on equity (ROE), 52, 182, 183, 185, 187–189, 195, 202
risk management, 106, 135, 144
risk sharing, 181
r-norm(s), 33–37
rules as a game, 12

S
sanction(s), 13, 30, 34, 36
  r-sanction(s), 34, 36
  s-sanction(s), 34, 36
savings to investment, 136, 184
scientific investigation, 22
scientific knowledge, 71
Searle, John, 10, 25–29, 33, 38, 45, 48, 49, 56, 59
Securities and Exchange Commission (SEC), 113, 142, 155
self-fulfilling performativity, 52, 53, 56, 206
self-interest, 16, 20
self-referring system, 47
semantics, 71
semiotic (analysis/perspective), 69, 70
shared belief, 14
shared mental model(s), 16–19, 21, 24
shareholder primacy, 206
s-norm(s), 33–37
social construct(s), 2, 9, 16, 21, 26, 30, 54, 55, 204, 211
social dynamics/dynamism, 1, 4, 57, 67, 68, 73, 77, 79, 216
social knowledge, 50
social meaning(s), 76
social movement, 74
social ontology, 2, 4, 5, 9, 10, 25, 27, 30, 59, 67, 211
social relation(s), 76
social scientific research, 21, 22
social scientist(s), 5, 11, 34, 45, 47, 49, 52, 54, 56–58, 63, 84, 178, 211
soft law, 202, 203
Soros, George, 55, 56, 61
soundness of financial institutions, 151
speech act(s), 48–50, 56, 58, 70
standard-setting, 3, 4, 45, 68, 69, 76, 81, 89, 97, 113, 115, 117, 126, 154, 159, 162, 170, 213, 215
Statement of Financial Accounting Standards (SFAS)
  SFAS 157, 154, 158, 159
status function(s), 26–29, 48, 56, 75
strong corporate governance, 185
structured narrative, 84
subjective judgment, 37
suffix(es), 68, 71–75
summary representation(s), 14
Summers, Lawrence, 104, 105
syntax, 71

T
tacit knowledge, 10
Takeda, Ryuji, 144–147, 153
theatrical persuasion, 48
token institution(s), 19–21
Tokyo Agreement, 118, 119, 122, 142, 165
transaction economics, 14
translation, 24, 57, 86, 159, 180, 184
trendsetter(s), 89
Tuomela, Raimo, 27, 32–34, 36, 38, 45, 60
Tweedie, David, 119, 142, 169

U
uncertainty(ies), 3, 17, 18, 36, 38, 47, 55, 61–63, 72, 82, 106, 126, 133, 177, 211, 212
understandability, 84, 153
unrealized gains, 149, 153

W
Westernization, 73, 75
Wimbledon effect, 102
World Bank, 117

Y
Yamada, Tatsumi, 125, 143, 151, 155, 156, 164, 165, 168–170, 190

SPRINGER NATURE

GPSR Compliance

The European Union's (EU) General Product Safety Regulation (GPSR) is a set of rules that requires consumer products to be safe and our obligations to ensure this.

If you have any concerns about our products, you can contact us on ProductSafety@springernature.com

In case Publisher is established outside the EU, the EU authorized representative is:

Springer Nature Customer Service Center GmbH
Europaplatz 3
69115 Heidelberg, Germany

The manufacturer's authorised representative in the EU is Springer Nature Customer Service Centre GmbH, Europaplatz 3, 69115 Heidelberg, Germany. If you have any concerns regarding our products, please contact ProductSafety@springernature.com

Printed and bound by CPI Group (UK) Ltd, Croydon, CR0 4YY
01/10/2026
02225854-0004